The Collected Works of J. Krishnamurti

Volume I

1933 - 1934

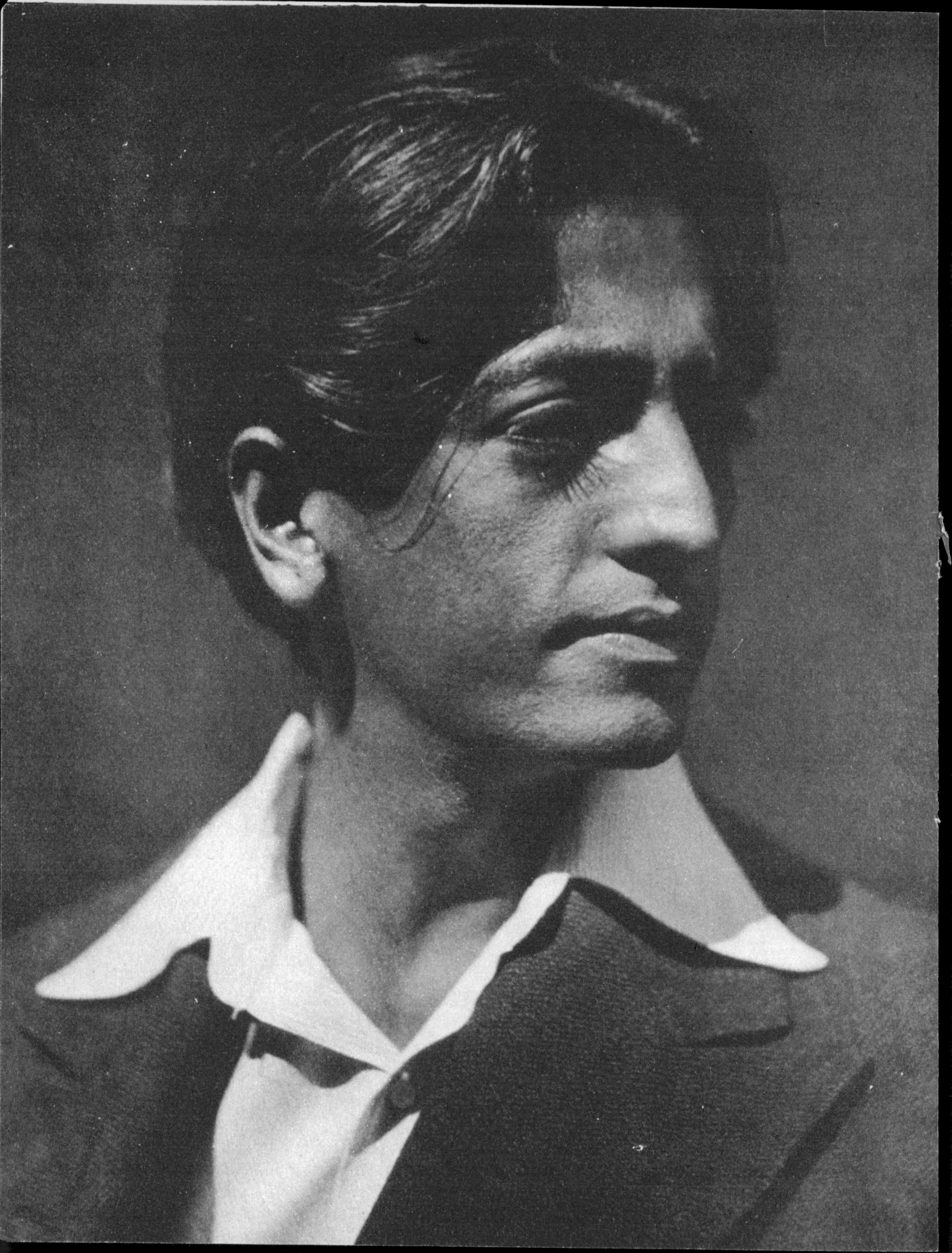

The Collected Works of J. Krishnamurti

Volume I

1933 - 1934

The Art of Listening

MOTILAL BANARSIDASS PUBLISHERS
PRIVATE LIMITED • DELHI

First Indian Edition : Delhi, 2007
First Published : USA, 1991

In Association With
KRISHNAMURTI FOUNDATION OF AMERICA
P.O. Box 1560, Ojai, California 93024 U.S.A
E-mail: kfa@kfa.org. Website: www.kfa.org

ISBN: 978-81-208-3241-1 (Vol. I)
ISBN: 978-81-208-3090-5 (18 Vols. Set)

MOTILAL BANARSIDASS
41 U.A. Bungalow Road, Jawahar Nagar, Delhi 110 007
8 Mahalaxmi Chamber, 22 Bhulabhai Desai Road, Mumbai 400 026
203 Royapettah High Road, Mylapore, Chennai 600 004
236, 9th Main III Block, Jayanagar, Bangalore 560 011
Sanas Plaza, 1302 Baji Rao Road, Pune 411 002
8 Camac Street, Kolkata 700 017
Ashok Rajpath, Patna 800 004
Chowk, Varanasi 221 001

Photo: J Krishnamurti, ca 1935 by Edwin Gledhill

Printed in India
AT NICE PRINTING PRESS,
3, RASHID MARKET EXTENSION, GALI NO. 4, DELHI 110 051
AND PUBLISHED BY NARENDRA PRAKASH JAIN FOR
MOTILAL BANARSIDASS PUBLISHERS PRIVATE LIMITED,
BUNGALOW ROAD, DELHI 110 007

Contents

Preface

Jiddu Krishnamurti was born in 1895 of Brahmin parents in south India. At the age of fourteen he was proclaimed the coming World Teacher by Annie Besant, then president of the Theosophical Society, an international organization that emphasized the unity of world religions. Mrs. Besant adopted the boy and took him to England, where he was educated and prepared for his coming role. In 1911 a new worldwide organization was formed with Krishnamurti as its head, solely to prepare its members for his advent as World Teacher. In 1929, after many years of questioning himself and the destiny imposed upon him, Krishnamurti disbanded this organization, saying:

Truth is a pathless land, and you cannot approach it by any path whatsoever, by any religion, by any sect. Truth, being limitless, unconditioned, unapproachable by any path whatsoever, cannot be organized; nor should any organization be formed to lead or to coerce people along any particular path. My only concern is to set men absolutely, unconditionally free.

Until the end of his life at the age of ninety, Krishnamurti traveled the world speaking as a private person. The rejection of all spiritual and psychological authority, including his own, is a fundamental theme. A major concern is the social structure and how it conditions the individual. The emphasis in his talks and writings is on the psychological barriers that prevent clarity of perception. In the mirror of relationship, each of us can come to understand the content of his own consciousness, which is common to all humanity. We can do this, not analytically, but directly in a manner Krishnamurti describes at length. In observing this content we discover within ourselves the division of the observer and what is observed. He points out that this division, which prevents direct perception, is the root of human conflict.

His central vision did not waver after 1929, but Krishnamurti strove for the rest of his life to make his language even more simple and clear. There is a development in his exposition. From year to year he used new terms and new approaches to his subject, with different nuances.

Because his subject is all-embracing, the *Collected Works* are of compelling interest. Within his talks in any one year, Krishnamurti was not able to cover the whole range of his vision, but broad amplifications of particular themes are found throughout these volumes. In them he lays the foundations of many of the concepts he used in later years.

The *Collected Works* contain Krishnamurti's previously published talks, discussions, answers to specific questions, and writings for the years 1933 through 1967. They are an authentic record of his teachings, taken from transcripts of verbatim shorthand reports and tape recordings.

The Krishnamurti Foundation of America, a California charitable trust, has among its purposes the publication and distribution of Krishnamurti books, videocassettes, films and tape recordings. The production of the *Collected Works* is one of these activities.

Alpino, Italy, 1933

First Talk at Alpino

Friends,

I should like you to make a living discovery, not a discovery induced by the description of others. If someone, for instance, had told you about the scenery here, you would come with your minds prepared by that description, and then perhaps you would be disappointed by the reality. No one can describe reality. You must experience it, see it, feel the whole atmosphere of it. When you see its beauty and loveliness, you experience a renewing, a quickening of joy.

Most people who think that they are seeking truth have already prepared their minds for its reception by studying descriptions of what they are seeking. When you examine religions and philosophies, you find that they have all tried to describe reality; they have tried to describe truth for your guidance.

Now I am not going to try to describe what to me is truth, for that would be an impossible attempt. One cannot describe or give to another the fullness of an experience. Each one must live it for himself.

Like most people, you have read, listened and imitated; you have tried to find out what others have said concerning truth and God, concerning life and immortality. So you have a picture in your mind, and now you want to compare that picture with what I am going to say. That is, your mind is seeking merely descriptions; you do not try to find out anew, but only try to compare. But since I shall not try to describe truth, for it cannot be described, naturally there will be confusion in your mind.

When you hold before yourself a picture that you are trying to copy, an ideal that you are trying to follow, you can never face an experience fully; you are never frank, never truthful as regards yourself and your own actions; you are always protecting yourself with an ideal. If you really probe into your own mind and heart, you will discover that you come here to get something new; a new idea, a new sensation, a new explanation of life, in order that you may mold your own life according to that. Therefore you are really searching for a satisfactory explanation. You have not come with an attitude of freshness, so that by your own perception, your own intensity, you may discover the joy of natural and spontaneous action. Most of you are merely seeking a descriptive explanation of truth, thinking that if you can find out what truth is, you can then mold your lives according to that eternal light.

If that be the motive of your search, then it is not a search for truth. It is rather for consolation, for comfort; it is but an attempt to escape the innumerable conflicts and struggles that you must face every day.

Out of suffering is born the urge to seek truth; in suffering lies the cause of the insistent inquiry, the search for truth. Yet when you suffer—as everyone does suffer—you seek an immediate remedy and comfort. When you feel momentary physical pain, you obtain a palliative at the nearest drug store to lessen your suffering. So also, when you experience momentary mental or emotional anguish, you seek consolation, and you imagine that trying to find relief from pain is the search for truth. In that way you are continually seeking a compensation for your pains, a compensation for the effort you are thus forced to make. You evade the main cause of suffering and thereby live an illusory life.

So those people who are always proclaiming that they are searching for truth are in reality missing it. They have found their lives to be insufficient, incomplete, lacking in love, and think that by trying to seek truth they will find satisfaction and comfort. If you frankly say to yourself that you are seeking only consolation and compensation for the difficulties of life, you will be able to grapple with the problem intelligently. But as long as you pretend to yourself that you are seeking something more than mere compensation, you cannot see the matter clearly. The first thing to find out, then, is whether you are really seeking, fundamentally seeking truth.

A man who is seeking truth is not a disciple of truth. Suppose that you say to me, "I have had no love in my life; it has been a poor life, a life of continuous pain; therefore, in order to gain comfort, I seek truth." Then I must point out that your search for comfort is an utter delusion. There is no such thing in life as comfort and security. The first thing to understand is that you must be absolutely frank.

But you yourself are not certain what you really want: you want comfort, consolation, compensation, and yet, at the same time, you want something that is infinitely greater than compensation and comfort. You are so confused in your own mind that one moment you look to an authority who offers you compensation and comfort, and the next moment you turn to another who denies you comfort. So your life becomes a refined hypocritical existence, a life of confusion. Try to find out what you really think; do not pretend to think what you believe you ought to think; then, if you are conscious, fully alive in what you are doing, you will know for yourself, without self-analysis, what you really desire. If you are fully responsible in your acts, you will then know without self-analysis what you are really seeking. This process of finding out does not necessitate great willpower, great strength, but only the interest to discover what you think, to discover whether you are really honest or living in illusion.

In talking to groups of listeners all over the world, I find that more and more people seem not to understand what I am saying, because they come with fixed ideas; they listen with their biased attitude, without trying to find out what I have to say, but only expecting to find what they secretly desire. It is vain to say, "Here is a new ideal after which I must mold myself." Rather find out what you really feel and think.

How can you find out what you really feel and think? From my point of view, you can do that only by being aware of your whole life. Then you will discover to what extent you are a slave to your ideals, and by discovering that, you will see that you have created ideals merely for your consolation.

Where there is duality, where there are opposites, there must be the consciousness of incompleteness. The mind is caught up in opposites, such as punishment and reward, good and bad, past and future, gain and loss. Thought is caught up in this duality, and therefore there is incompleteness in action.

This incompleteness creates suffering, the conflict of choice, effort, and authority, and the escape from the unessential to the essential.

When you feel that you are incomplete, you feel empty, and from that feeling of emptiness arises suffering; out of that incompleteness you create standards, ideals, to sustain you in your emptiness, and you establish these standards and ideals as your external authority. What is the inner cause of the external authority that you create for yourself? First, you feel incomplete, and you suffer from that incompleteness. As long as you do not understand the cause of authority, you are but an imitative machine, and where there is imitation there cannot be the rich fulfillment of life.

To understand the cause of authority you must follow the mental and emotional process which creates it. First of all, you feel empty, and in order to get rid of that feeling you make an effort; by that effort you only create opposites; you create a duality which but increases the incompleteness and the emptiness. You are responsible for such external authorities as religion, politics, morality, for such authorities as economic and social standards. Out of your emptiness, out of your incompleteness, you have created these external standards from which you now try to free yourself. By evolving, by developing, by growing away from them you want to create an inner law for yourself. As you come to understand external standards, you want to liberate yourself from them, and to develop your own inner standard. This inner standard, which you call "spiritual reality," you identify with a cosmic law, which means that you create but another division, another duality.

So you first create an external law, and then you seek to outgrow it by developing an inner law, which you identify with the universe, with the whole. That is what is happening. You are still conscious of your limited egotism, which you now identify with a great illusion, calling it cosmic. So when you say, "I am obeying my inner law," you are but using an expression to cover your desire to escape. To me, the man who is bound either by an external or an inner law is confined in a prison; he is held by an illusion. Therefore such a man cannot understand spontaneous, natural, healthy action.

Now why do you create inner laws for yourself? Is it not because the struggle in everyday life is so great, so inharmonious, that you want to escape from it and to create an inner law which shall become your comfort? And you become a slave to that inner authority, that inner standard, because you have rejected only the outward picture, and have created in its place an inner picture to which you are a slave.

By this method you will not attain true discernment, and discernment is quite other than choice. Choice must exist where there is duality. When the mind is incomplete and is conscious of that incompleteness, it tries to escape from it and therefore creates an opposite to that incompleteness. That opposite can be either an external or an inner standard, and when one has established such a standard, he judges every action, every experience by that standard, and therefore lives in a continual state of choice. Choice is born only of resistance. If there is discernment, there is no effort.

So to me this whole conception of making an effort toward truth, toward reality, this idea of making a sustained endeavor, is utterly false. As long as you are incomplete you will experience suffering, and hence you will be engaged in choice, in effort, in the ceaseless struggle for what you call "spiritual attainment." So I say, when mind is caught up in authority, it cannot have true understanding, true thought. And since the minds of most of you are caught up in authority—which is but an escape from understanding, from discernment—you cannot face the experience of life completely. Therefore you live a dual life, a life of pretense, of hypocrisy, a life in which there is no moment of completeness.

July 1, 1933

First Talk at Stresa

Friends,

In my talks I am not going to weave an intellectual theory. I am going to speak of my own experience which is not born of intellectual ideas, but which is real. Please do not think of me as a philosopher expounding a new set of ideas with which your intellect can juggle. That is not what I want to offer you. Rather, I should like to explain that truth, the life of fullness and richness, cannot be realized through any person, through imitation, or through any form of authority.

Most of us feel occasionally that there is a true life, an eternal something, but the moments in which we feel that are so rare that this eternal something recedes more and more into the background and seems to us less and less a reality.

Now to me there is reality; there is an eternal living reality—call it God, immortality, eternity, or what you will. There is something living, creative, which cannot be described, because reality eludes all description. No description of truth can be lasting, for it can only be an illusion of words. You cannot know of love through the description of another; to know love, you yourself must have experienced it. You cannot know the taste of salt until you have tasted salt for yourself. Yet we spend our time looking for a description of truth instead of trying to find out the manner of its realization. I say that I cannot describe, I cannot put into words, that living reality which is beyond all idea of progress, all idea of growth. Beware of the man who tries to describe that living reality, for it cannot be described; it must be experienced, lived.

This realization of truth, of the eternal, is not in the movement of time, which is but a habit of the mind. When you say that you will realize it in the course of time, that is, in some future, then you are only postponing that comprehension which must ever be in the present. But if the mind understands the completeness of life, and is free from the division of time into the past, present, and future, then there comes the realization of that living, eternal reality.

But since all minds are caught up in the division of time, since they think of time as past, present, and future, there arises conflict. Again, because we have divided action into the past, present, and future, because to us action is not complete in itself, but is rather something propelled by motives, by fear, by guides, by reward or punishment, our minds are incapable of understanding the continuous whole. Only when the mind is free of the division of time can true action result. When action is born of completeness, not in the division of time, then that action is harmonious and is freed from the trammels of society, classes, races, religions and acquisitiveness.

To put it differently, action must become truly individual. Now I am not using that word *individual* in the sense of placing the individual against the many. By individual action I mean action that is born of complete comprehension, complete understanding by the individual, understanding not imposed by others. Where that understanding exists, there is true individuality, true aloneness—not the aloneness of escape into solitude, but the aloneness that is born of the full comprehension of the experiences of life. For the completeness of action, the mind must be free of this idea of time as yesterday, today, and tomorrow. If the mind is not liberated from that division, then conflict arises and leads to suffering and to the search for escapes from that suffering.

I say that there is a living reality, an immortality, an eternity that cannot be described; it can be understood only in the fullness of your own individual action, not as a part of a structure, not as a part of a social, political, or religious machine. Therefore you must experience true individuality before you can understand what is true. As long as you do not act from that eternal source, there must be conflict; there must be division and continual strife.

Now each of us knows conflict, struggle, sorrow, lack of harmony. These are the elements that largely make up our lives, and from them we try, consciously or unconsciously, to escape. But few know for themselves the cause of conflict. Intellectually they may know the cause, but that knowledge is merely superficial. To know the cause is to be aware of it with both mind and heart.

Since few are aware of the deep cause of their suffering, they feel the desire to escape from the suffering, and this desire for escape has created and vitalized our moral, social, and religious systems. Here I have not time to go into details, but if you will think the matter over, you will see that our religious systems throughout the world are based on this idea of postponement and evasion, this searching for mediators and comforters. Because we are not responsible for our own acts, because we are seeking escape from our suffering, we create systems and authorities which will give us comfort and shelter.

What, then, is the cause of conflict? Why does one suffer? Why does one have to struggle ceaselessly? To me, conflict is the impeded flow of spontaneous action, of harmonious thought and feeling. When thought and emotion are inharmonious, there is conflict in action; that is, when mind and heart are in a state of discord, they create an impediment to the expression of harmonious action, and hence conflict. Such impediment to harmonious action is caused by the desire to escape, by the continual avoidance of facing life wholly, by meeting life always with the weight of tradition—be it religious, political, or social. This incapacity to face experience in its completeness creates conflict, and the desire to escape from it.

If you consider your thoughts and the acts springing from them, you will see that where there is the desire to escape there must be the search for security; because you find conflict in life with all its actions, its affections, its thoughts, you want to escape from that conflict to a satisfactory security, to a permanency. So your whole action is based on this desire for security. But actually, there is no security in life—neither physical nor intellectual, neither emotional nor spiritual. If you feel you are secure, you can never find that living reality; yet most of you are seeking security.

Some of you are seeking physical security through wealth, comfort, and the power over others that wealth gives you; you are interested in social differences and social privileges that assure you of a position from which you derive satisfaction. Physical security is a crude form of security, but since it has been impossible for the majority of mankind to attain that security, man has turned to the subtle form of security which he calls spiritual or religious. Because of the desire to escape from conflict, you seek and establish security—physical or spiritual. The longing for physical security shows itself in the desire to have a substantial bank account, a good position, the desire to be considered somebody in the town, the striving for degrees and titles and all such meaningless stupidities.

Then some of you become dissatisfied with physical security and turn to security of a more subtle form. It is security still, but merely a little less obvious, and you call it spiritual. But I see no real difference between the two. When you are satiated with physical security or when you cannot attain it, you turn to what you call spiritual security. And when you turn to that, you establish and vitalize those things which you call religion and organized spiritual beliefs. Because you seek security you establish a form of religion, a system of philosophical thought in which you are caught, to which you become a slave. Therefore, from my point of view, religions with all their intermediaries, their ceremonies, their priests, destroy creative understanding and pervert judgment.

One form of religious security is the belief in reincarnation, the belief in future lives, with all that that belief implies. I say that when a man is caught up in any belief he cannot know the fullness of life. A man who lives fully is acting from that source in which there is no reaction, but only action; but the man who is seeking security, escape, must hold to a belief because from that he derives continual support and encouragement for his lack of comprehension.

Then there is the security created by man in the idea of God. Many people ask me whether I believe in God, whether there is a God. You cannot discuss it. Most of our conceptions of God, of reality, of truth, are merely speculative imitations. Therefore they are utterly false, and all our religions are based on such falsities. A man who has lived all his life in a prison can only speculate about freedom; a man who has never experienced the ecstasy of freedom cannot know freedom. So it is of little avail to discuss God, truth; but if you have the intelligence, the intensity to destroy the barriers around you, then you will know for yourself the fulfillment of life. You will then no longer be a slave in a social or religious system.

Again, there is the security through service. That is, you like to lose yourself in the bog of activity, in work. Through this activity, this security, you seek to escape from facing your own incessant struggles.

So security is but escape. And since most people are trying to escape, they have made themselves into machines of habit in order to avoid conflict. They create religious beliefs, ideas; they worship the image of an imitation which they call God; they try to forget their inability to face the struggle by losing themselves in work. All these are ways of escape.

Now in order to safeguard security, you create authority. Isn't that so? To receive comfort, you must have someone or some system to give you comfort. To have security, there must be a person, an idea, a belief, a tradition, that gives you the assurance of security. So in our attempt to find security, we set up an authority and become slaves to that authority. In our search for security we set up religious ideals that we, in our fear, have created; we seek security through priests or spiritual guides whom we call teachers or masters. Or, again, we seek our authority in the power of tradition—social, economic, or political.

We ourselves, individually, have established these authorities. They did not come into being spontaneously. Through centuries we have been establishing them, and our minds have become crippled, perverted through their influence.

Or, suppose that we have discarded external authorities; then we have developed an inner authority which we call intuitional, spiritual authority—but which, to me, differs little from the external. That is, when the mind is caught up in authority—whether external or inner—it cannot be free, and therefore it cannot know true discernment. Hence, where there is authority born of the search for security, in that authority are the roots of egotism.

Now what have we done? Out of our weakness, our desire for power, our search for security, we have established spiritual authorities. And in this security, which we call immortality, we want to dwell eternally. If you look at that desire calmly, discerningly, you will see that it is nothing but a refined form of egotism. Where there is a division of thought, where there is the idea of 'I', the idea of 'mine' and 'yours', there cannot be completeness in action, and therefore there cannot be the understanding of living reality.

But—and I hope you understand this—that living reality, that totality, expresses itself in the action of individuality. I have explained what I mean by individuality: the state in which action takes place through understanding, liberated from all standards—social, economic, or spiritual. That is what I call true individuality, because it is action born of the fullness of understanding, whereas egotism has its roots in security, in tradition, in belief. Therefore action induced by egotism is ever incomplete, is ever bound up with ceaseless struggle, with suffering and pain.

These are a few of the impediments and hindrances that prevent man from realizing that supreme reality. That living reality you can understand only when you have freed yourself from these hindrances. The freedom of completeness is not in the escape from bondage, but in the understanding of action, which is the harmony of mind and heart.

Let me explain this more clearly. Most thinking people are intellectually aware of many hindrances. For instance, if you consider such securities as wealth, which you accumulate as a protection, or spiritual ideas in which you try to take shelter, you will see their utter futility.

Now if you examine these securities, you may intellectually see their falseness; but to me, that intellectual consciousness of impediment is not full awareness at all. It is merely an intellectual conception, not a full consciousness. Full consciousness exists only when you are aware, both emotionally and mentally, of these hindrances. If you are thinking of these hindrances now, you are probably considering them only intellectually, and you say, "Tell me a way by which I can get rid of these impediments." That is, you are merely trying to conquer impediments, and thereby you are creating another set of resistances. I hope I have made this clear. I can tell you that security is futile, that it has no significance, and you may intellectually admit this; but as you have been accustomed to struggle for security, when you go from here you will merely continue that struggle, but now, against security; thereby you merely seek a new way, a new method, a new technique, which is but a renewed desire for security in another form.

To me there is no such thing as a technique for living, a technique for the realization of truth. If there were such a technique for you to learn, you would merely be enslaved by another system.

The realization of truth comes only when there is completeness of action without effort. And the cessation of effort comes through the awareness of hindrances—not when you try to conquer them. That is, when you are fully conscious, fully aware in your heart and mind, when you are aware with your whole being, then through that awareness you will be free from hindrances. Experiment and you will see. Everything that you have conquered has enslaved you. Only when you have understood an impediment with your whole being, only when you have really understood the illusion of security, you will no longer struggle against it. But if you are only intellectually conscious of hindrances, then you will continue to struggle against them.

Your conception of life is based on this principle. Your striving for spiritual achievement, spiritual growth, is the outcome of your desire for further securities, further aggrandizement, further glory, and hence this continual and ceaseless struggle.

So I say, do not seek a way, a method. There is no method, no way to truth. Do not seek a way, but become aware of the impediments. Awareness is not merely intellectual; it is both mental and emotional; it is completeness of action. Then, in that flame of awareness, all these impediments fall away because you penetrate them. Then you can perceive directly, without choice, that which is true. Your action will then be born out of completeness, not out of the incompleteness of security; and in that completeness, in that harmony of mind and heart, is the realization of the eternal.

July 2, 1933

Second Talk at Alpino

Friends,

Today I am going to talk about what is called evolution. It is a subject difficult to discuss, and you may misunderstand what I am going to say. If you don't quite understand me, please ask me questions afterwards.

To most of us the idea of evolution implies a series of achievements, that is, achievements born of continual choice between what we call the unessential and the essential. It implies leaving the unessential and moving towards the essential. This series of continual achievements resulting from choice we call evolution. Our whole structure of thought is based on this idea of advancement and spiritual attainment, on the idea of growing more and more into the essential, as the result of continual choice. So then, we think of action as merely a series of achievements, don't we?

Now when we consider growth or evolution as a series of achievements, naturally our actions are never complete; they are always growing from the lower to the higher, always climbing, advancing. Therefore, if we live under that conception, our action enslaves us; our action is a constant, ceaseless, infinite effort, and that effort is always turned toward a security. Naturally, when there is this search for security, there is fear, and this fear creates the continual consciousness of what we call the 'I'. Isn't that so? The minds of most of us are caught up in this idea of achievement, attainment, climbing higher and higher, that is, in the idea of choosing between the essential and the unessential. And since this choice, this advancement which we call action, is but a ceaseless struggle, a continual effort, our lives are also a ceaseless effort and not a free, spontaneous flow of action.

I want to differentiate between action and achievement or attainment. Achievement is a finality, whereas action, to me, is infinite. You will understand that distinction as I continue. But first, let us understand that this is what we mean by evolution: a continual movement through choice, towards what we call the essential, ever pursuing greater and greater achievement.

The highest bliss—and to me this is not a mere theory—is to live without effort. Now I am going to explain what I mean by effort. For most of you, effort is but choice. You live by choice; you have to choose. But why do you choose? Why is there a necessity that urges you, impels you, forces you to choose? I say that this necessity for choice exists as long as one is conscious of emptiness or loneliness within oneself; that incompleteness forces you to choose, to make an effort.

Now the question is not how to fill that emptiness, but rather, what is the cause of that emptiness. To me, emptiness is action born of choice, in search of gain. Emptiness results when action is born of choice. And when there is emptiness, the question arises, "How can I fill that void? How can I get rid of that loneliness, that feeling of incompleteness?" To me, it is not a question of filling the void, for you can never fill it. Yet that is what most people are trying to do. Through sensation, excitement, or pleasure, through tenderness or forgetfulness, they are trying to fill that void, to lessen that feeling of emptiness. But they will never fill that emptiness, because they are trying to fill it with action born of choice.

Emptiness exists as long as action is based on choice, on like and dislike, attraction and repulsion. You choose because you don't like this and you like that; you are not satisfied with this but you want to satisfy yourself with that. Or you are afraid of something and run away from it. For most people action is based on attraction and repulsion, and therefore on fear.

Now what happens when you discard this and choose that? You are basing your action merely on attraction or repulsion, and thereby you are creating an opposite. Hence there is this continual choice which implies effort. As long as you make a choice, as long as choice exists, there must be duality. You may think that you have chosen the essential; but because your choice is born out of attraction and repulsion, want and fear, it merely creates another unessential.

That is what your life is. One day you want this—you choose it because you like it and want it because it gives you joy and satisfaction. The next day you are surfeited with it; it means nothing more to you, and you discard it in order to choose something else. So your choice is based on continuous sensation; you choose through the consciousness of duality, and this choice merely perpetuates the opposites.

As long as you choose between opposites, there is no discernment, and hence there must be effort, ceaseless effort, continual opposites and duality. Your choice, therefore, is ceaseless, and your effort is continuous. Your action is always finite, always in terms of achievement, and hence that emptiness which you feel will always exist. But if the mind is free of choice, if it has the capacity to discern, then action is infinite.

I shall explain this again. As I have said, if you say, "I want this thing," in that choosing you have created an opposite. Again, after that choice you create another opposite, and so you go on from one opposite to another through a process of continual effort. That process is your life, and in that there is ceaseless struggle and pain, conflict and suffering. If you realize that, if you really feel with your whole being—that is, emotionally as well as mentally—the futility of choice, then you no longer choose; then there is discernment; then there is intuitive response which is free from choice, and that is awareness.

If you are aware that your choice born of opposites but creates another opposite, then you perceive what is true. But most of you have not the intensity of desire nor the awareness, because you want the opposite, because you want sensation. Therefore you never attain discernment; you never attain that rich, full awareness that liberates the mind from opposites. In that freedom from opposites, action is no longer an achievement, but a fulfillment; it is born of discernment which is infinite. Then action springs from your own fullness, and in such action there is no choice and hence no effort.

To know such fullness, such reality, you must be in a state of intense awareness, which you can attain only when you are faced by a crisis. Most of you are faced by some kind of crisis, with regard to money, or people, or love, or death; and when you are caught up in such a crisis you have to choose, to decide. How do you decide? Your decision springs from fear, want, sensation. So you are merely postponing; you are choosing what is convenient, what is pleasant, and therefore you are merely creating another shadow through which you have to pass. Only when you feel the absurdity of your present existence, feel it not just intellectually, but with your whole heart and mind—when you really feel the absurdity of this continual choice—then out of that awareness is born discernment. Then you do not choose: you act. It is easy to give examples, but I shall give none, for they are often confusing.

So to me, awareness does not result from the struggle to be aware; it comes of its own accord when you are conscious with your whole being, when you realize the futility of choice. At present you choose between two things, two courses of action; you make a choice between this and that; one you understand, the other you do not. With the result of such choice, you hope to fill your life. You act according to your wants, your desires. Naturally, when that desire is fulfilled, action has come to an end. Then, since you are still lonely, you look for another action, another fulfillment. Each one of you is faced with a duality in action, a choice between doing this or that; but when you are aware of the futility of choice, when you are aware with your whole being, without effort, then you will truly discern.

You can test this only when you are really in a crisis; you cannot test it intellectually, when sitting at your ease and imagining a mental conflict. You can learn its truth only when you are face to face with an insistent demand for choice, when you have to make a decision, when your whole being demands action. If in that moment you realize with your whole being, if in that moment you are aware of the futility of choice, then out of that comes the flower of intuition, the flower of discernment. Action born of that is infinite; then action is life itself. Then there is no division between action and actor; all is continuous. There is no temporary fulfillment which is soon over.

Question: Please explain what you mean by saying that self-discipline is useless. What do you mean by self-discipline?

KRISHNAMURTI: If you have understood what I have been saying, you will see the futility of self-discipline. But I shall explain this again, and try to make it clear.

Why do you think that you must discipline yourself? To what do you want to discipline yourself? When you say, "I must discipline myself," you hold before yourself a standard to which you think you must conform. Self-discipline exists as long as you want to fill the emptiness within you; it exists as long as you hold a certain description of what God is, what truth is, as long as you cherish certain sets of moral standards which you force yourself to accept as guides. That is, your action is regulated, controlled, by the desire to conform. But if action is born of discernment, then there is no discipline.

Please understand what I mean by discernment. Don't say, "I have learned to play the piano. Doesn't that involve discipline?" Or, "I have studied mathematics. Is not that discipline?" I am not talking about the study of technique, which cannot be called discipline. I am talking about conduct in life. Have I made that clear? I am afraid most of you have not understood this, for to be free of the idea of self-discipline is most difficult, since from childhood we have been slaves of discipline, of control. To get rid of the idea of discipline does not mean that you must go to the opposite, that you must be chaotic. What I say is that when there is discernment, there need be no self-discipline; then there is no self-discipline.

Most of you are caught up in the habit of discipline. First of all, you hold a mental picture of what is right, of what is true, of what good character should be. To this mental picture you try to fit your actions. You act merely according to a mental picture that you hold. As long as you have a preconceived idea of what is true—and most of you have this idea—you must act according to that. Most of you are unconscious that you are acting according to a pattern, but when you become aware that you are acting thus, then you no longer copy or imitate; then your own action reveals what is true.

You know, our physical training, our religious and moral training, tend to mold us after a pattern. From childhood, most of us have been trained to fit into a pattern—social, religious, economic—and most of us are unconscious of this. Discipline has become a habit, and you are unconscious of that habit. Only when you become aware that you are disciplining yourself to a pattern, will your action be born of discernment.

So first of all, you must realize why you discipline yourself, not why you should or should not discipline. What has happened to man through all the centuries of self-discipline? He has become more of a machine and less of a human being; he has merely attained greater skill in imitation, in being a machine. Self-discipline, that is, conforming to a mental picture established either by you yourself or by someone else, does not bring about harmony; it only creates chaos.

What happens when you attempt to discipline yourself? Your action is ever creating emptiness within you because you are trying to fit your actions to a pattern. But if you become aware that you are acting according to a pattern—a pattern of your own or some one else's making—then you will perceive the falseness of imitation and your action then will be born of discernment, that is, from the harmony of your mind and heart.

Now, mentally you want to act in a certain way, but emotionally you do not desire the same end, and hence conflict results. In order to conquer that conflict you seek security in authority, and that authority becomes your pattern. Hence, you do not act what you really feel and think; your action is motivated by fear, by desire for security, and from such action is born self-discipline. Do you understand?

You know, understanding with the whole intensity of your being is a very different thing from understanding merely intellectually. When people say, "I understand," they usually understand only intellectually. But intellectual analysis will not free you from this habit of self-discipline. When you are acting, do not say, "I must see if this act is born of self-discipline, if it is according to a pattern." Such an attempt only prevents true action. But if, in your acting, you are aware of the imitation, then your action will be spontaneous.

As I have said, if you examine every act to determine whether it is born of self-discipline, of imitation, your action becomes more and more limited; then there is hindrance, resistance. You do not truly act at all. But if you become aware, with your whole being, of the futility of imitation, the futility of conformity, then your action will not be imitative, hampered, bound. The more you analyze your action, the less you act. Isn't that so? To me, analysis of action does not free the mind of imitation, which is conformity, self-discipline; what frees the mind of imitation is being aware with your whole being in your action.

To me, self-analysis frustrates action, it destroys complete living. Perhaps you do not agree with this, but please listen to what I have to say before you decide whether or not you agree. I say that this continuous process of self-analysis, which is self-discipline, constantly puts a limitation on the free flow of life, which is action. For self-discipline is based on the idea of achievement, not on the idea of the completeness of action. Do you see the distinction? In the one there is a series of achievements and therefore always a finality; whereas in the other, action is born of discernment, and such action is harmonious and therefore infinite. Have I made this clear?

Watch yourself the next time you say, "I must not." Self-discipline, the "I must," the "I must not," is based on the idea of achievement. When you realize the futility of achievement—when you realize this with your whole being, emotionally as well as intellectually—then there is no longer an "I must" and an "I must not."

Now you are caught up in this attempt to conform to a picture in your mind, you have the habit of thinking "I must" or "I must not." Therefore, the next time you say this, become aware of yourself, and in that awareness you will discern what is true, and free yourself from the hindrance of "I must" and "I must not."

Question: You say that nobody can help anyone else. Why then are you going around the world addressing people?

KRISHNAMURTI: Need that be answered? It implies a great deal if you understand it. You know, most of us want to acquire wisdom or truth through another, through some outside agency. No one else can make you into an artist; only you yourself can do that. That is what I want to say: I can give you paint, brushes, and canvas, but you yourself have to become the artist, the painter. I cannot make you into one. Now in your attempts to become spiritual, most of you seek teachers, saviors, but I say that no one in the world can free you from the conflict of sorrow. Someone can give you the materials, the tools, but no one can give you that flame of creative living.

You know, we think in terms of technique, but technique does not come first. You must first have the flame of desire, and then technique follows. "But," you say, "let me learn. If I am taught the technique of painting, then I shall be able to paint." There are many books that describe the technique of painting, but merely learning technique will never make you a creative artist. Only when you stand entirely alone, without technique, without masters, only then can you find truth.

Let us understand this first of all. Now you are basing your ideas on conformity. You think that there is a standard, a way, by which you can find truth; but if you examine, you will discover that there is no path that leads to truth. In order to be led to truth, you must know what truth is, and your leader must know what it is. Isn't that so? I say that a man who teaches truth may have it, but if he offers to lead you to truth and you are led, then both are in illusion. How can you know truth if you are still held by illusion? If truth is there, it expresses itself. A great poet has the desire, the flame for creative writing, and he writes. If you have the desire, you learn the technique.

I feel that no one can lead another to truth, because truth is infinite; it is a pathless land, and no one can tell you how to find it. No one can teach you to be an artist; another can only give you the brushes and canvas and show you the colors to use. Nobody taught me, I assure you, nor have I learned what I am saying from books. But I have watched, I have struggled, and I have tried to find out. It is only when you are absolutely naked, free from all techniques, free from all teachers, that you find out.

July 4, 1933

Third Talk at Alpino

Friends,

In these talks I have been trying to show that where action involves effort, self-control—and I have explained what I mean by these terms—there must be diminution and limitation of life, but where action is effortless, spontaneous, there is completeness of life. What I say, however, concerns the fullness of life itself, not the chaos of misunderstood liberation. I shall again explain what I mean by effortless action.

When you are conscious of incompleteness, you have the desire to find a goal or an end which will be your authority, and thereby you hope to fill that emptiness, that incompleteness. Most of us are continually seeking a goal, an end, an image, an ideal for our comfort. We are ceaselessly working towards that goal because we are conscious of the struggle which arises from incompleteness. But if we understood incompleteness itself, then we would no longer seek a goal, which is but substitution.

To understand incompleteness and its cause you must find out why you seek a goal. Why do you work towards a goal? Why do you want to discipline yourself according to a pattern? Because the incompleteness, of which you are more or less conscious, gives rise to continued effort, continued struggle, from which the mind tries to escape by establishing the authority of a comforting ideal which it hopes will serve as a guide. Thereby action in itself has no significance; it becomes merely a stepping-stone towards an end, a goal. In your search for truth you use action merely as a means towards an end, and the significance of action is lost. You make a great effort to attain a goal, and the importance of your action lies in the end which it achieves—not in the action itself.

Most people are caught up in the search for reward, in the attempt to escape punishment. They are working for results; they are urged forward by a motive, and therefore their action cannot be complete. Most of you are caught in this prison of incompleteness, and therefore you have to become conscious of that prison.

If you don't understand what I mean, please interrupt me, and I shall explain again.

I say that you must become conscious that you are a prisoner; you must become aware that you are continually trying to escape from incompleteness and that your search for truth is but an escape. What you call the search for truth, for God, through self-discipline and achievement, is but an escape from incompleteness.

The cause of incompleteness is in the very search for attainment, but you are continually escaping from this cause. Action born of self-discipline, action born of fear or of the desire for achievement, is the cause of incompleteness. Now when you become aware that such action is itself the cause of incompleteness, you are freed of that incompleteness. The moment you become aware of poison, the poison ceases to be a problem to you. It is a problem only as long as you are unaware of its action in your life.

But most people do not know the cause of their incompleteness, and from this ignorance arises ceaseless effort. When they become aware of the cause—which is the search for achievement—then in that awareness there is completeness, completeness that demands no effort. In your action then there is no effort, no self-analysis, no discipline.

From incompleteness arises the search for comfort, for authority, and the attempt to reach this goal deprives action of its intrinsic significance. But when you become fully aware with your mind and your heart of the cause of incompleteness, then incompleteness ceases. Out of this awareness comes action that is infinite because it has significance in itself.

To put it differently, as long as mind and heart are caught up in want, in desire, there must be emptiness. You want things, ideas, persons, only when you are conscious of your own emptiness, and that wanting creates a choice. When there is craving there must be choice, and choice precipitates you into the conflict of experiences. You have the capacity to choose, and thereby you limit yourself by your choice. Only when the mind is free from choice is there liberation.

All want, all craving, is blinding, and your choice is born of fear, of the desire for consolation, comfort, reward, or as the result of cunning calculation. Because of the emptiness within you, there is want. Since your choice is always based on the idea of gain, there can be no true discernment, no true perception; there is only want. When you choose, as you do choose, your choice merely creates another set of circumstances which results in further conflict and choice. Your choice, which is born of limitation, sets up a further series of limitations, and these limitations create the consciousness which is the 'I', the ego. The multiplication of choice you call experiences. You look to these experiences to deliver you from bondage, but they can never deliver you from bondage because you think of experiences as a continual movement of acquisition.

Let me illustrate this by an example, which will perhaps convey my thought. Suppose that you lose by death someone whom you love very much. That death is a fact. Now at once you experience a sense of loss, a craving to be again near that person. You want your friend back, and since you cannot have him again, your mind creates or accepts an idea to satisfy that emotional craving.

The person whom you love has been taken from you. Then, because you suffer, because you are aware of an intense emptiness, a loneliness, you want to have your friend again. That is, you want to end your suffering, or put it aside, or forget it; you want to deaden the consciousness of that emptiness, which is hidden when you are with the friend whom you love. Your want arises from the desire for comfort; but since you cannot have the comfort of his presence, you think of some idea that may satisfy you—reincarnation, life after death, the unity of all life. In such ideas—I do not say that they are right or wrong, we will discuss them another time—in such ideas, I say, you take comfort. Because you cannot have the person whom you love, you take mental consolation in such ideas. That is, without true discernment, you accept any idea, any principle, that seems for the moment to satisfy you, to put aside that consciousness of emptiness which causes suffering.

So your action is based on the idea of consolation, on the idea of multiplication of experiences; your action is determined by choice which has its roots in want. But the moment you become aware with your mind and heart, with your whole being, of the futility of want, then emptiness ceases. Now you are only partly conscious of this emptiness, so you try to get satisfaction by reading novels, by losing yourself in the diversions that man has created in the name of civilization; and this search for sensation you call experience.

You must realize with your heart as well as with your mind that the cause of emptiness is craving, which results in choice, and prevents true discernment. When you become aware of this, there is then cessation of want.

As I have said, when one feels an emptiness, a want, one accepts without true discernment. And most of the actions that make up our lives are based on this feeling of want. We may think that our choices are based on reason, on discernment; we may think that we weigh possibilities and calculate chances before making a choice. Yet because there is in us a longing, a want, a craving, we cannot know true perception or discernment. When you realize this, when you become aware of it with your whole being, emotionally as well as with the mind, when you realize the futility of want, then want ceases; then you are freed from that feeling of emptiness. In that flame of awareness there is no discipline, no effort.

But we do not perceive this fully; we do not become aware, because we experience a pleasure in want, because we are continually hoping that the pleasure in want shall dominate the pain. We strive to attain the pleasure even though we know it is not free from pain. If you become fully aware of the whole significance of this, you have wrought a miracle for yourself; then you will experience freedom from want, and therefore liberation from choice; then you will no longer be that limited consciousness, the 'I'.

Where there is dependency or the looking to another for support, for encouragement, where there is reliance on another, there is loneliness. In your looking to another for fulfillment, for happiness or well-being, in your looking to another for consolation, in your dependence on any person or idea as an authority in matters of religion—in all this there is utter loneliness. Because you are thus dependent and hence lonely, you seek comfort, or a way of escape; you seek authority and support from another to give you consolation. But when you become aware of the falseness of all this, when you become aware with your heart as well as with your mind, then there is cessation of loneliness, for then you no longer rely on another for your happiness.

So where there is choice there can be no discernment, for discernment is choiceless. Where there is choice and the capacity to choose, there is only limitation. Only when choice ceases is there liberation, fullness, richness of action, which is life itself. Creation is choiceless, as life is choiceless, as understanding is choiceless. Likewise is truth; it is a continuous action, an ever-becoming, in which there is no choice. It is pure discernment.

Question: How can we get rid of incompleteness without forming some ideal of completeness? After the realization of completeness there may be no need for an ideal, but before the realization of completeness some ideal seems inevitable, although it will have to be provisional and will change according to the growth of understanding.

KRISHNAMURTI: Your very saying that you need an ideal in order to overcome incompleteness shows that you are merely trying to superimpose that ideal on incompleteness. That is what most of you are trying to do. It is only when you find out the cause of incompleteness and are aware of that cause that you become complete. But you do not find out the cause. You do not understand what I am saying, or rather, you understand only with your minds, only intellectually. Anyone can do that, but really to understand demands action.

Now you feel incompleteness, and therefore you seek an ideal, the ideal of completeness. That is, you are seeking an opposite to incompleteness, and in wanting that opposite you merely create another opposite. This may sound puzzling, but it is not. You are continually seeking what seems to you the essential. One day you think this essential; you choose it, strive for it, and possess it, but meanwhile it has already become the unessential. Now if the mind is free from all sense of duality, free from the idea of essential and nonessential, then you are not confronted by the problem of choice; then you act from the fullness of discernment, and you no longer seek the image of completeness.

Why do you cling to the ideal of freedom when you are in a prison? You create or invent that ideal of freedom because you cannot escape from your prison. So also with your ideals, your gods, your religions: they are the creation of the desire for escape into comfort. You yourself have made the world into a prison, a prison of suffering and conflict; and because the world is such a prison, you create an ideal god, an ideal freedom, an ideal truth. And these ideals, these opposites, are but attempts at emotional and mental escape. Your ideals are means of escape from the prison in which you are confined. But if you become conscious of that prison, if you become aware of the fact that you are trying to escape, then that awareness destroys the prison; then, instead of pursuing freedom, you will know freedom.

Freedom does not come to him who seeks freedom. Truth is not found by him who searches for truth. Only when you realize with your whole mind and heart the condition of the prison in which you live, when you realize the significance of that prison, only then are you free, naturally and without effort. This realization can come only when you are in a great crisis, but most of you try to avoid crises. Or, when you are confronted by a crisis, you at once seek comfort in the idea of religion, the idea of God, the idea of evolution; you turn to priests, to spiritual guides, for consolation; you seek diversion in amusements. All of these are but escapes from conflict. But if you really confront the crisis before you, if you realize the futility, the falseness of escape as a mere means of postponement of action, then in that awareness is born the flower of discernment.

So you must become aware in action, which will reveal the hidden pursuits of craving. But this awareness does not result from analysis. Analysis merely limits action. Have I answered that question?

Question: You have enumerated the successive steps of the process of creating authorities. Will you enumerate the steps of the inverse process, the process of liberating oneself from all authority?

KRISHNAMURTI: I am afraid the question is wrongly stated. You do not ask what creates authority, but how to free yourself from authority. Please, let me say this again: once you are aware of the cause of authority, you are free from that authority. The cause of the creation of authority is the important thing—not the steps leading to authority or the steps leading to the overthrow of authority.

Why do you create authority? What is the cause of your creating authority? It is, as I have said, the search for security, and I shall have to say this so often that it will become almost a formula for you. Now you are searching for a security in which you think you will need to make no effort, where you will not need to struggle with your neighbor. But you will not attain this state of security by searching for it. There is a state which is fulfillment, which is the assurance of bliss, a state in which you act from life; but that state you attain only when you no longer seek security. Only when you realize with your whole being that there is no such thing as security in life, only when you are free from this constant search, can there be fulfillment.

So you create authority in the shape of ideals, in the shape of religious, social, economic systems, all based on the search for individual security. And you yourself are therefore responsible for the creation of authority, to which you have become a slave. Authority does not exist by itself. It has no existence apart from him who creates it. You have created it, and until you are aware with your whole being of the cause of its creation, you will be a slave to it. And you can become aware of that cause only when you are acting, not through self-analysis or intellectual discussion.

Question: I do not want a set of rules for being "aware," but I should very much like to understand awareness. Must not great effort be made to be aware of each thought as it arises, before one arrives at the state of effortlessness?

KRISHNAMURTI: Why do you want to be aware? What is the need of being aware? If you are perfectly satisfied as you are, continue in that way. When you say, "I must be aware," you are merely making awareness another end to be attained, and by that means you will never become aware. You have disposed of one set of rules, and now you are creating another set, instead of trying to be aware when you are in a great crisis, when you are suffering.

As long as you seek comfort and security, as long as you are at your ease, you merely consider the matter intellectually, and say, "I must be aware." But when in the midst of suffering you try to find out the significance of suffering, when you do not try to escape from it, when in a crisis you arrive at a decision—not born of choice, but of action itself—then you really become aware. But when you are trying to escape, your attempt to be aware is futile. You don't really want to be aware, you don't want to discover the cause of suffering; your whole concern is with escape.

You come here and listen to my telling you that to escape from conflict is futile. Yet you desire to escape. So you really mean, "How can we do both?" Surreptitiously, cunningly, in the back of your minds you want the religions, the gods, the means of escape that you have cleverly invented and built up through the centuries. Yet you listen to me when I say that you will never find truth through the guidance of another, through escape, through the search for security, which results only in eternal loneliness. Then you ask, "How are we to attain both? How are we to compromise between escape and awareness?" You have confused the two and you seek a compromise; therefore you ask, "How am I to become aware?" But if, instead of this, you frankly say to yourself, "I want to escape, I want comfort," then you will find exploiters to give you what you want. You yourself have created exploiters because of your desire to escape. Find out what you want, become aware of what you crave; then the question of awareness will not arise. Because you are lonely you want consolation. But if you seek consolation, be honest, be frank, be aware of what you want and conscious that you are seeking it. Then we can understand the matter.

I can tell you that from dependence on another, from the search for comfort, results eternal loneliness. I can make this plain to you, and you, in turn, may agree or disagree. I can show you that in want there is eternal emptiness and nothingness. But you derive satisfaction from sensation, from pleasure, from passing joys that fill your wants, your desires. Then, when I show you the falsity of want, you do not know how to act. So, as a compromise, you begin to discipline yourself, and this attempt to discipline destroys your creative living. When you really perceive the absurdity, the emptiness of want then that want falls away from you without your effort. But as long as you are enslaved to the idea of choice, you have to make an effort, and from this arises, as an opposite, the desire for awareness, the problem of living without effort.

Question: You speak to man, but man has first been a child. How can we educate a child without discipline?

KRISHNAMURTI: Do you agree that discipline is futile? Do you feel the futility of discipline?

Comment: But you start from the point at which man is already man. I want to begin with the child as a child.

KRISHNAMURTI: We are all children; all of us have to begin, not with others, but with ourselves. When we do this, then we shall find out the right way with children.

You cannot begin with children because you are the parents of children, you must begin with yourselves. Say that you have a child. You believe in authority and train him according to that belief; but if you understood the futility of authority, you would liberate him from it. So first of all, you yourselves have to find out the significance of authority in your life.

What I say is very simple. I say that authority is created when the mind seeks comfort in security. Therefore, begin with yourselves. Begin with your own garden, not with someone else's. You want to create a new system of thought, a new system of ideas, a new system of behavior; but you cannot create something new by reforming something old. You must break away from the old in order to begin the new; but you can break away from the old only when you understand the cause of the old.

July 6, 1933

Second Talk at Stresa

Question: It has been said that you are really enchaining the individual, not liberating him. Is this true?

KRISHNAMURTI: After I have answered this question, you yourself can find out whether I am liberating the individual or enchaining him.

Let us take the individual as he is. What do we mean by the individual? A person who is controlled and dominated by his fears, his disappointments, his cravings, which create a certain set of circumstances that enslave him and force him to fit into a social structure. That is what we mean by an individual. Through our fears, our superstitions, our vanities and our cravings, we have created a certain set of circumstances to which we have become slaves. We have almost lost our individuality, our uniqueness. When you examine your action in daily life, you will see that it is but a reaction to a set of standards, a series of ideas.

Please follow what I am saying, and do not say that I urge man to free himself so that he can do what he likes—so that he can bring about ruin and disaster.

First of all I want to make it clear that we are but reactions to a set of standards and ideas which we have created through our suffering and fear, through our ignorance, our desire for possession. This reaction we call individual action, but to me, it is not action at all. It is a constant reaction in which there is no positive action.

I shall put it differently. At present, man is but the emptiness of reaction, nothing more. He does not act from the fullness of his nature, from his completeness, from his wisdom; he acts merely from a reaction. I maintain that chaos, utter destruction, is taking place in the world because we are not acting from our fullness, but from our fear, from the lack of understanding. Once we become aware of the fact that what we call individuality is but a series of reactions in which there is no fullness of action; once we understand that that individuality is but a series of reactions in which there is a continual emptiness, a void, then we will act harmoniously.

How are you going to find out the value of a certain standard that you hold? You will not find out by acting in opposition to that standard, but by weighing and balancing what you really think and feel against what that standard demands. You will find that the standard demands certain actions, while your own instinctive action tends in another direction. Then what are you going to do? If you do what your instinct demands, your action will lead to chaos, because our instincts have been perverted through centuries of what we call education—education that is entirely false. Your own instinct demands one type of action, but society, which we, individually, have created through centuries, society to which we have become slaves, demands another kind of action. And when you act in accordance with the set of standards demanded by society you are not acting through the fullness of comprehension.

By really pondering over the demands of your instincts and the demands of society, you will find out how you can act in wisdom. That action liberates the individual; it does not enchain him. But the liberation of the individual demands great earnestness, great searching into the depth of action; it is not the result of action born of a momentary impulse.

So you have to recognize what you now are. However well educated you may be, you are only partly a true individual; the greater part of you is determined by the reaction to society, which you have created. You are but a cog in a tremendous machine which you call society, religion, politics, and as long as you are such a cog, your action is born of limitation; it leads only to disharmony and conflict. It is your action that has resulted in our present chaos. But if you acted out of your own fullness you would discover the true worth of society and the instinct causing your action; then your action would be harmonious, not a compromise.

First of all, then, you must become conscious of the false values which have been established through the centuries and to which you have become a slave; you must become conscious of values, to find out whether they are false or true, and this you must do for yourself. No one can do it for you—and herein lies the greatness and glory of man. Thus, by discovering the right value of standards, you liberate the mind from the false standards handed down through ages. But such liberation does not mean impetuous, instinctive action leading to chaos; it means action born of the full harmony of mind and heart.

Question: You have never lived the life of a poor man; you have always had the invisible security of your rich friends. You speak of the absolute giving up of every kind of security in life, but millions of people live without such security. You say that one cannot realize that which one has not experienced; consequently, you cannot know what poverty and physical insecurity really are.

KRISHNAMURTI: This is a question frequently asked me; I have often answered it before, but I shall answer it again.

First of all, when I speak of security I mean the security that the mind establishes for its own comfort. Physical security, some degree of physical comfort, man must have in order to exist. So do not confuse the two. Now each one of you is seeking not only a physical but also a mental security, and in that search you are establishing authority. When you understand the falsity of the security which you seek, then that security ceases to have any value; then you realize that although there must be a minimum of physical security, even that security can have but little value. Then you no longer concentrate your whole mind and heart on the constant acquisition of physical security.

I shall put it differently, and I hope it will be clear; but whatever one says can be easily misunderstood. One has to pass through the illusion of words in order to discover the thought that another wishes to convey. I hope you will try to do that during this talk.

I say that your pursuit of virtue, which is merely the opposite of that which you call vice, is but a search for security. Because you have a set of standards in your mind, you pursue virtue for the satisfaction that you get from it; for to you virtue is merely a means of acquiring security. You do not try to acquire virtue for its own intrinsic value, but for what it gives you in return. Your actions, therefore, are concerned merely with the pursuit of virtue; in themselves they are valueless. Your mind is constantly seeking virtue in order to obtain through it something else, and thus your action is always a stepping-stone to some further acquisition.

Perhaps most of you here are seeking a spiritual rather than a physical security. You seek spiritual security either because you already possess physical security—a large bank account, a secure position, a high place in society—or because you cannot attain physical security and therefore turn to spiritual security as a substitute. But to me there is no such thing as security, a shelter in which your mind and emotion can take comfort. When you realize this, when your mind is free from the idea of comfort, then you will not cling to security as you do now.

You ask me how I can understand poverty when I have not experienced it. The answer is simple. Since I am seeking neither physical nor mental security, it matters nothing to me whether I am given food by my friends, or work for it. It is of very little importance to me whether I travel or do not travel. If I am asked, I come; if I am not asked, it makes little difference to me. Because I am rich in myself (and I do not say this with conceit), because I do not seek security, I have few physical needs. But if I were seeking physical comfort, I would emphasize the physical needs, I would emphasize poverty.

Let us look at this differently. Most of our quarrels throughout the world concern possession and nonpossession; they are concerned with the acquisition of this and the protection of that. Now why do we lay such emphasis on possession? We do it because possession gives us power, pleasure, satisfaction; it gives us a certain assurance of individuality and affords us scope for our action, our ambition. We lay emphasis on possession because of what we derive from it.

But if we become rich in ourselves, then life will flow through us harmoniously; then possession or poverty will no longer be of great importance to us. Because we lay emphasis on possession, we lose the richness of life; whereas, if we were complete in ourselves, we should find out the intrinsic value of all things and live in the harmony of mind and heart.

Question: It has been said that you are the manifestation of the Christ in our times. What have you to say to this? If it is true, why do you not talk of love and compassion?

KRISHNAMURTI: My friends, why do you ask such a question? Why do you ask whether I am the manifestation of Christ? You ask because you want me to assure you that I am, or that I am not the Christ, so that you can judge what I say according to the standard that you have. There are two reasons why you ask this question: you think that you know what the Christ is, and therefore you say, "I will act accordingly"; or, if I say that I am the Christ, then you think that what I say must be true. I am not evading the question, but I am not going to tell you who I am. That is of very little importance, and, moreover, how can you know what or who I am even if I tell you? Such speculation is of very little importance. So let us not be concerned about who I am, but let us look at the reason for your asking this question.

You want to know who I am because you are uncertain about yourselves. I am not saying whether I am or whether I am not the Christ. I am not giving you a categorical answer, because to me the question is not important. What is important is whether what I am saying is true, and this does not depend on what I am. It is something that you can find out only by freeing yourselves from your prejudices and standards. You cannot attain real freedom from prejudice by looking towards an authority, by working towards an end, yet that is what you are doing; surreptitiously, sedulously, you are searching for an authority, and in that search you are but making yourselves into imitative machines.

You ask why I do not speak of love, of compassion. Does the flower talk about its perfume? It simply is. I have spoken about love; but to me the important thing is not to discuss what love is or what compassion is, but to free the mind from all the limitations that prevent the natural flow of what we call love and compassion. What love is, what compassion is, you yourself will know when your mind and heart are free from the limitation which we call egotism, self-consciousness; then you will know without asking, without discussion. You question me now because you think that then you can act according to what you discover from me, that then you will have an authority for your action.

So I say again, the real question is not why I do not talk about love and compassion, but rather, what prevents the natural harmonious living of man, the fullness of action which is love. I have talked about the many barriers that prevent our natural living, and I have explained that such living does not mean instinctive, chaotic action, but rich, full living. Rich, natural living has been prevented through centuries of conformity, through centuries of what we call education, which has been but a process of turning out so many human machines. But when you understand the cause of these hindrances and barriers which you have created for yourself through fear in your search for security, then you free yourself from them; then there is love. But this is a realization that cannot be discussed. We do not discuss the sunshine. It is there; we feel its warmth and perceive its penetrating beauty. Only when the sun is hidden do we discuss the sunshine. And so with love and compassion.

Question: You have never given us a clear conception of the mystery of death and of the life after death, yet you constantly speak of immortality. Surely you believe in life after death?

KRISHNAMURTI: You want to know categorically whether there is or is not annihilation after death: that is the wrong approach to the problem. I hope you will follow what I say, for otherwise my answer will not be clear to you, and you will think that I have not answered your question. Please interrupt me if you do not understand.

What do you mean when you speak of death? Your sorrow for the death of another, and the fear of your own death. Sorrow is awakened by the death of another. When your friend dies, you become conscious of loneliness because you have relied on him, because you and he have complemented each other, because you have understood each other, supported and encouraged each other. So when your friend is gone, you are conscious of emptiness; you want that person back to fill the part in your life that he filled before.

You want your friend again, but since you cannot have him, you turn to various intellectual ideas, to various emotional concepts, which you think will give you satisfaction. You look to such ideas for consolation, for comfort, instead of finding out the cause of your suffering and freeing yourself eternally from the idea of death. You turn to a series of consolations and satisfactions which gradually diminish your intense suffering; yet, when death returns, you experience the same suffering over again.

Death comes and causes you intense sorrow. One whom you greatly love has gone, and his absence accentuates your loneliness. But instead of seeking the cause of that loneliness, you try to escape from it through mental and emotional satisfactions. What is the cause of that loneliness? Reliance on another, the incompleteness of your own life, the continual attempt to avoid life. You do not want to discover the true value of facts; instead, you attribute a value to that which is but an intellectual concept. Thus, the loss of a friend causes you suffering because that loss makes you fully conscious of your loneliness.

Then there is the fear of one's own death. I want to know if I shall live after my death, if I shall reincarnate, if there is a continuance for me in some form. I am concerned with these hopes and fears because I have known no rich moment during my life; I have known no single day without conflict, no single day in which I have felt complete, as a flower. Therefore I have this intense desire for fulfillment, a desire that involves the idea of time.

What do we mean when we talk about the 'I'? You are conscious of the 'I' only when you are caught in the conflict of choice, in the conflict of duality. In this conflict you become conscious of yourself, and you identify yourself with the one or the other, and from this continual identification results the idea of 'I'. Please consider this with your heart and mind, for it is not a philosophical idea which can be simply accepted or rejected.

I say that through the conflict of choice, the mind has established memory, many layers of memory; it has become identified with these layers, and it calls itself the 'I', the ego. And hence arises the question, "What will happen to me when I die? Shall I have an opportunity to live again? Is there a future fulfillment?" To me, these questions are born of craving and confusion. What is important is the freeing of the mind from this conflict of choice, for only when you have thus freed yourself can there be immortality.

For most people the idea of immortality is the continuance of the 'I', without end, through time. But I say such a concept is false. "Then," you answer, "there must be total annihilation." I say that is not true either. Your belief that total annihilation must follow the cessation of the limited consciousness we call the 'I', is false. You cannot understand immortality that way, for your mind is caught up in opposites. Immortality is free from all opposites; it is harmonious action in which the mind is utterly freed from conflict of the 'I'.

I say there is immortality, immortality which transcends all our conceptions, theories, and beliefs. Only when you have full individual comprehension of opposites, will you be free from opposites. As long as the mind creates conflict through choice, there must be consciousness as memory which is the 'I', and it is the 'I' which fears death and longs for its own continuance. Hence there is not the capacity to understand the fullness of action in the present, which is immortality.

A certain Brahmin, according to an old Indian legend, decided to give away some of his possessions in the performance of a religious sacrifice. Now this Brahmin had a little son who watched his father and plied him with many questions until the father became annoyed. At last the son asked, "To whom are you going to give me?" And the father replied in anger, "I shall give you to Death." Now it was held in ancient times that whatever was said had to be carried out;

so the Brahmin had to send his son to Death, in accordance with his rashly spoken words. As the boy made his way to the house of Death, he listened to what many teachers had to say about death and life after death. When he arrived at the house of Death, he found that Death was absent; so he waited for three days without food, in accordance with the ancient custom which forbade eating in the absence of the host. When at last Death arrived, he apologized humbly for having kept a Brahmin waiting, and as a token of regret he granted the boy any three wishes that he might desire.

For his first wish the boy asked to be returned to his father; for his second, he requested that he be instructed in certain ceremonial rites. But the boy's third wish was not a request but a question: "Tell me, Death," he asked, "the truth about annihilation. Of the teachers to whom I have listened on my way here, some say that there is annihilation; others say that there is continuity. Tell me, O Death, what is true?" "Do not ask me that question," replied Death. But the boy insisted. So in answer to the question, Death taught the boy the meaning of immortality. Death did not tell him whether there is continuity, whether there is life after death, or whether there is annihilation; Death taught him rather the meaning of immortality.

You want to know whether there is continuity. Some scientists are now proving that there is. Religions affirm it, many people believe it, and you may believe it if you choose. But to me, it is of little importance. There will always be conflict between life and death. Only when you know immortality is there neither beginning nor end; only then does action imply fulfillment, and only then is it infinite. So I say again, the idea of reincarnation is of little importance. In the 'I' there is nothing lasting; the 'I' is composed of a series of memories involving conflict. You cannot make that 'I' immortal. Your whole basis of thought is a series of achievements and therefore a continuous effort, a continuous limitation of consciousness. Yet you hope in that way to realize immortality, to feel the ecstasy of the infinite.

I say that immortality is reality. You cannot discuss it; you can know it in your action, action born of the fullness, the richness, of wisdom; but that fullness, that richness, you cannot attain by listening to a spiritual guide or by reading a book of instruction. Wisdom comes only when there is fullness of action, when there is complete awareness of your whole being in action; then you will see that all the books and teachers that pretend to guide you to wisdom can teach you nothing. You can know that which is immortal, everlasting, only when your mind is free from all sense of individuality which is created by the limited consciousness, which is the 'I'.

Question: What are the causes of the misunderstanding which makes us ask you questions instead of acting and living?

KRISHNAMURTI: It is good to question, but how do you receive the answers? You ask a question, and receive a reply. But what do you do with that reply? You have asked me what there is after death, and I have given you my answer. Now what will you do with that answer? Will you store it in some corner of your brain and let it remain there? You have intellectual granaries in which you collect ideas that you do not understand, but which you hope will serve you in trouble and sorrow. But if you understand, if you give yourself heart and mind to what I say, then you will act; then action will be born of your own fullness.

Now there are two ways of asking a question: you may ask a question when you are in the intensity of suffering, or you may ask a question intellectually, when you are bored and at your ease. One day you want to know intellectually; another day you ask because you suffer and want to know the reason for the suffering. You can really know only when you question in the intensity of suffering, when you do not desire to escape from suffering, when you meet it face to face; only then will you know the value of my answer, its human value for man.

Question: Exactly what do you mean by action without aim? If it is the immediate response of our whole being in which aim and action are one, how can all the action of our daily life be without aim?

KRISHNAMURTI: You yourself have given the answer to the question, but you have given it without understanding. What will you do in your daily life without an aim? In your daily life you may have a plan. But when you experience intense suffering, when you are caught in a great crisis that demands immediate decision, then you act without aim; then there is no motive in your action, because you are trying to find out the cause of suffering with your whole being. But most of you are not inclined to act fully. You are constantly trying to escape from suffering, you try to avoid suffering; you do not want to confront it.

I shall explain what I mean in another way. If you are a Christian, you look at life from a particular point of view; if you are a Hindu, you look at it from another angle. In other words, the background to your mind colors your view of life, and all that you perceive is seen only through that colored view. Thus you never see life as it really is; you look at it only through a screen of prejudice, and therefore your action must ever be incomplete, it must ever have a motive. But if your mind is free from all prejudice, then you meet life as it is; then you meet life fully, without the search for a reward or the attempt to escape from punishment.

Question: What is the relationship between technique and life, and why do most of us mistake the one for the other?

KRISHNAMURTI: Life, truth, is to be lived; but expression demands a technique. Now in order to paint, you need to learn a technique; but a great artist, if he felt the flame of creative impulse, would not be a slave to technique. If you are rich within yourself, your life is simple. But you want to arrive at that complete richness through such external means as the simplicity of dress, the simplicity of dwelling, through asceticism and self-discipline. In other words, the simplicity that results from inner richness you want to obtain by means of technique. There is no technique that will guide you to simplicity; there is no path that will lead you to the land of truth. When you understand that with your whole being, then technique will take its proper place in your life.

July 8, 1933

Fourth Talk at Alpino

Friends,

Before answering some of the questions that have been asked me, I shall give a brief talk concerning memory and time.

When you meet an experience wholly, completely, without bias or prejudice, it leaves no scar of memory. Every one of you goes through experiences, and if you meet them completely, with your whole being, then the mind is not caught up in the wave of memory. When your action is incomplete, when you do not meet an experience fully, but through the barriers of tradition, prejudice, or fear, then that action is followed by the gnawing of memory.

As long as there is this scar of memory, there must be the division of time as past, present, and future. As long as the mind is tethered to the idea that action must be divided into the past, present, and future, there is identification through time and therefore a continuity from which arises the fear of death, the fear of the loss of love. To understand timeless reality, timeless life, action must be complete. But you cannot become aware of this timeless reality by searching for it; you cannot acquire it by asking, "How can I obtain this consciousness?"

Now what is it that causes memory? What is it that prevents your acting completely, harmoniously, richly in every experience of life? Incomplete action arises when mind and heart are limited by hindrances, by barriers. If mind and heart are free, then you will meet every experience fully. But most of you are surrounded by barriers—the barriers of security, authority, fear, postponement. And since you have these barriers, you naturally act within them, and therefore you are unable to act completely. But when you become aware of these barriers, when you become aware with your heart and mind in the midst of a crisis, that awareness frees your mind without effort from the barriers that have been preventing your complete action.

Thus, as long as there is conflict, there is memory. That is, when your action is born of incompleteness, then the memory of that action conditions the present. Such memory produces conflict in the present and creates the idea of consistency. You admire the man who is consistent, the man who has established a principle and acts in accordance with that principle. You attach the idea of nobility and virtue to a person who is consistent. Now consistency results from memory. That is, because you have not acted completely, because you have not understood the whole significance of experience in the present, you establish artificially a principle according to which you resolve to live tomorrow. Therefore your mind is being guided, trained, controlled by the lack of understanding, which you call consistency.

Now please don't go to the other extreme, to the opposite, and think that you must be utterly inconsistent. I am not urging you to be inconsistent; I am talking of your freeing yourself from the fetish of consistency which you have set up, freeing yourself from the idea that you must fit into a pattern. You have established the principle of consistency because you have not understood; from your lack of understanding you evolve the idea that you must be consistent, and you measure any experience that confronts you by the idea that you have established, by the idea or principle that is born only through the lack of understanding.

So consistency, living according to a pattern, exists as long as your life lacks richness, as long as your action is not complete. If you observe your own mind in action, you will see that you are continually trying to be consistent. You say, "I must," or "I must not."

I hope that you have understood what I have said in my former talks; otherwise what I say today will have little meaning for you.

I repeat that this idea of consistency is born when you do not meet life wholly, completely, when you meet life through a memory; and when you constantly follow a pattern, you are but increasing the consistency of that memory. You have created the idea of consistency by your refusal to meet freely, openly, and without prejudice, every experience of life. That is, you are always meeting experiences partially, and out of that arises conflict.

To overcome that conflict you say that you must have a principle; you establish a principle, an ideal, and strive to condition your action by it. That is, you are constantly trying to imitate; you are trying to control your daily experience, the actions of your everyday life, through the idea of consistency. But when you really understand this, when you understand it with your heart and mind, with your complete being, then you will see the falsity of imitation and of being consistent. When you are aware of this, you begin to free your mind without effort from this long-established habit of consistency, though this does not mean that you must become inconsistent.

To me, then, consistency is the sign of memory, memory that results from lack of true comprehension of experience. And that memory creates the idea of time; it creates the idea of the present, past, and future, on which all our actions are based. We consider what we were yesterday, what we shall be tomorrow. Such an idea of time will exist as long as mind and heart are divided. As long as action is not born of completeness, there must be the division of time. Time is but an illusion, it is but the incompleteness of action.

A mind that is trying to mold itself after an ideal, to be consistent to a principle, naturally creates conflict, because it constantly limits itself in action. In that there is no freedom; in that there is no comprehension of experience. In meeting life in that way you are meeting it only partially; you are choosing, and in that choosing you lose the full significance of experience. You live incompletely, and hence you seek comfort in the idea of reincarnation; hence your question, "What happens to me when I die?" Since you do not live fully in your daily life, you say, "I must have a future, more time in which to live completely."

Do not seek to remedy that incompleteness, but become aware of the cause that prevents you from living completely. You will find that this cause is imitation, conformity, consistency, the search for security which gives birth to authority. All these keep you from the completeness of action because, under their limitation, action becomes but a series of achievements leading to an end, and hence to continued conflict and suffering.

Only when you meet experiences without barriers will you find continual joy; then you will no longer be burdened by the weight of memory that prevents action. Then you will live in the completeness of time. That to me is immortality.

Question: Meditation and the discipline of mind have greatly helped me in life. Now by listening to your teaching I am greatly confused, because it discards all self-discipline. Has meditation likewise no meaning to you? Or have you a new way of meditation to offer us?

KRISHNAMURTI: As I have already explained, where there is choice there must be conflict, because choice is based on want. Where there is want there is no discernment, and therefore your choice merely creates a further obstacle. When you suffer, you want happiness, comfort, you want to escape from suffering; but since want prevents discernment, you blindly accept any idea, any belief that you think will give you relief from conflict. You may think that you reason in making your choice, but you do not.

In this way you have set up ideas which you call noble, worthy, admirable, and you force your mind to conform to these ideas; or you concentrate on a particular picture or image, and thereby you create a division in your action. You try to control your action through meditation, through choice. If you do not understand what I am saying, please interrupt me, so that we can discuss it.

As I have said, when you experience sorrow, you immediately begin to search for the opposite. You want to be comforted, and in your search you accept any comfort, any palliative, that will give you momentary satisfaction. You may think that you reason before you accept such comfort, such relief, but in reality you accept it blindly, without reason, for where there is want there cannot be true discernment.

Now meditation, for most people, is based on the idea of choice. In India, the idea is carried to its extreme. There the man who can sit still for a long period of time, dwelling continuously on one idea, is considered spiritual. But, actually, what has he done? He has discarded all ideas except the one that he has deliberately chosen, and his choice gives him satisfaction. He has trained his mind to concentrate on this one idea, this one picture; he controls and thereby limits his mind and hopes to overcome conflict.

Now to me, this idea of meditation—of course I have not described it in detail—is utterly absurd. It is not really meditation; it is a clever escape from conflict, an intellectual feat that has nothing whatever to do with true living. You have trained your mind to conform to a certain rule according to which you hope to meet life. But you will never meet life as long as you are held in a mold. Life will pass you by because you have already limited your mind by your own choice.

Why do you feel that you must meditate? Do you mean by meditation, concentration? If you are really interested, then you do not struggle, force yourself to concentrate. Only when you are not interested do you have to force yourself brutally and violently. But in forcing yourself, you destroy your mind, and then your mind is no longer free, nor is your emotion. Both are crippled. I say that there is a joy, a peace, in meditation without effort, and that can come only when your mind is freed from all choice, when your mind is no longer creating a division in action.

We have tried to train the mind and heart to follow a tradition, a way of life, but through such training we have not understood, we have merely created opposites. Now I am not saying that action must be impetuous, chaotic. What I say is that when the mind is caught up in division, that division will continue to exist even though you strive to suppress it by means of consistency to a principle, even though you try to dominate and overcome it by establishing an ideal. What you call the spiritual life is a continual effort, a ceaseless striving, by which the mind tries to cling to one idea, one image; it is a life, therefore, which is not full, complete.

After listening to this talk you may say, "I have been told that I should live fully, completely; that I must not be bound by an ideal, a principle; that I must not be consistent—therefore I shall do what I like." Now that is not the idea that I wish to leave with you in this last talk. I am not talking about action that is merely impetuous, impulsive, thoughtless: I am talking about action that is complete, which is ecstasy. And I say that you cannot act fully by forcing your mind, by strenuously molding your mind, by living in conformity with an idea, a principle, or a goal.

Have you ever considered the person who meditates? He is a person who chooses. He chooses that which he likes, that which will give him what he calls help. So what he is really seeking is something that will give him comfort, satisfaction—a kind of dead peace, a stagnation. And yet, the man who is able to meditate we call a great man, a spiritual man.

Our whole effort is concerned with this superimposition of what we call right ideas on what we consider wrong ideas, and by this attempt we continually create a division in action. We do not free the mind from division; we do not understand that that continuous choice born of want, of emptiness, of craving, is the cause of this division. When we experience a feeling of emptiness, we want to fill that emptiness, that void; when we experience incompleteness, we want to escape that incompleteness which causes suffering. For this purpose we invent an intellectual satisfaction which we call meditation.

Now you will say that I have given you no constructive or positive instruction. Beware of the man who offers you positive methods, for he is giving you merely his pattern, his mold. If you really live, if you try to free the mind and heart from all limitation—not through self-analysis and introspection, but through awareness in action—then the obstacles that now hinder you from the completeness of life will fall away. This awareness is the joy of meditation—meditation that is not the effort of an hour, but which is action, which is life itself.

You ask me, "Have you a new way of meditation to offer us?" Now you meditate in order to achieve a result. You meditate with the idea of gain, just as you live with the idea of reaching a spiritual height, a spiritual altitude. You may strive for that spiritual height; but I assure you that, though you may appear to attain it, you will still experience the feeling of emptiness. Your meditation has no value in itself, as your action has no value in itself, because you are constantly looking for a culmination, a reward. Only when mind and heart are free of this idea of achievement, this idea born of effort, choice, and gain—only when you are free of that idea, I say, is there an eternal life which is not a finality, but an ever-becoming, an ever-renewing.

Question: I recognize a conflict within me, yet that conflict does not create a crisis, a consuming flame within me, urging me to resolve that conflict and realize truth. How would you act in my place?

KRISHNAMURTI: The questioner says that he recognizes the conflict within him, but that that conflict causes no crisis and therefore no action. I feel that is the case with the majority of people. You ask what you should do. Whatever you try to do, you do intellectually, and therefore falsely. It is only when you are really willing to face your conflict and understand it fully, that you will experience a crisis. But because such a crisis demands action, most of you are unwilling to face it.

I cannot push you into the crisis. Conflict exists in you, but you want to escape that conflict; you want to find a means whereby you can avoid it, postpone it. So when you say, "I cannot resolve my conflict into a crisis," your words merely show that your mind is trying to avoid the conflict—and the freedom that results from facing it completely. As long as your mind is carefully, surreptitiously avoiding conflict, as long as it is searching for comfort through escape, no one can help you to complete action, no one can push you into a crisis that will resolve your conflict. When you once realize this—not see it merely intellectually, but also feel the truth of it—then your conflict will create the flame which will consume it.

Question: This is what I have gathered from listening to you: one becomes aware only in a crisis; a crisis involves suffering. So if one is to be aware all the time, one must live continuously in a state of crisis, that is, a state of mental suffering and agony. This is a doctrine of pessimism, not of the happiness and ecstasy of which you speak.

KRISHNAMURTI: I am afraid you haven't listened to what I have been saying. You know, there are two ways of listening: there is the mere listening to words, as you listen when you are not really interested, when you are not trying to fathom the depths of a problem; and there is the listening which catches the real significance of what is being said, the listening that requires a keen, alert mind. I think that you have not really listened to what I have been saying.

First of all, if there is no conflict, if your life has in it no crises and you are perfectly happy, then why bother about conflicts and crises? If you are not suffering, then I am very glad! Our whole system of life is arranged so that you may escape from suffering. But the man who faces the cause of suffering, and is thereby freed from that suffering, you call a pessimist.

I shall again explain briefly what I have been saying, so that you will understand. Each one of you is conscious of a great void, an emptiness within you, and being conscious of that emptiness, you either try to fill it or to run away from it; and both acts amount to the same thing. You choose what will fill that emptiness, and this choosing you call progress or experience. But your choice is based on sensation, on craving, and hence involves neither discernment, nor intelligence, nor wisdom. You choose today that which gives you a greater satisfaction, a greater sensation than you receive from yesterday's choice. So what you call choice is merely your way of running away from the emptiness within you, and hence you are merely postponing the understanding of the cause of suffering.

Thus, the movement from sorrow to sorrow, from sensation to sensation, you call evolution, growth. One day you choose a hat that gives you satisfaction; the next day you tire of that satisfaction, and want another—a car, a house, or you want what you call love. Later on, as you become tired of these, you want the idea or the image of a god. So you progress from the wanting of a hat to the wanting of a god, and therein you think you have made admirable spiritual advancement. Yet all these choices are based merely on sensation, and all that you have done is to change your objects of choice.

Where there is choice there must be conflict, because choice is based on craving, on the desire to complete the emptiness within you or to escape from that emptiness. Instead of trying to understand the cause of suffering, you are constantly trying to conquer that suffering or to escape from it, which is the same thing. But I say, find out the cause of your suffering. That cause, you will discover, is continual want, continual craving that blinds discernment. If you understand that—if you understand it not just intellectually, but with your whole being—then your action will be free from the limitation of choice; then you are really living, living naturally, harmoniously, not individualistically, in utter chaos, as now. If you live fully, your life does not result in discord, because your action is born of richness and not of poverty.

Question: How can I know action and illusion from which it springs if I do not probe action and examine it? How can we hope to know and recognize our barriers if we do not examine them? Then why not analyze action?

KRISHNAMURTI: Please, since my time is limited, this is the last question that I shall be able to answer.

Have you tried to analyze your action? Then, when you were analyzing it, that action was already dead. If you try to analyze your movement when you are dancing, you put an end to that movement; but if your movement is born of full awareness, full consciousness, then you know what your movement is in the very action of that movement; you know without attempting to analyze. Have I made that clear?

I say that if you analyze action, you will never act; your action will become slowly restricted and will finally result in the death of action. The same thing applies to your mind, your thought, your emotion. When you begin to analyze, you put an end to movement; when you try to dissect an intense feeling, that feeling dies. But if you are aware with your heart and mind, if you are fully conscious of your action, then you will know the source from which action springs. When we act, we are acting partially, we are not acting with our whole being. Hence, in our attempt to balance the mind against the heart, in our attempt to dominate the one by the other, we think that we must analyze our action.

Now what I am trying to explain requires an understanding that cannot be given to you through words. Only in the moment of true awareness can you become conscious of this struggle for domination; then, if you are interested in acting harmoniously, completely, you become aware that your action has been influenced by your fear of public opinion, by the standards of a social system, by the concepts of civilization. Then you become aware of your fears and prejudices without analyzing them; and the moment you become aware in action, these fears and prejudices disappear.

When you are aware with your mind and heart of the necessity for complete action, you act harmoniously. Then all your fears, your barriers, your desire for power, for attainment—all these reveal themselves, and the shadows of disharmony fade away.

July 9, 1933

Ommen, Holland, 1933

First Talk at Ommen

If it is possible, I want this camp during these three weeks to be different from the other camps that we have held so far. During these three weeks I will try to make my ideas clear, and please try to understand their full significance; please do not go away, after this camp, with merely a new set of illusions, covering up the old. If what I say is not clear, ask questions, and I shall explain again and again—it does not matter how often.

If we all thought alike, you would not be here in this gathering. But during these talks I am going to try to explain the differences, so that we understand each other. Let us be frank; let us not try to agree over things that we do not understand. At present I feel that you are not sure what I think. But to find out what I think you must first be sure of what you yourselves think, which is much easier than finding out what I think. During these past many camps up to now, I feel that we have never tried to find out what each one really thinks. You have never been quite sure of what I think, nor of what you yourselves think.

The important point is not whether you are bound by old traditions or old systems of thought, but that you are really aware of what you are thinking, that you are quite certain of your own thought. Then, if I say something which is opposed to what you think, there can be no compromise. For all compromise destroys the fullness of action. This does not mean that you must adopt my ideas and force yourself to look at life as I do. Please do not think that in the combination of your ideas and mine, you are going to realize a unified whole. It is in the fulfillment of a true thought that there can ever be completeness. I am afraid most of you are trying to compromise. This, among other things, I shall try to explain during these three weeks.

If you are contented and happy with life, you would not come here. The majority of you are here because you perceive there is so much cruelty, suffering in the world and as you yourself are a part of it, you want to find out if there is a true and lasting understanding of this terrifying chaos. For without this comprehension there is a constant dread of utter emptiness of mind and heart. This we can discuss simply, frankly, only when you know for yourselves what you really think; but if you don't know what you think, then, I fear, you will not understand what I am trying to say.

Many of you come to these meetings with the desire to find a new set of beliefs and systems in which you can take comforting shelter. But I cannot give them to you, as there are no shelters or escapes from life. These beliefs are snares and illusions, destroying, utterly, understanding. You are unconsciously ever wanting these comforting illusions, and naturally what I say must cause bewilderment, disappointment. You listen to what I say, but my words leave you in great confusion.

Now before I continue with what I want to say, please let me make one or two points clear. I am not talking to an audience with one mind, one heart, one belief; I am not talking to a group of people who come here for pleasure or out of habit, or to a nucleus of listeners with sectarian spirit. I am not talking to an assemblage of mere reformers. I am not addressing a group; I am talking to individuals. For only when you are entirely alone are you able to discern what is true.

Let me repeat that I am not a reformer. I am not here to remake you, to force you to follow a new set of beliefs. Please understand the significance of this. Most of you want to shape yourselves after a certain pattern, to conform to a set of ideas, beliefs. Now this attempt to force the mind and heart after a belief, a pattern, must inevitably create conflict and suffering. So I am not creating a new system for you to follow, I am not offering you a new set of beliefs which shall act as your guide.

People want to fit into a mold because they think that living according to a pattern can be easier, safer, and without suffering, than living without one. They struggle to force their mental and emotional lives to fit into the grooves of a set system. Then, having conformed, they try to force others to reshape their lives. And this they call helping and reforming the world, serving mankind, and other fine-sounding phrases.

Now I do not desire to reform you. But what I want to do is to help you perceive the barriers that surround you, and when you have discerned them, you can be rid of them yourself, and not reshape yourself to fit some other pattern. When you yourself break through these patterns and systems, your action becomes spontaneous. Then it is no longer bound by mere custom, it is no longer born of mere habit. When you free your mind and heart from the many barriers that shut them in, then there is the flow of reality.

Now your existence may be quite placid and contented, which may be taken for a life of understanding, but in reality you may have merely protected yourself against problems and conflicts through beliefs, ideals, and explanations. But you are conscious of life only when there is conflict, pain, suffering, out of which alone comes the true understanding of life. For instance, a sprained ankle, as long as it is carefully bandaged and not used, it may give you no pain; but when it is used, blood surges through it, causing pain. So, likewise, you have many twisted ideas and perverted judgments of which you are wholly unconscious. They reveal themselves only through conflict and suffering, if you do not escape from them. When you become mentally and emotionally aware of these barriers, without reshaping yourself after another pattern, the freedom from these limitations is a spontaneous and an intelligent progress without self-imposed discipline and control.

Most people think only in terms of reform, but not in complete change, revolution. People insist, for instance, on the value of discipline. They believe that they can reform themselves only through rigid self-control. They believe either in an artificial discipline externally imposed, as by society, religion, or economic conditions; or in an inner discipline according to which they govern themselves. Either a man adopts an external standard as a beacon by which he guides his thoughts, or he creates an inner standard which guides his actions. That is the case with the majority of people. I don't believe in reforming discipline. To me discipline is merely destructive; it is a narrowing down of the heart and mind. Later on we shall come back to this point. I talk of it here merely to point out that, from my point of view, there cannot be reformation with regard to discipline. Since you believe in it, since the structure of your thought is based on discipline, on control, on authority, there naturally arises confusion between what I say and your convictions.

Discovering that former beliefs, traditions, and ideals have no longer any deep significance, you are seeking new ideals, ethics, and new conceptions to replace the old. So you go from one teacher to another, from one sect or religion to another, hoping that by putting together many finites there will be the infinite, like the bee that gathers honey. Either there is a search for a change that will yield a new and further sensation, or else there is a desire for deep, inner security, only through a new system of beliefs, ideals, and through its exponents. Which of these are you seeking? If you are seeking neither of these, sensation nor security, then there is in you a deep longing to understand life itself, realizing that from this understanding alone can there be a new conception of morality and of action. But to fully grasp the significance of this, the mind must be free from the desire for security and sensation. This is one of the most difficult tasks, to keep the mind and heart from conformity and accumulative knowledge which becomes merely a safeguard against the ever-changing present or against the future. The reserve fund of these safeguards creates the limited consciousness of the 'I'. Between these protective safeguards and the movement of life there must inevitably arise conflict. To escape from this conflict the mind creates further security and illusions, getting more and more entangled and limited. Take the case of a wealthy man: he is afraid of the emptiness that would exist in his life if he lost his possessions. As he dreads this, he tries to make himself more and more secure by the continual attempt to increase his possessions.

To free yourself from the pursuit of security and power, you mentally create its opposite. But in doing this you are merely creating another set of securities, only calling it by different names. This opposite is nothing more than another form of security, even though it is called love, humility, service, following truth.

To this new opposite, you try to be sincere, glorifying it as peace, humility, service, as opposed to security, power. You abandon a certain set of ideas, a certain group of concepts and create new ones which become your security. And these you safeguard as carefully as the rich man guards his treasure, both by the group as well as by the individual. So you have changed, if this is a change at all, merely from one set of ideas to another with different names, but under the new covering there are the same desires and hopes for security.

To me there is no such thing as security; and yet that is what almost everyone is constantly seeking, even though each one may disguise it by a different word. With conscious or unconscious desire for some kind of security, certainty, you come to listen to me; you take my words and build out of them the structure of your longing. Out of this contradiction, there arises confusion and the appearance of the negative quality of what I am saying.

For this reason, discover what it is you are seeking. If you find that you really want security, then go into it profoundly, with your whole being, completely. Then you will understand that there is no such thing as security. When you discover that, you may turn to the opposite; you may try deliberately to become insecure, which would only be another form of security. The more you delve into your security, the looser and looser it becomes. It has no substance. It would lose its grip on you, but you are afraid to let it because you dread the emptiness that may then come upon your mind and heart.

To truly find out for yourself what it is that you are seeking, there must be frankness and not sincerity. You can be sincere to an idea but that idea may be an illusion, utterly false. The foolish are sincere to an idea or to something. After all, there is no great difference between the foolish who are sincere to a single idea and those who try to be sincere to many ideas. Sincerity implies duality. It implies the actor, and the thing or person or idea to which he is trying to be sincere. Out of this duality there arises a hypocritical contradiction. Frankness admits no duality and hence there is not always that striving to be something which again breeds hypocrisy. Sincerity often conceals shallowness, but frankness, that open recognition of *what is*, uncovers great richness.

Now in your attempt to find out what your true desires are, do not try to control your thought and emotion. Rather, let the mind be so eagerly conscious that all the impediments, the bonds which now weigh down your thought will reveal themselves. In discovering these hindrances you will understand the pursuit of your hidden desires. The man who is held in bondage can be free only when his bonds are destroyed. So the realization of that which is can come about only when the mind is utterly free from the hindrances that it has and is creating for itself.

By being frank you can find out your own limitations, your own complicated illusions. But if you are merely sincere you can never find them out, because you are constantly trying to be true to an ideal which prevents the understanding of the actual. It is only when the mind has disentangled from illusion that there is the ecstasy of enduring life.

July 27, 1933

Second Talk at Ommen

Friends,

To understand the constant movement of life, the mind must be free from the burden of explanatory knowledge; it must be free from the attempt to hold the self-protective lessons of experience. It must meet life anew every day, and in that meeting there is understanding.

Most of us, I think, realize consciously or unconsciously that there is an emptiness, an insufficiency in our lives, and we try to run away from that insufficiency, through sensation, through forgetfulness, or through work. In the search for sensation we go from one experience to another; we desire greater variety in sensation, and this movement of sensation we call experience. Yet that empty void, that loneliness, does not cease to exist. We are simply trying to get away from it through experience, and this attempt to escape, this effort to fill it with experience, with mere knowledge, only creates greater insufficiency. Where there is an emptiness there is always a craving and a grasping.

Where there is wanting there can never be discernment. Choice, which is based on want, can never bring about discernment. Choice is the conflict of the opposites. In choosing between opposites, you merely create further opposites. What is considered to be the essential becomes the unessential, and this movement is not progress. Choice creates the opposites. As long as the mind is caught in this system of opposites there can never be discernment. Wanting prevents discernment. Where there is want there is emptiness. You cannot destroy it, get rid of it, but you have to discover the cause that creates want. Now because there is insufficiency in yourself, you try to fill that emptiness through sensation of various kinds, from the gross forms to the most subtle. Want exists only when there is not the right understanding of values. When you realize this with your whole being, then you will begin to discern the intrinsic value of all things; then you will no longer perceive values as merely the result of opposites.

When there is want, action must be incomplete. Now that incompleteness further increases the emptiness of mind and heart.

In awareness is discernment, in which there is no choice. Choice is a ceaseless struggle, a constant conflict.

Question: Please explain clearly what you mean by frankness as distinguished from sincerity. Do you mean that we must first be absolutely true in ourselves in what we do, feel, and think, in order to understand life in the whole?

KRISHNAMURTI: What I mean by sincerity is this: You have an ideal, a preconception, or a pattern in your mind, in accordance with which you shape your thought and conduct. You try to be sincere to that ideal or principle. So a person who so shapes his life, who holds rigidly to an idea or principle, you call "sincere." The more closely he lives according to that principle (and principles, ideals must be limited) the more sincere he is. But to me, such a person can never understand the flow of reality.

Now frankness is openness, which reveals actuality, the present, without any bias. Only by being intelligently frank can you find out your own limitation. You cannot do this by merely being sincere to an ideal, to a hope. You can discover your little vanities, hindrances, and conceits only through absolute frankness.

First you must find out what you are: only then will you know how to act with regard to what you discover.

Most people think according to a certain pattern or principle, or their thought is influenced or controlled by environment, which must naturally hinder the flow of reality. To discover these hindrances, mind must become aware of its own thoughts, and in intelligently allowing them freedom, you will then begin to discern the secretive fears and hopes that are constantly throwing up barriers against the full expression of life which causes suffering. This needs great frankness and awakened desire to understand, but if there is want, intelligent comprehension of the present is destroyed. This lack of discernment creates duality in action, and this incompleteness is the cause of suffering.

Question: I have found that in the process of getting rid of personal barriers one feels the urge for self-discipline. Yet you say that you do not believe in self-discipline. What do you mean by self-discipline?

KRISHNAMURTI: I wonder if you have asked this question really to find out what I think, or are you so strongly in favor of self-discipline that you feel you have to oppose what I have to say with regard to it? If you are steadfastly opposed to what I say, then that is the end of the discussion. Because I talk about the futility of self-discipline, don't think that you must not have self-discipline. The majority of you assembled here have already made up your minds that self-discipline is essential. You have practiced it for years. Your system and beliefs demand it; your religions insist upon it; your sacred books cry aloud concerning it, and you yourselves hold it to be of great value. But if you want to find out what I think about it, you must try to understand the whole significance of self-discipline and not merely a part of it.

A mind that is being consistent must submit itself to self-discipline. Now why has it to be consistent? Isn't it because it cannot understand the swift movement of the present? Isn't it because it cannot follow the rapid change and significance of experience? Because the mind cannot meet experience, life completely, wholly, it resorts to a standard, to authority behind which it takes shelter, afraid to meet the unknown. For the understanding of experience, there is no precedent. The mind tries to live in the vibrant fullness of today with the burden of dead yesterdays. Thus the present action is being forced into the channels of the past. Out of this there arises the dictum, born of fear, "I must," or "I must not."

Look to the lack of understanding that demands self-discipline, and not to the best method of discipline. You are one thing today, and another thing tomorrow. You are different today from what you will be tomorrow. Yet the mind is forcing and twisting itself to follow a certain rule, and thereby you are creating a conflict. Thus there is never completeness in action, that true fulfillment.

Consistency involves memory; it involves the remembrance of a certain ideal, a certain pattern which is predetermined, based on self-protection and on fear. The memory of that which is already dead disciplines you. Now if you are constantly acting in accordance with that memory, how can you live spontaneously, or follow the swift wanderings of truth? There must be the understanding of the significance of the desire to be consistent—the cause, before abandoning self-discipline, the result.

Because one does not meet every incident of life wholly, there arises conflict which creates memory. Mind identifies itself with this suffering, out of which it creates for itself a self-protective principle, and by this measure all experiences are judged and controlled. It is in suffering only that the mind tries to escape, consciously or unconsciously, to the pattern, and from this there arises the defensive "I must" and "I must not."

If you can discern the cause of fear, which brings forth these self-protective ideals which demand consistency and the rigid following of a discipline, then without the effort of overcoming the fear, the mind will free itself from it.

As there is great separation between thought and action, there must be conflict, suffering; and self-discipline is thought necessary to bridge this gulf, to realize completeness. Through self-discipline, there can never be completeness of action. It is to be realized only when the mind is free from self-protective barriers, prejudices, and fears. The mere adjustment to a pattern through self-discipline, control, destroys the significance and the revealing depth of action; thus the mind and heart gradually become barren and vainly empty.

"I have found that in the process of getting rid of our personal barriers, one feels the urge for self-discipline." What is conquered is not lasting. Only through understanding of the cause of limitations do they disappear, yielding place to intelligence. Where there is an overcoming, there is bondage. In conquering there is no intelligence; there is only subjugation and hidden decay. All conquering indicates the attraction of something beyond, but the cause of limitation still remains. It is only in the intelligent understanding of the cause of hindrances that there is freedom from suffering.

Your attempt to overcome limitations is urged by the desire for reward. So you have not overcome your barrier at all. You have disciplined yourself merely in order to get something else. And because you are thinking of what you will get in return for your action, for your self-discipline, your action and your discipline have no value at all.

Question: Must one be free of craving in order to attain liberation? If so, how can liberation be attained without the exercise of self-control and self-discipline?

KRISHNAMURTI: Craving without understanding creates conflict, and to escape from this suffering there is a search for truth, happiness, liberation. So instead of looking for liberation, for truth, let us concern ourselves with that which is more familiar to us, conflict and suffering, with the actuality rather than with illusions which offer us convenient escapes, shelters. So let us concern ourselves with the cause of suffering. The very desire, conscious or unconscious, to avoid suffering, to find a substitute for it and to cultivate its opposite, brings about the lack of comprehension of the present. The many prejudices, limitations, that the mind has built around itself in its search for self-protections, create sorrow when they come into contact with the ever-living quality of experience. This suffering is not to be overcome through self-discipline and self-control, but when the mind frees itself from the self-protective limitations and illusions, there is the ecstasy of life. This liberation from the false, from the stupid, is not to be realized through self-analysis, but in the awareness of action itself. Self-discipline is but conformity to an established form of escape, an ideal, and in this there is no intelligence. Awareness, that discernment without conformity, without compulsion, reveals the illusions and hindrances which are concealed, preventing the mind from the fullness of action, which alone makes of life an eternal becoming.

Question: In the discussion gathering it was stated that a man could get rid of his hindrances by understanding them. Consequently, we must assume that if we feel that our hindrances have not yet disappeared, it is because we have not yet totally understood them. Many of us feel that hindrances increase when we make an effort to understand them.

KRISHNAMURTI: Naturally they do, because you make an effort to rid yourself of the many hindrances in order to gain truth, happiness or liberation. You lay the emphasis on liberation, truth, because it offers an escape and so the hindrances increase and flourish.

Why do you make an effort to understand your hindrances? If you are deeply desirous of finding out your hindrances, you don't make an effort, do you? But because there is not this consuming desire, you force yourself to make an effort.

Want cripples discernment, causing misery and anguish. Effort is made to overcome this, without understanding its cause. Want is the result of false values. You cannot understand right values when the mind is hindered by prejudices and fears. You must become aware of these prejudices and fears. But such consciousness, such awareness, is not born of effort, but of intense, purposive desire to understand the cause which obstructs pure discernment.

The desire for security is an impediment to discernment, but if you intelligently pursue it, you will find out for yourself its true significance. But perhaps your mind perceives the illusory nature of security, but still there is an intense desire for it. Out of this contradiction there arises conflict and suffering, incompleteness of action. To overcome this incompleteness, you begin to control yourself, discipline yourself. But this does not in any way eliminate conflict. This contradiction exists because you do not deeply desire to discern the true significance of security, with its comforting ideals and illusions. Until there is this burning desire to understand, you must continue with suffering, put up with all the innumerable stupidities and exploitations.

July 28, 1933

Third Talk at Ommen

I was pointing out yesterday that where there is choice there must be conflict and any action born out of choice must be limited. Man is free to choose and thereby we are limited, because we have the capacity to choose. Our capacity limits our discernment and it is only when you are free of choice that there is true liberation. So action born out of choice is limited.

Most of our action is based either through an external influence of society, of laws, morality, etc., and that action, which is reaction, must inherently be limited. Then we escape from that external reaction and develop our own, individual, temperamental reaction, which again creates reaction, the 'I' and the non 'I'.

So when you examine most of your actions frankly, then you will see that they are born either out of fear of punishment or reward. Our actions are based on this, and hence cannot have spontaneity. I am using this word in a quite different meaning. I will try to explain it.

A man of superficial feelings, of superficial thought is spontaneous; he is too spontaneous. He has no fear, no consideration. So he is acting in a certain way out of an impulse; so in a certain way he acts spontaneously. In people who are not burdened with the fear of what society says, of what the neighbors say, because they are acting from their own impulses, there is a certain spontaneity, but I do not call that real spontaneity. That action is thoughtless action. To me, spontaneous action comes only when mind and heart are in perfect harmony. That needs tremendous fullness, complete rightness, not a superficial action.

To realize, and to let action be born out of that realization, we must question the standards developed by society, otherwise you can never find out whether you are acting through exterior influences or through reaction, which you have established for yourself as your own standard. To have an external standard to which one reacts, and to have an inner standard to which one reacts are both false because the inner standard which one develops is but a reaction. It is not the fullness. To realize what I call spontaneous, rich, full action, one must question the value which society has set about us and thereby discover that true significance.

And to question truly the problem, there must be a great crisis. You cannot discover it intellectually. It must become an intense problem. It is only when you are in a crisis that you come to discover the right values, not when you are merely superficially examining. Most of us want to avoid a direct frank questioning of standards: religious, social demands, social standards, class distinction. So you can only find out true values, the true significance, when you question it in a crisis. Now most of us want to avoid or take as accepted any problem, or run away from it. Hence we never discover its true significance.

If you are in a crisis of any kind, when you have to decide something vital, real, what do you do? You approach it with your whole being, not only mentally or emotionally, but harmoniously. Out of that there is a decision that is not born out of choice. Please think on it and you will see. When you are in a crisis, you are not seeking a solution. Search for a solution is merely escape. You can easily find a solution, an escape, but to discover the true significance of the problem, of the crisis, you must come with a fullness, with your mind and heart in complete union. When there is a crisis, when you have to decide something very important, you begin to think, and gradually out of that, the decision is born and there is no choice. You don't weigh the opposites; on the contrary. You do that only when you do not calculate, when there is a direct discernment only, when the problem is a real, vital problem.

One must live intensely all the time with full consciousness, facing everything, as it comes, frankly, not sincerely. That is what I explained yesterday, so that every incident is regarded intrinsically for its own sake, not in comparison with what you are going to get out of it. So you discover individually the true significance of all the standards which society has imposed on each individual.

So, in discovering the right significance you either break away from society and the whole structure of society, or you may find for yourself that you agree with society. That depends on the intensity, vitality, frankness with which you approach the problem.

Take the question of possession and nonpossession of property. Through centuries, the law has allowed you to possess land, property, children, wife, jewels. It is allowed and we have created that problem through centuries of craving, greed, desire for power, and we have become slaves of that legislation. Then another legislation will come that says you shall not possess. Then you will become the slaves of that legislation also, whereas if you understand the true significance of the problem, then you are free of possession and nonpossession. I shall explain that. If it is not clear, ask me questions.

So, in discovering right values, action is born out of completeness, that is harmonious, spontaneous, and that action is of life itself, and therefore it is infinite. To me action is not achievement. An action which is born out of a desire for achievement is no true action, it is limitation; whereas action born out of the spontaneity of fullness is infinite. As we are free to choose and our action is born out of that choice and there is no discernment; our action is limited; it is not spontaneous. Whereas when action is born through the discernment of right values (which comes only when you question intensely as in a crisis), then such action is infinite and spontaneous, because it is not born out of choice.

Question: What would you think of a camp without you, where the people could come to a certain general explanation of what they have found in you, and of what they are missing in you?

KRISHNAMURTI: Why not? If you want to meet here when I am not here, what is the harm? I don't quite understand why this question is put. Sir, are you saying you have to come together to find out what I have said and what I am, and what you are missing or getting, and in order to discover that you must come together? Cannot you discern for yourself individually, now? I don't think that is the implication of the question. Can there be a camp without me? I do not understand why not. I am not going to be here next year, and if Mr. Folkersma and others decide it, I don't see why you should not do it.

Question: Is your opinion of not being able to help anybody not illogical and even contradictory to your convictions, for by coming here you give the impression of being able to help. After all, your writings are sufficient.

KRISHNAMURTI: I will explain what I mean by not being able to help. Most people want to be influenced in one way or the other, and they think by coming to a religious teacher they will be influenced in a right direction through the aura, atmosphere, etc. Being influenced along a particular line, I call detrimental. I do not want to influence anyone. What the majority of people want is for me to give them strength, power, will to push them along right lines, to encourage them. I do not intend to help anyone that way because I think it is utterly false. To discover what is everlastingly true, you must be absolutely free of all influences. You must stand in the integrity of the aloneness and then you will find out. Whereas what I can do by talking and writing is to point out. I cannot fundamentally help. To me it is an erroneous idea that another can give you that living truth. None can give it to you. It must be born out of your own comprehension, out of your own experience. Experience is not going from one incident to another, but the comprehension of that incident with all its significance at the right moment, with the right attention, with the right attitude.

I can make things clear (at least I can try to) and point out what to me are utter fallacies, and it is for you to act on that if you desire, out of your own thinking, out of your own comprehension, uninfluenced, without fear. Most religious leaders and organizations tend to increase and to emphasize the subtle fears and nonacceptance of opportunities which create fears, and subtle influences which you divide along a certain line. Those things to me are utterly false. So I do not hold that my position is illogical. I am acting from that aloneness, from that eternal thing. I do not want to influence and I don't want you to follow me. I say to understand life you must come to it with a choiceless mind, a mind that is free of time, that is no longer being consistent, which does not mean that it is inconsistent, or must be inconsistent.

Question: Can you take for granted that life or truth or God or whatever name you give to the highest, has made such a hopeless mistake by letting us have absolutely wrong use of mind and reason, as your opinion would make us suppose?

KRISHNAMURTI: We have got the capacity to reason, the capacity to feel, and it does not matter who created it. Who created it is not the important thing for the moment. What is important is that the wrong use of such reason, such feeling has brought about such chaotic conditions in the world.

Question: Just as in former years many people tried to make you out a Theosophist—if rather an erring one—now there exists the opinion that you are something like an ultra-idealistic and glorified communist. This opinion has been broadly hinted at in print and it would be good to clear up the point. The idea expressed is, that you are the ideal spiritual communist of a communism that perhaps will never exist in the material world, but rather of the "higher plane" kind of communism, that will always be the aspiration of its true leaders. What have you to say to that? But please be very plain and clear.

KRISHNAMURTI: I don't think I am a communist or a fascist; I approach the whole thing quite differently. The problem of possession and nonpossession, and all the complications in the world will have their right significance when men approach them rightly, not by choosing or by emphasizing whether you must possess or not possess, that is of very little importance. If man is complete in himself, these things will have very little value.

If man is complete in himself, self-sufficient, then all these problems will have minor importance and therefore will be solved. My whole attitude is to show to the individual, to each of you, how to be complete for yourselves, and then these problems will be solved without your even discussing them. I feel because we are incomplete, because there is no real spiritual existence, real completeness, then you look to all these things to give you strength, happiness, security, and hence these problems become tremendously increased out of proportion. The more you investigate, the more you will see that this is a false emphasis. It is first necessary to understand. You say bread is necessary to be complete, to live. Don't put bread or completeness first, but approach the whole thing rightly. You cannot live by bread alone, nor can you live by spirituality alone, but if you understand the true significance of living, both have their right place. Now please, I am not giving solace to the bourgeois, nor encouraging the people who have given up their possessions. Possessions, accumulations, the question of inheriting, all these things will have lost their savor if in yourself you are complete; and that is far more difficult, that needs far greater vitality, greater discernment, than the struggle for possessions which are easy to acquire.

As I say, I don't belong to the communist party, nor do I belong to the fascist party. I am a human being, and I say that is far more important than to what party I belong. If one is a complete human being, one is divine, and then no party, no system is of value. One is like the wind that is pliable and fits in with all things; in oneself one is complete.

Question: You abhor power. What does that word signify to you? I differentiate between power used in three ways: 1. To injure or exploit or hamper the growth of another for one's own aggrandizement. 2. Presumptuously to interfere in an endeavor to help. 3. Opportunely to share one's knowledge or power with others. Does your use of the term "power" include or exclude No. 3?

KRISHNAMURTI: Your question is like an examination paper. I have answered this question in my first talk. When there is search for security, economically, emotionally, or mentally, then there is search for power, because you derive comfort from the security and domination not only over yourself, but also over others. We are unconsciously seeking comfort and comfort implies limitations, consistency to the principles of yesterday which have become the principles of today, and we are living according to the edicts of the desire for security. Hence we do not comprehend the incidents, pictures, and images of life. So, if one understands the cause of this search for security, then the desire for power ceases. As I said, the cause of the search for security is this lack of sufficiency, this aching loneliness, and you hope to cover up this loneliness by having greater and greater security, and thereby you create more and more fear.

Question: As I live day by day, I don't feel I get much nearer to liberation; but looking back, say to the last camp, I feel that I have eliminated various unessentials and got nearer to an understanding of life. Is liberation a gradual thing?

KRISHNAMURTI: I see, you look at liberation as a finality, as a thing to be achieved. As I said the other day, what is achieved is not lasting. Liberation is not a thing to be gained; it is not a portal to which you get nearer and nearer by action. Action itself is liberation, when action itself is spontaneous, whole, complete, born out of that full aloneness. You may have changed since the last camp. I have too. Your hair may become gray, so has mine. We are getting older; we may get rid of certain forms of thought and have some others, but this surely is not a measure by which you judge liberation, is it? You will know that liberation is complete when it is harmonious, choiceless, and out of that comes the perfume of eternal life.

Liberation has to be achieved by action and through action; whereas you regard action as having no meaning; that action is merely a stepping stone to reward. It is not through action that liberation is realized but in action itself. I hope you see the signification of this. We are kind because we want to come to a righteous understanding. Such a kindness has no value. Likewise we say we will be righteous, but if we will be righteous to obtain liberation, that is but merchandise.

Hence your action is always based on fear, reward or punishment, and the significance of the action is lost. So love has no meaning; tenderness, thoughts, affection, none of these have a meaning. You are concerned with achieving liberation, which is a mere idea. It is but an idea, and therefore false, and you cannot understand liberation if you are looking all the time from a point of view of time: today, yesterday, tomorrow, what did I do yesterday, and what shall I do tomorrow? You ask, "Is liberation a gradual thing?" It is not, because there is no time. I will put it differently. Consistency is time, and you can only understand liberation when your mind is free of time, not if you are comparing what you did yesterday and are going to do tomorrow or today. It is still caught up in the idea of time. Time exists so long as there is incomplete understanding of action which creates memory. Time exists so long as your action is not complete, either influenced externally or in imitation of a standard which creates conflict. Out of that memory the mind gets identified, and hence the question, "Is liberation a gradual process?"

You know, it is like a man who has twisted his ankle. If you untwist it, then life flows freely, without pain, without subjective consciousness. Likewise, if your mind and heart are free from all hindrances that create conflict, pain, and struggle, then there is a flow of eternal life. Your search after liberation itself is a hindrance, because your search is after something you must already know, and you cannot know if you are in prison, if you are in pain, in conflict. So you can't seek that which is, but you can free yourself from that which holds you, through comprehending, not through conquering.

To me, perfection, liberation, or eternal reality is not to be gained on a scale of experience, what you call progress. It does not lie at the ultimate height of all experience. But if you are fully awake, if your attention is given at the right moment when you are extremely sensitive, then you will understand the significance of experience and the whole substance of life.

We think liberation or the idea of God or truth or perfection is a matter of occupation. Yesterday I was that, today I am this, tomorrow I shall be something else. Or yesterday I have changed, today I will change, all with regard to a certain pattern, a certain standard. You have established that standard, and you are molding yourself according to that. Surely, that is no liberation. That is a glorified form of prejudice. Whereas perfection comes or is when the mind is free from all standards, from all comparison; when the mind discerns immediately. And you can only discern, as I said, truly, lastingly, when you have discovered true values. No one can give you true values, and you will only discover them when you are in crisis, when your whole life is in a crisis. It is not necessary to strain after it, i.e. have a crisis every second of the day until the mind is free from all crises, from all problems. Before that, you cannot understand the everlasting; you can only understand when the mind is free from choice.

Question: How about the person who has no conflicts, but who is also lazy, inert. Does he not have to discipline himself, make himself do something, in order to understand?

KRISHNAMURTI: Surely, the lazy person has his own reward. Why should he be lazy? I think, certainly, it is stupid to be lazy, because one does not understand. If you are lazy and it gives you satisfaction and contentment like a cow, what harm is there? If you are satisfied, if you are content, you may be lazy. But unfortunately there is no such person. He may be lazy, but there is something going on, eating his heart out, and gradually that laziness covers up his pain. So he dies. He is living, though he is dead.

You ask me, "Does he not have to discipline himself?" That is such a false thing. If he wants to be lazy, he does not want to discipline himself in order to be active. You think by discipline, naturally, you will be active, but that is such a false activity; it is like moving a thing from one place to another, which is what most people consider to be action, doing something. Please don't misunderstand. One must work. I am not for the man who sits quietly with his sure income. One must live, and therefore living is action, and no amount of discipline will awaken him to real action. What will awaken him is the continual conflict with life. It will shake him out of his laziness. What are you to do? You cannot shake him up. You can if you are a reformer, and reform him to a certain mold, which you have done.

Question: You have said that we must not reconcile nor compromise between your point of view and our own illusions, and the systems of thought we have accepted. You say many things which seem vitally true. I have also heard other teachers, e.g. Dr. Besant, expound ideas which also seem true, and which my experience partly confirms. I do not want to reconcile these different teachings in the sense of forcing them together, but I do not see how various concepts which are true can be without an ultimate and natural plan of synthesis.

KRISHNAMURTI: You know, we think truth has many aspects, like colored glass, that in all these images there is one light, with different shades covering it. To me, all that, if I may say so, is nonsense. Please don't think I am dogmatic. That is invented by a mind which wants to be tolerant to other aspects. I am talking of completeness. In completeness, in that fullness, there is no idea of putting two and two together, of compromising, of taking understanding from other teachers, or from myself, and hence this question does not arise at all.

I use the word compromise with regard to certain things, and I explained what they are, and I gave the example of self-discipline. You hear me talking about the futility of self-discipline, and you hear another talking with the same insistence about the rightness of self-discipline. Now you try to combine and produce something new. Whereas I say, find out what its intrinsic worth is, without prejudice. You will only be prejudiced as long as you are looking for that prejudice, what you are going to get out of it. I used that word compromise with regard to that.

Question: What is the best way in which to maintain the attitude of awareness?

KRISHNAMURTI: I am going on to that tomorrow or after tomorrow, or next week, more fully, but I will briefly explain.

First of all, it is not a question of maintaining. Have you ever been in a room with a snake? Your attention, your whole intense concentration is maintained naturally through fear of being bitten. You don't say, "How am I to maintain my attention?" Awareness is that approach to life with your whole mind and heart in perfect harmony. That only arises when there is a crisis that demands your instant attention, your whole interest.

Now, you are not interested in what I am talking about. Most people are not interested; that is why these questions arise. I know it by your faces and by the questions. If you are interested, intent to find out, not between the opposites, but the significance of things, only at that moment is there awareness. You will find out the answer immediately. I assure you it is awfully simple; don't make this awareness so complicated. I have heard so many explanations of what to me is a very simple thing, and how complicated it is made year by year because your mind is so burdened with knowledge and you are only talking out of your knowledge, and applying that awareness to that knowledge.

Please forget everything that you have learned, read in books, and approach what I am saying very simply, freshly, frankly. Then you will see that it is utterly simple. There is awareness only when your whole being is awake and questioning, your whole being is mind as well as heart, not merely mind or merely heart, and when you approach everything in that way, then there is no problem or solution or ways of conquering or disciplining. Then you are acting from your whole being, spontaneously, naturally, without conflict, without effort.

July 29, 1933

Fourth Talk at Ommen

You know, life is a tremendous mystery and most of us create a false mystery, an illusion, and try to penetrate that illusion hoping that it will be real.

We prefer the mystery of an illusion to the mystery of reality, and life is a mystery which cannot be understood, if mind and heart are caught up in an illusion. So all illusion must cease before one can penetrate that innermost sanctuary that one calls life. I am trying to show the manner it can be penetrated, not the way, because I do not believe there is such a thing as a way. There is no path to truth. It is an uncharted land. It is an uncharted land and you must come to it entirely naked, unprepared, you cannot have it charted, laid down; you must come to it wholly, unprepared, free, naked. Then you will understand it.

Now to me, there is a living ecstasy which may be called God, reality, that is a timeless becoming. It is not an end which is to be gained, achieved, or conquered. It is a thing that is continually moving, changing, alive; it cannot be described. To discover it, to understand it, to penetrate it, the mind must be free of this idea of achievement. You cannot think of truth in terms of gains or in terms of success or conquering. Please, this is not rhetorical. Don't listen to me with a rhetorical mind. And as most minds are crippled by this idea of conquering, achieving, catching hold, our whole system of thought is based on it.

To understand that living reality, the mind must be wholly free of this idea of achievement, because achievement involves time; that which you are going to gain implies a future and a present and a past. A mind and a heart that is caught up in time cannot understand that endless becoming. So achievement, gain, conquering, and success, truth, as a reward for righteous action implies an effort, indicates that you must make a tremendous volition, develop a will, character, in order to attain, in order to be rewarded for your effort. And where there is an effort there is a duality; the thing which you conquer and the conqueror. Where there is duality there is an opposite, an antithesis, as good and bad, pain and pleasure, reward and punishment. As long as there is duality in mind there is effort to escape from one to the other. This effort gives birth to the consciousness of the 'I', self-consciousness, and hence there arises suffering, pain, and the idea of time broken up into past, present, and future. Where mind is continually seeking advancement, achievement, success, conquering a virtue, or an end, there is the implication of duality, which creates a consciousness of the 'I'. From that there arises suffering. So to overcome the suffering, we resort to forgetfulness, because most people are caught up in suffering. With that suffering, with that continual uncertainty and lack of comprehension, which created a void, an emptiness, we are all the time trying to forget it, to run away from it or trying to conquer it through self-discipline. This forgetfulness, this running away or disciplining oneself, further increases that duality and then there is that strain of conquest, and the battle takes place. This is a process each one goes through consciously or unconsciously. The result is that you have set up an end to be conquered, which you consider to be true, an ideal of perfection, of God, of truth, of life; and you are always straining to discipline yourself to conquer it, to train your mind to dwell constantly on that idea and to function in it. So you create in your mind a duality, an observer, a controller, and the thing which is observed and controlled. So you develop a higher mind and a lower mind, a higher emotion and a lower emotion, because your mind is suffocated, gripped in this duality.

Hence naturally there is continual disharmony, which creates conflict and you are caught up in this circle. That is what is happening; that is obvious. That is what is taking place in each one: this establishment of an idea, which we call truth or God, which is impossible because you cannot understand it, you cannot picture it as a whole until you are completely free of it. You can have an occasional glimpse, but if you cling to that glimpse, you are destroying the full comprehension of the present. So we begin to establish what we consider truth, which is born out of prejudice, because we always choose that which we consider to be truth out of like and dislike, what gives you satisfaction, mentally, emotionally, or any other way. So you distinguish between right action and wrong action—the right action being dominated by the higher mind, the mind that is continually observing, conquering, guiding, and, hence, creates in itself a duality, the 'I' and the non 'I'. This is not another philosophy. It is what happens with each of us. That is how the process of self-discipline takes place. Now, to me, this is entirely erroneous. The whole process of approach is entirely wrong, because it indicates a ceaseless effort, and as I say, where there is effort there is no understanding of truth. Truth does not come through effort. It must be born naturally when you remove all hindrances, when you are free from all barriers created by effort. What creates this duality in us? Action. Action born out of the desire for want, gain; action born out of fear, punishment; that creates a duality. And, as I say, it is only action itself which is life, which is eternal. So when the mind is caught up by the bondage of a reward, or a punishment, or a motive, or the search after truth, action has lost its significance, and instead of action there is always the sense of achievement as opposed to action. To me action is infinite, everlasting, enduring; whereas achievement has a finality. So it is only when the mind and heart are free from all hindrances, that life can flow easily, spontaneously, naturally, frankly. It is like a twisted ankle, which causes pain and when the ankle is put back in its place, life flows naturally again through it. So in the same way, when you free the mind from all hindrances, from all barriers, then life flows through it easily. That is eternal action, but these hindrances are not to be conquered. You cannot say I am going to conquer my hindrance, I am going to overcome it, translate it, transmute it. If you are thinking in terms of gain, then you are looking to sensation, and action based on sensation does not give this true discernment.

What gives true discernment is action without choice. If action is based on achievement, then that action has no significance, that action is of time and therefore creates conflict; whereas if there is action not from a reward, not from a punishment, not from fear, then action itself is inherently true and therefore enduring. What destroys action in its true significance, is want, is this continual craving, which creates loneliness. Where there is want, one is conscious of loneliness, emptiness, a void, and immediately one wants something to fill that; so one goes on accumulating more and more, and the emptiness is still there. The cause of loneliness is want, because wherever there is want, there is no discernment. Want blinds and cripples the mind and heart from true understanding. You can only want, crave, when the mind is burdened with false values. The moment you understand a thing, wholly, completely in all its significance, there is no more want. You are part of it, whether the understanding of an experience, or a thing, or an idea, or an emotion. So wanting perverts judgment, true discernment, which is the cause of loneliness.

Now, I am going to explain something, which I hope will make what I am saying clear. Most people agree mentally; mentally you have followed. If you have followed what I have said the last three days, you will have followed that where there is want, there is lack of discernment. You will agree intellectually, but emotionally you are still wanting, and hence there is conflict. The mind imposes itself on the emotions that want and hence the continual battle, the strain of what you call spirituality; the trying to force together the two elements that are warring with each other. So mind is convinced of the futility of comfort or of want; intellectually it is assured of its falseness; sensationally it still wants it, it is seeking sedulously and is unconsciously absorbed with it. Then what do you do? There it is, there are two elements in you, one that says no comfort, no security, no want, that intellectually, mentally sees the fallacy of it, and emotionally all the time holding, as is the case with love, what you call love, as a husband, a wife, a lover, which is a possessive thing but intellectually you despise what you are doing. What do you do? What does one do? One either gives it up as a hopeless thing, or else tries to dominate. Mentally, you suppress the other, continually suffocate the search for comfort, the search for security, the search for want, so out of that there is discipline, there is the controller and the controlled and the desire to accumulate virtues to strengthen its own assurance, and there is this continual domination going on. Now if you emotionally pursue the want, if you emotionally think security is essential for your well-being, pursue it, don't try to dominate it. Investigate it, try to plumb its full depths and in the discovery, in the penetration of want, you will discover the futility of want. I am afraid it is simple and you will miss it. If you want a thing, approach it wholly both with your mind and heart; look at it intellectually and emotionally. If you want comfort with all its implications of power, domination, take it with both your whole heart and mind, don't separate your mind from want. Now you are intellectually developing and therefore your mind's response is always intellectual which is the curse of modern education. Whereas, when you approach it wholly both with your mind and your heart, then you will find the true significance of want, that is, when you are fully aware of this hindrance. Want is a hindrance, from my point of view. Probably it is not from yours. But to understand, whatever it is you want, approach it wholly as a harmonious being, not a conflicting being, whether it is jewels, cars, your wife, husband, even God, truth. Then you will approach it as a human being, not as a split individual. Hence you never try to conquer any hindrance: you penetrate it, understand it, gather its significance, and then you are free from that particular hindrance, without effort. Effort only exists when there is contradiction in yourself between want and nonwant, an observer who is observing the thing which wants.

That is why, to me, all discipline which you have imposed on yourself, all meditation (what you call meditation) appears so destructive. Otherwise you will never understand the joy of eternity, the ecstasy of life in all its spontaneity, with all its natural feelings and expressions. If you hate, approach it not with a mind that says, "I must not hate," and at the same time with a feeling of hate; approach it with all your being and you will see how quickly it disappears—like the morning mist which is dispelled by the sun. It is because we do not approach everything so inherently with our whole being, that we pursue virtues, develop character, will, discipline, and search out reward.

Please, experiment with it. I am afraid you don't experiment, because you have already made up your mind that discipline is necessary, control is essential, reward is worthwhile; otherwise, if there is no achievement, what is life? All these clichés are so instilled, drilled into your mind, that you don't experiment with what I am saying, or you become sentimental. Experiment for a day and you will understand that you can live harmoniously, completely, with action that is infinite, not in terms of achievement.

Question: In awareness, must there not be effort? If I find that I have habits that are useless, it requires effort to eliminate them, does it not? Yet, you speak of awareness as being effortless, spontaneous.

KRISHNAMURTI: Effort exists as long as you are trying to conquer something, as long as you are seeking an achievement with success at the end of it; whereas awareness is not born of gain or achievement or success, because achievement, success, implies time, choice. Awareness is choiceless, timeless. I have explained this very carefully during the last few days. Don't mystify what I am saying; it is very simple. When you realize with your whole being that a habit or an idea or an emotion is futile, then you don't make an effort. The habit may continue, but the decision is finished and the habit will gradually wear out. It is childish. I am sure you have experimented with it, and have found it so. Say you have a habit of scratching yourself. If you are fully conscious of it, if you are aware of it with your whole being, there is a decision. The habit may continue for a while, but it will disappear of its own accord. But now you are not fully conscious of the habit and you try to dominate it, and hence there is a continual desire to control your habit. Awareness is direct discernment without choice. You can only discern directly, perceive immediately when you approach the problem, that habit, or a crisis, with your whole being. Therefore it requires intense watchfulness, alertness. You do these things when you are interested in them. Now you are not interested in these things; the majority of people is not interested in what I am talking about. Why are they not interested? Because they like sensation, they want security, comfort, pleasure. Not that I am saying that you must not have these things; don't jump to the opposite. Those things take minor importance when you are complete. I don't mean that you must not have clothes, food, shelter, but they are not the first things; they have their right place. So please first find out, not what it is to be aware, but if you want to pursue that with all your being. If you want security, comfort; if you are craving all the time for achievement, success, virtue, approach it wholly; not with a tired, wearisome feeling, wanting and not wanting, seeing the absurdity of it intellectually and at the same time emotionally running after it. So, you cannot know awareness, nor can you maintain it if you are not interested enough to act wholly with both mind and heart, with your whole being. When you are interested, then out of that comes the flame of awareness. Then it is not a question of maintaining it all the time; it is there when the moment comes, when you approach everything fully; and then you are free of that particular impediment.

Question: I come to Star Camp because it is the most enjoyable way of spending a summer holiday that I know. During a summer holiday one gets more detached and takes stock. For that I do not want a lot of frivolities—there are cinemas all the year round. In taking stock, your challenge is a valuable part of the holiday. Is such a reason for coming of no value from your standpoint?

KRISHNAMURTI: First of all before I answer that question, let me say that when I smile, I am not laughing at the questioner, because humor is quite impersonal. It has nothing to do with you and me. So please, I am not laughing at the questioner. When the audience laughs, I am sure it is the same thing, they are not laughing at the questioner. The question implied that only during a certain part of the year you can take stock, not at other times. During these holidays at the Star Camp you have time and leisure and my challenge helps you to take stock. It is like setting aside one hour of the day to meditate; the rest of the day there is no time. That is, your circumstances don't allow you to take stock the rest of the year. You are so surrounded by family worries, by people, town, by activities, that you have no time to take stock. Here you have time; it is a beautiful place, though it occasionally rains, but here you can take stock.

What a false way of looking at it. Why cannot you take stock while living in the world? Because the world is too much? You are part of it. The world is not too much, you like to play with the toys of the world, and so you have no time nor interest nor leisure. This is not the moment to take stock these ten days, or three weeks. So, what you have done is to divide life as possible and not possible. The possible at the Starcamp and the impossible in daily life. Why is it not possible in your daily life? Because you have created it, individually you have created your daily life and you have become a slave to it and therefore you say I cannot take stock. I say, you can only take stock there and not here. Here you are stimulated by me. That is naturally a false sensation. This has been going on every year. Please don't think I am harsh. On the contrary, if you were alive in your circumstances, you would break the circumstances and take stock in them. Now you don't want to break the circumstances and therefore you come here to find out, keeping the circumstances the whole time and at the same time trying to arrive at truth. You can't do it. It is like a man that is having a lovely holiday in summertime. He sees mountains, tranquil lakes, and goes back to the beastly office. He hates it, but his mind is continually going back to that loveliness of the summer. Why not break the office routine, why not recreate afresh, anew, instead of all the time having a double life? Don't give false reasons of responsibility and don't say I cannot because of my mother and so on. The circumstances have been created by you through fear; you can only recreate them yourself and no one else can. That is what happens with the man who has summer holidays. He goes back to the daily surroundings and thereby he gradually destroys his sensitiveness. When he breaks the circumstances he finds out true values. Don't say I am afraid of hurting people, of changing circumstances, of responsibility. To find truth there must be no father or mother, nothing to stand in the way, no relationship, no responsibility. But please don't take the opposite and say, "Good, I will give up all my responsibilities"—which is such an easy, cowardly way of doing it. In acting completely, then you will find out, that no relationship, no bondage can stand in your way. To act completely you must be complete. Your whole being must live and then nothing can stand in your way, no circumstances, whether a town or a camp.

Question: Sometimes I hate everybody and everything. Can you advise me how to prevent this terrible feeling from surging up, because in those moments I am quite unable to get out of it.

KRISHNAMURTI: Approach it, as I have said, with your whole being, as you approach love. When you love someone intensely, you do it with your whole substance, with your whole being, in that there is no conflict, in that you don't say, how am I to get out. In the same way, with hate, transient pleasures—all these things are to be approached wholly. You will then not get rid of them, but you will penetrate and find out their full significance, their true value and from that there is action. So please don't regard these things as something to be rid of, to be conquered. That approach prevents complete action and hence there is conflict; and you cannot surmount it, conquer it. It only creates further duality, further opposites. But if you approach it both with your heart and your mind then it dissolves itself; then you can understand it fully, then a new element is born.

Question: Thinking over what you said, I know that I am clinging to certain things. For instance, I am fond of jewels. I know, that if I lost my ring, I would cheerfully accept the inevitable, but I would not like to give it to another person. So I am far from detached. I know (perhaps only mentally) that I would be happier, or live more easily without these material things. Yet, I have the desire to possess them, and I have lots of other desires. How can I get rid of them?

KRISHNAMURTI: If you want jewels, have jewels. Why do you want to get rid of them? Why do you want to give them to others? I am afraid you don't follow what I have been talking about the last four days. You see, there is no such thing for me as renunciation. When you understand a thing, then it drops off. The outside person may call it renunciation, but for one that acts harmoniously it is no renunciation. It is natural action. The world praises such a man and says what a wonderful man, calls him noble, spiritually puts him on a pedestal and worships him, because they themselves cannot do that. So, if you are still caught up in the sensation of jewels, possessions, what is wrong? There are millions of people who are slaves of possession. You are only another kind of a slave to another kind of possession. But you object to it because you are afraid of loss; you are afraid of becoming again lonely. You desire possessions, houses, and land, etc. because these things give you a certain security, a certain happiness and you are afraid of losing the sensation of possession which gives you happiness.

Why are you a slave to that happiness of possession? Is it because in yourself there is no richness, in yourself there is no potential life dynamic? Therefore you rely on all these tawdry things and say, how much you must own and how much you must not own. In yourself there is so much poverty that you rely on external possessions. Whereas if you were rich, you would not want all these things. Then you will have your houses, clothes, but they will have a minor importance. Then you are a law unto yourself, you are free from all law, because you are complete. A thing that is harmonious is eternal because it is free from all transiency. So approach everything with all your being and out of that the supreme act is born. With regard to everything, your clothes, your jewels, your houses, your properties, your wife and children, then you will know the infinite act.

Question: You said, "Man, being free, is limited." Is the liberated man limited? If yes, this means he is limited like the free man. Please explain.

KRISHNAMURTI: The liberated man is without choice, yet he acts from that aloneness, not from himself, but from that eternal aloneness. I am using that word not in the sense of retiring from the world, but that aloneness of true values which is eternal, neither yours nor mine. To such a man there is no choice, but to the man who is not liberated there is choice, and therefore he is limited. He is free to choose according to his likes and dislikes; therefore he chooses, and thereby he is limited. Your choice is based on like and dislike and you are free in this like and dislike, therefore it is limited. But if you are without choice then you are truly liberated; then your action is divine; then you are pure action, that lovely thing.

So where action is born out of choice there must be limitation, because whatever act is born of an opposite must create another series of opposites and hence you are caught in this continual duality of opposites and hence ceaseless effort, ceaseless limitation. You may break down one limitation, but erect another.

If I am afraid, I am seeking courage. Then my courage is the opposite of fear, which does not free one of fear. I only escaped to what I call courage. But if I am free of fear, fear itself, then I am free of both courage and fear. So where there is choice there is conflict all the time as yesterday, today and tomorrow; and where action is without choice, time is a whole, there is no yesterday, today, and tomorrow. That is eternity, that is immortality.

July 30, 1933

Fifth Talk at Ommen

The vast majority of people come to listen to me or go to a church or search out teachers in order to be helped, to be guided or to gain something which will give them satisfaction. In other words when we talk of being helped, we want and we desire to come to a certain state of mentality, in which we shall find satisfaction. So we are always looking for a result, when we talk of being helped. To me, as I explained a few days ago, to be helped in this manner is absolutely transient and worthless.

So having gained what we seek, either happiness, a solution to a problem or the satisfaction of achievement or success, then we want to propagate and we want to coerce others to that pattern to which we have arrived. We want to coerce other people, to awaken other people to that point of view. We call that helping the world, bringing another to a particular point of view in which we have found satisfaction, and which has given us a certain contentment, which has given a sense of success, a sensation. So, having gained something, you ask yourself, "What shall I do with it? How shall I use it? In what manner can I use it to bring other people to the same attitude of mind?"

So one is concerned with the result, not with what one has. You are concerned with how you shall use what you gain, and thereby with propaganda, talk, your convictions, you are urging others to come to your point of view. This has no value at all because you only want them to come to a certain point of view which you have arrived at and which has given you satisfaction. Action then has no value at all. To bring other people to a certain point of view, to awaken others to a certain result, is to me the formation of a sect. To awaken people to a certain point of view and to propagate for that point of view, you are concerned not with sowing that which you have, but with the result of your sowing.

If you have something in your basket, if you have your hands full, your mind and heart free, then you are concerned with sowing, not with the result which you may reap. When most people want to help, that is exactly what they are seeking. They want a result. Thereby you are concerned not with the chief thing, which is the sowing, but what you shall reap. Please see this point because I have listened to people, their questions have shown me, that you look at everything from a sectarian point of view, from a group point of view. You try to awaken other people to a certain point of view, to a certain pattern, to a certain result, which you yourself have achieved, or you consider how you shall sow that which you have. All this, to me, shows a very limited mind and such a mind cannot understand the swiftness of wisdom.

Now we are concerned with the result of sowing, because we are not sure what we are sowing. We want conviction from others to encourage us, to show that we have it. That gives us a sensation.

What I want to show this morning is that if you have come here to be helped to discover a solution, or to gain something, I am afraid you will be disappointed, because what you gain you lose. If you seek a result, it is transient. If you seek a solution, you are trying to run away from the cause of the problem. In other words, a result or a gain or the idea of achievement is but a certain comfort in which you take shelter, which becomes your security, and which you call truth. Hence your action, which alone can reveal the full significance of life, is utterly denied. You only seek a result, when there is an emptiness, an aching insufficiency.

Why do we seek a result? Why do we seek achievement? Because we cannot meet life or experience or every incident of the day completely, with a freshness. Because we have not the capacity to meet all things freshly, newly, spontaneously. Our minds are so burdened with memory, we are incapable of meeting anything fresh. We always meet events with ready-made reactions, born of yesterday's memories.

When the mind and the heart are burdened with a memory of incompleteness, then we seek a result, a success, an achievement. Whereas when you meet all things anew, with a freshness, with an eagerness, not with that ready-made reaction, that jaded memory, then that action will give you its full significance. You no longer seek a result, an achievement. You no longer run away from sensation. In action itself there is the full significance, and that is wisdom.

To follow that wisdom, your heart and mind must be entirely free from the search for a result. When one recognizes that; when one becomes aware in action, that one is continually seeking a result, a success, an achievement, a gain; when you really understand with your mind as well as with your heart, then your everyday action reveals in what manner your mind and your heart are caught up. But now you are acting without consciousness, or full understanding of why you are doing it.

Most of our actions are based on a motive, achievement, success or fear. When you become conscious of that not only mentally, but emotionally as well, then that action of which you are conscious, aware, frees itself from the result which you are seeking. I will try to put it differently.

Don't say, "I must not seek a result." Don't say, "I must not have achievement, or I must not seek shelter." If you say that, you are creating another set of shelters. In the "must not" there is a shelter, there is a security. So do not say that. Become aware if your action is the result of that search, of the want to gain security. When you become aware in action, then action itself will show you its full significance. After all, wisdom is not a thing to be gained out of books.

I cannot transmit wisdom to you. Wisdom is born in the fullness of action and you can only act fully or understand action completely, when your mind and heart are free from this continual desire for a result. So if you say you must not seek an achievement or a success, you do not understand action. Whereas you will understand action with all its significance, if you become aware of the cause of your action.

Now to become aware of the cause of action, is not to go through self-analysis. To me self-analysis is destructive. But to be fully conscious, to be awake, both mentally and emotionally, when you are acting, then you will know the cause of your action. When you are conscious of your action, then you will understand the full significance of your search for a result, which will of its own accord reveal its transience. What I want to show is, what I want to explain is, that we should be concerned with sowing, not with its result. And the result will be right, if you sow rightly.

Now we are concerned with the result of our sowing, and hence valuelessness of our action, and we do that because we are empty, because there is no sufficiency in each one of us. So we are concerned with all the results of our action. Such a mind cannot understand wisdom or the swiftness of truth. A mind that can meet all things afresh, anew, without the burden of memory, such a mind, in its fullness, in its plenitude, is only concerned with sowing.

Question: Some people call you a mystic, as opposite to an occultist, as they call it, because you do not lay so much emphasis on the improvement of the "bodies." Please will you change this bad reputation of yours, for it gives me a lot of work, even quarrels, to defend you. I am tired of it.

KRISHNAMURTI: First of all don't defend another, especially with regard to this kind of thing. You know, when there is completeness there is no division, there are no opposites. It is only when the mind is insufficient in itself, it creates opposites, as mysticism and occultism. To me, a man who is caught up in mysticism as opposed to occultism, can never understand what the truth is. You cannot divide life up as mystic and occult. It is a complete whole, it is a fullness, a plenitude. You cannot break it up and say, this is one side of it, and that is the other. It is only when the mind and heart are entirely free from all opposites that you will understand what that enduring action is. We create opposites because we choose, and our choice is always based on "dislike" and "like," on a prejudice. Therefore there is no direct discernment and opposites are created. I choose this, because I like it. Therefore in choosing what I like, I create another opposite which I don't like, and so I am caught up continually in this circle of likes and dislikes. And we choose because we are urged through the desire to gain, to achieve. Therefore such a desire blinds our choice, and hence we create opposites in which we are caught up.

Question: Can you describe briefly: a.) how the world looks to you, as one who has attained the ecstasy of living? b.) how it would look to you, were all, or many of your hearers and readers to realize liberation and live completely. If this is not possible, the reason why would doubtless be interesting and instructive.

KRISHNAMURTI: Do you know, I never thought about it. I never thought what it would look like, the world, if we all obtained liberation, what would be the result. Whether we should have perfect communism or perfect fascism. You see, I do not know first of all why the questioner has put it.

There are one or two possibilities why he has put it. He wants to know what the world looks like as a result of a few people's achievement. That is, he wants to force others to a certain pattern, not let people be free in themselves. Therefore I have never examined for myself what the result would be. I am concerned with sowing, not with reaping and who shall benefit.

If you are a prisoner, I am not concerned in describing what freedom is. My chief concern is to show what creates the prison and for you to break it down, if you are interested. If you are not, of course that is your own affair.

If you say that truth must be useful, it must be beneficial to others, then you do not understand. It will be, but if it is your concern, it will not be. That is why this question is put to me. You want to know what the result will be. It is impossible to tell you, because the result can never be discovered, because it will always be changing. It is not a set thing to which you come. At present one is a slave to so many legislations, one is a cog in a huge machine, spiritual, economical, social, in every way. When you are really free, that is, when you discover its true value, not run away from it or break away from it; when you discover the true value of this social standard in which you are a prisoner, then you will be free of all legislation, and you will not conform. There will be no idea of conformity to truth or to a description of truth, which this questioner desires.

Question: To a loving honeymoon couple the world is, at least temporarily, transformed into a beautiful one, by their happiness. Does this in any way illustrate what you mean by the world problem being the individual problem?

KRISHNAMURTI: You know, when we are caught up in a sensation, that sensation gives us so much pleasure that the world takes on a different hue. We have covered the world with a particular sensation which we have. In our transiency of happiness, we look at the world through that film of happiness.

What I mean by the world problem as being the individual problem is this: We have created through centuries, through particular desires, cravings, a certain set of rules, standards, to which we have unconsciously become slaves. We have through centuries sought security, economic, social, spiritual, in every way. To that security, which we have individually created, we have become slaves. We are unconscious wholly of that slavery. When you begin to question and to find out the true values of that social standard, of those prison bars that hold you, and by questioning and discovering the true value, you as an individual, free yourself from it. That is what I mean by world problem and individual problem. You may, through fear, create another set of rules, standards, that man shall not possess or have any security. What have you done? You have only moved from possession to nonpossession. That has become your prison. Whereas, if you truly discovered the value, the true significance of possession, which is born out of fear, then you will be free of possession and nonpossession as opposites. Then you will be free of all legislation, of all false standards, that society has set up. And you can only be that, when you are wholly individual, not individualistic.

To me, the true individual is one who discovers true values, eternal values of all things—and I say there are eternal values which neither I nor another can give you. No one can give you true values. You have to find out for yourself and when you have discovered the true value of all things, then you will act in your aloneness, in your sufficiency, in your completeness. In that there is ecstasy. But if you are merely satisfied to live as a cog in the machine, then there is nothing to be said. I do not want you to awaken to a certain standard. I would wish that, if I wanted you to conform. You can only discover true values, when you are really in a crisis, when you are really demanding. Most spiritual people, at least people who think they are spiritual, try to demand a satisfaction. They are all the time avoiding this demand which shows the true significance of all their actions and thoughts. That can only come if there is tremendous discontent, not when the mind is dulled to sleep by contentment or the picture of peace, which you call truth.

Now don't turn round and say, "If I wake up to this prison, will it have an influence in the world? Will the world be any better, because I, as an individual have discovered the true value? Will the world benefit by it?" Then you are not discovering true value. You are only discovering what will be useful for the world. If you discover the true value, it will be beyond this, it will be eternal, and therefore applicable to all men.

Question: In order to achieve "release of life," should we acknowledge a duality, a separation between "life" and our physical, emotional, and mental inertia, in order to face the latter as something to be dissolved?

KRISHNAMURTI: Why do you have to acknowledge something of which you are conscious? If you are not conscious of separation, then there is no conflict. If you are not aware of duality, then there is no struggle. There is a harmonious reaction. But as most people are aware of that conflict, why need there be an acknowledgment of separation? You see, you don't acknowledge the separation which causes conflict, because you are seeking a solution of the conflict. Because we are trying to escape from the conflict, we are not aware that there is duality in our actions. Because we are seeking comfort, security, running away from this fear of loneliness, we have to mentally acknowledge the existence of a duality. When there is a conflict, what happens? You want to seek an escape from it, a way out of it. You never find out what is the cause of this conflict. You will find out the true cause of the conflict, when you are conscious or when you are aware fully, not when you inquire mentally what is the cause of the conflict. You will find out the cause of conflict, of pain and suffering, only when you really want to find out with your mind as well as with your heart. Now most people only want to find out the cause mentally, and therefore whatever they discover will only be false, because they do not approach the cause fully. You approach the cause only fully, when there is a crisis, when it consumes you, when all your escapes are blocked. That is why I said become conscious, become aware, then you will see how your mind is trying to escape from facing the cause, or trying to see a solution, running away, forgetting. So you gradually begin to stop up all those avenues of escape and security, and then you will face it with your whole being. That is true awareness. In that, you will find out the true cause.

Question: Sometimes I am totally indifferent, nothing interests me; I even do not want to be happy. How could I get out of this condition of inertia?

KRISHNAMURTI: There are two possibilities. One that you are physically, mentally, emotionally tired. Or, which is more probable, you have filled your mind and your heart with a lot of rubbish, as you fill a wastepaper basket. When the mind is full with useless, transient things, it can get very tired and that is probably the main reason—sheer exhaustion from the collection of useless things, like the rich man has. Now you have collected it. The next thing is to empty it. That is if you are interested. If you empty that mind of useless things, you will discover the everlasting. If your action is born from that rubbish, then your action will ever be futile and worthless, finite. If your action is born from that transient useless rubbish, which you have collected, false values, that action will have no value at all.

So you have to discover if you are acting from that rubbish. That is why I say: Become fully aware of your action, of what you are doing, and then you will discover true value in that rubbish itself. You do not have to get rid of it or start another wastepaper basket and fill it up again with more rubbish.

I hope you follow this, because that is what has happened to the majority of people. They have gone out in search of true values, of the truth, and they have collected and have been choosing. This is essential; this is not essential. They have accumulated, their mental granaries are full with things which they have considered of value, but which have turned to ashes. Hence there is sheer exhaustion, fatigue.

Now do not destroy that granary and start another. You will, if you destroy it or try to conquer it. But if you become conscious, aware, if you see, if you observe both emotionally and mentally, that your actions are born from that memory, from that granary, from that collection, that accumulation, then you will see immediately, instantaneously, the cause of your action, and then you will know for yourself, instantaneously, the true value of that cause.

This is not a trick which you have to learn by heart and then it becomes another security, another phrase, about which you meditate and lose yourself. It is really very simple, if you really want to find out whether you are acting from rubbish and therefore your action is valueless, or whether you are acting completely and hence action is infinite.

You have memories, ideas, which you have stored up for ages. And you are acting from those. And hence you do not meet anything freshly, anew. Now, if you become aware that you are thus acting, your action itself will reveal the cause. And in that discovery lies the true significance of your act, and then all action is free from motive. There is a repletion, there is a fullness, and in that there is ecstasy.

Question: Please tell me how to bring up children.

KRISHNAMURTI: To me the child is not the important thing. The child is not important at all. It is the mother and the father and the teacher who are important, not the child. This is not just a clever statement. The child is there to be formed anyhow, as you will, a pliable thing like putty. So it is not how you are to bring up the child. It is what you are yourself, whether you are the teacher, mother, or father. Have you followed that? Then comes whether you as a parent believe in authority. If you are fully conscious of the futility of authority, then you will for yourself find out the true way. When you know for yourself the sheer valuelessness of authority, then you will find out how to discipline the child rightly.

See what the significance of having no authority means. You have authority only when there is fear. When you are free of fear you are acting from completeness, which does not mean the opposite, lack of authority, which is a negation. After all, that is how we bring up a child, don't we?—on authority, "must and must not," "don't and do," or give wrong explanations of things which we ourselves fear.

The other day a mother told her child, when asked about death, that there is reincarnation, and the child was satisfied. What have you done, when you have given such an explanation? You have created a security for yourself in reincarnation, and you have merely transferred it to the child. And so you have already begun to build in that child's mind the idea of security. So you have established an authority. When you understand the significance of what authority means, then you will not make the child licentious or let it do exactly what it likes. That is not the point. You know that this is such an immense subject that one must take things one by one. First of all authority.

Authority implies conformity to a certain regulation, certain moral law, a certain standard—the true significance of which you, the parent or the teacher, have not yourself tested. So you say, "This is right and this is wrong," and you have helped to build up, based on authority, certain ideas in the mind. So what you are doing now is merely transferring, transmitting to that child all the false values which you yourself have accumulated.

I say there will be false values as long as you are not examining, so long as you as an individual have not found out the true significance. So, when you say you are bringing up the child, you are merely handing down to it all your false conceptions. Therefore I say, find out for yourself if you as an individual, as a mother or a father or a teacher, really believe in authority.

You know authority does not just mean "Do," or "Do not," you must find out the whole significance of it—authority of spirituality, the authority of laws—authority with all its nuances. Then when you have found out for yourself, or are in the process of finding out the true significance for yourself, you are creating for the child a new condition. You cannot help doing so. Not that you are going to succeed at once with the complete freedom from authority, because you yourself are not free from it. But if you are really attempting to free your mind from false values, there is a pliability, a swiftness, an adjustment. Then you will be able to meet the child.

August 3, 1933

Sixth Talk at Ommen

There is so much sorrow, so much suffering, and one becomes so conscious of that insufficiency to do anything about it that one begins to seek what truth is. Because one suffers, one thinks one can find out the end of all sorrow, and so one goes out in search of that completeness or of that truth, God, or whatever name you like to give to it. To me the very search is inherently not true. To me a person who seeks truth, who sets out in search of truth, will never find it, because his search for truth, for that completeness, will be born out of an opposite. So when we seek truth, we are seeking that understanding or that completeness away from that which we are. If we are in conflict, if we are in great sorrow, or if we are aware of tremendous emptiness, we naturally seek its opposite and call that as an end, as a finality, as truth, as God. So our search for truth can only be born out of the opposite. Therefore the thing that we discover in our search can never be true and yet all of us are longing all the time, are struggling to attain truth, to find out what truth is. To me a man who seeks truth and the man who explains and describes truth are both false. The one is seeking truth out of an opposite and the other who describes it, who says, "I know," are both caught up in illusion. The man who says, "I know" must be limited. So beware of a person who says he knows, because truth is not a thing to be known; it is.

There are two different things. One is objective perception, and the other is inherently by itself, alone. So why are we continually caught up in the struggle, in the search for truth? I think it is because we hope that in realizing this truth, this completeness, this God, all our difficulties will be dissolved. Or because our difficulties are so great, our problems so innumerable that we try to escape, run away to something that we conceive to be true. For the majority of people, the search for truth is but an escape, and action born out of this escape, born with the desire to seek truth, can give no comprehension. In that there is no significance, in that there is no fullness. We are out to seek God, we are out to find what truth is. In that desire to find out, we act. To me that desire is born out of fear, out of desire to escape from our innumerable difficulties. Therefore our action, our daily living, our thoughts, our emotion, our earning money, all these have no inherent value, because our action has as a motive the desire to gain, the desire to achieve, to realize truth, and we act from that craving. Therefore action itself has lost its significance. If you are kind to me because I give you something in return, then surely your kindness has no meaning, because you are looking for a reward.

Now in the same way, we seek out truth and act from that search, our action has no meaning, because we rely for the understanding of action on a result, we look to the effect of action rather than to action itself. Our action then is judged by the effect, by the sensation, by praise from others, and its success. So action inherently loses its value, because we are all the time looking to a result, to a reward. In our search which is born out of fear, out of escape, out of search for a solution, our action loses its own intrinsic significance. Only in action itself lies the whole of eternity.

If we become aware that we are acting in this way, then we do not seek truth through action, but in action itself. To me, action is awareness in that which you are doing. When you are aware, the past memories, past hindrances, past things that you have not fully comprehended, come into activity, without your trying to analyze the subconscious. That is true awareness. While you are acting, if you are fully conscious of all its significance, in that lies the true understanding of that action.

Now we look through action to gain something. We say, through self-discipline we shall find truth; through righteous acts we shall realize completeness; through loving, through service, we shall realize God. So service, love, kindliness, righteousness, which we call action, all lose their significance because we are all the time looking for a reward at the other end.

When you become aware of this, when you understand it, not only intellectually, but emotionally as well, when you feel it, the futility of such an act, and when you become so aware, then while you are acting in everyday things, all the past memories, hindrances, will come into activity, and thereby you will be free without analyzing. Where there is self-analysis there is death to action. The more and more you analyze, the less and less you will ever act, naturally, fully, spontaneously. In this self-analysis there is greater and greater effort and therefore a limitation of action. In such action there is always the observer, the watcher and the thing that acts, and in such action there is always a duality.

In action born of self-analysis there is no harmony, no completeness. Such action can never give you its full significance. Whereas if you are fully aware in action, which to me is true action, then in that flame all your past hindrances, your memories, your lack of comprehension, comes into full being and you free your mind from that limitation.

To understand what I am saying, you will have to experiment. I have heard so many people say to me, "What you are saying is not practical, has no use."

First of all, to find out if it is practical you have to experiment with it; you have to try it. Then, when you try to understand what I am saying, you will say, "What you are saying is very complicated, I cannot understand it."

Now this is what I am saying. I am going to try and make it as simple as I can.

Our action has always a motive. Our action is born of a reaction, out of a memory, out of a search for reward, achievement or truth, or for the love of another or the love of one's country, etc. I say that such action born of conformity, of authority, cannot give you its full significance in which alone lies the whole of eternity. And as the actions of most people are based on that, I say, do not therefore go to the opposite and say, "I must find out from what I am reacting." Do not say, "I must act from myself alone, not from reaction."

I say: Become conscious, become aware in your action that you are acting in search of reward. That is very simple, is it not? Become fully aware in your action, that you are acting through a desire for a reward, achievement, success, or through fear, through escape. The moment you have become fully conscious of that, the cause disappears, because you will have understood it. You can only do that when your mind and heart are fully occupied, are fully harmonious with that act.

Question: If there is harmony between mind and heart in action, where does will come in?

KRISHNAMURTI: The questioner wants to know, "If action is born out of the harmony of mind and heart, where does will come in?" Now what do you mean by will? Is it not the exertion or the effort to overcome, conquer? Will is the very center of effort, effort directed with the desire to be consistent, effort with regard to conquering. So that when there is a conflict there must be effort, and out of conflict there is born will, a resistance to overcome that conflict. To put it differently, where there is conflict, there is a consciousness of the 'I'. The 'I' is identified with self-consciousness, with will. So will is synonymous with that self-consciousness, that conflict.

Why is there conflict? Why is each one of us in conflict? I think because we have in our minds this idea of continual progress, endeavor, a ceaseless series of achievements, that perfection lies not at right angles to these innumerable steps towards perfection. We think that perfection lies at the end of a series of achievements, successes. To me perfection lies at right angles to that idea.

Conflict arises also, because we are lonely, because we are conscious of that insufficiency, and we try, through choice, to fill up that insufficiency. So where there is choice, there must be effort and hence there must be will.

We hope through choice to discern. We hope that by choosing this against that we will have learned, our mind will have grown bigger, our heart more expanded, that we will be nearer perfection through our choice.

To me discernment is impossible through choice. To put it differently, through will you cannot discern, through will you cannot comprehend, because will is created through resistance.

We want character, we want virtue and to develop character and to possess virtue there must be effort. Whereas to me, a man of character, a man of will, can never understand the full freedom of life, because his character, his will, is based on resistance. Please, if I am using the wrong word, pass through the words.

Will is developed through distinction. In distinction there is no comprehension. Distinction creates resistance. Distinction, which is choice, must create resistance, and out of that resistance there is the consciousness of will.

It is like damming up a river. There is a swirl, strong movement, a whirlpool of water. Then that dam is removed, there is a free flow of water. To me that dam represents the struggle for virtue, this constant development of character. This continual struggle to choose is but a resistance born of distinction. So I say: Do not choose, but discern. Discernment does not lie between two choices, between this and that, but is the freedom of both. When you have to decide between two things, what do you do? You calculate, you weigh, so you are merely looking at the opposites. Whereas, what happens when you have to decide something vital, something immense, which demands your whole concentration, your whole interest? You do not calculate, you do not weigh. Your thought and your emotions act right together and there comes out of that a true discernment.

This is what happens in every case, when you have to do something vital. You do not choose, you act with a full heart. That is what you call intuition. I purposely do not use that word because from my point of view, it has been so much misrepresented. So in the development of will you create a further resistance, and therefore further distinction, and hence, a greater conflict of choice. Your struggle is infinite, your endeavor is continual.

When you are acting naturally, spontaneously, easily, there is no will. You are acting from that fullness. In that there is no will. You have not to make an effort, you have not to control, to discipline, you have not to restrict, you have not to choose—you act.

It is only when there is self-consciousness which is the result of conflict, the result of resistance born of distinction, that will comes into being.

Question: For people who are not able to protect themselves from complete abasement, such as feeblemindedness, victims of their passions, morphinists, etc., is it not to be regarded rather as a help to belong to a religion, sect, or the like?

KRISHNAMURTI: Look here, friends. If you are such people, you must have a drug. Then you must have religion, you must have sects. If you are babies, you must have nurses, and the nurses will keep you as babies. You say, "I am not feebleminded and not a victim to my passion, but someone else is. Is it not necessary for him?"

Why do you consider him? Are you afraid of him? Are you acting out of pity, compassion for him? You say, "I will give him what is necessary for him, a religion, a sect, and the like." You adopt a superior attitude, what you call a considerate attitude, and give him a religion, and say, "Is it not necessary for him?" So you keep him, by your giving him a drug, you keep him as feebleminded as ever. That is the attitude always of class distinctions. The man who says, "I will give you what is necessary," keeps you always at that level below him, keeps that distinction. This has always been so throughout the ages. The man who has knowledge treats the other as being an imbecile, and gives him what is necessary and keeps him there.

Or we go the other way. We say, "I will awaken that man below to a higher attitude," which is another form of pity. To me, if a sect, a religion, is a limitation for you, it is a limitation for everybody. If, as I hold, there can not be a mediator between truth and yourself, then a priest is unnecessary for you, as well as for the feebleminded man.

You see, we want people to awaken to a certain result, to a certain image, to a certain pattern. We do not want people to be awake and let them find out, but we want them to be awakened to a particular point of view. For me, the importance is not religions and sects and all the rest of it, but to awaken him to the cause of these things. When he becomes awake for himself, then he will break away from the cause, instead of your giving him a panacea, of your giving him the opiate that will, you hope, awaken him; it does not.

This same thing applies to self-discipline, to everything. So the proper question is: Do you need it? Do you need religion, sects, self-discipline, imposition of authority to keep you straight, to make you behave, so that your acts shall be righteous? That is the way I would put the question. Do I need it, not someone else? And in freeing myself from that prison, I will not only break down my own walls, but I will help another to break down his, too. Make him realize the cause, not help him to break down the walls, because he will build another wall if you merely help him to destroy the wall.

Question: You mention discernment as an act of pure intuition. What is pure intuition and how can one know that it is pure, true?

KRISHNAMURTI: As I said: discernment is choiceless. Think about it. So long as the mind is caught up in choice, there cannot be direct perception of what is true, because choice is based on like and dislike, on want, and all want blinds. Now an action born of such a want, such a choice must create conflict, and one can only become conscious of that conflict, not of what is true intuition. When you ask me to explain what true intuition is, I say: You will know it, when your action is free of choice.

We are so little accustomed to act easily, without conflict. We are so frightened, because we have acted and the consequences have been so disastrous, so painful; so we go about trying to find out what is true action, what is pure intuition, so that we can grasp it intellectually and mold our minds and hearts to that effect. When we realize, when we become fully aware that our very actions are born of this escape, this fear, when we really feel that, then out of that there comes a natural action in which there is no conflict.

Most of our intuition is based on sensation. We like an idea, it gives us satisfaction, pleasure, contentment, and we say, "It is an intuitive idea," and we cling to it, because we want that idea. Therefore it is no longer a pure idea, a pure thing in itself. It happens so often that one hears of the idea of reincarnation and you jump at it and say, "It is an intuitive idea; I feel it is true." It must be so and you call that an intuitive idea or intuition. It is not at all intuition. It is because you want this idea of reincarnation, because you feel satisfaction, comfort, postponement of your discernment in the present, and it encourages you to cling to that idea.

We are not discussing whether reincarnation is a fact or not. We will go into that another time. That is of very little importance. As long as there is a want, a desire for comfort, security, then there can be no intuition, no true intuition, so do not inquire what is intuition, so long as you are caught up in it. Become aware that you are caught up in it and free yourself, and in that act there is intuition; such an act is born of intuition. You may think what I am saying is a negative way of approaching life. It is not. What you have been doing is to me a negative way of living, establishing a picture and living according to that, which you call a positive way of living, which is but an escape.

The same thing is implied in this question: "What is intuition? How shall one know when it is pure?" You will know when it is pure when there are no conflicts, when there is full reason behind it as well as feeling. But to have such action born of that intuition your mind and heart must be entirely free from fear, achievement, success, and all the rest of it. So look to that first and not to what is intuition.

Question: I am in disharmony with my thoughts, feelings, actions, and therefore dissatisfied. The reason is there is no understanding between my husband and myself, but I cannot go away from him because he is ill. What is your advice, so that I may come to a better understanding?

KRISHNAMURTI: First of all, we cling to people, because we ourselves are empty. We hope the other will enrich us. That is the reason why we possess people. So that creates disharmony also. Now that is one side.

The questioner wants to know what she shall do, because she is dissatisfied, living with that person, the husband. Either you are relying on him for your sufficiency, which he does not supply, which makes you feel dissatisfied, or you want to give to him and he will not accept, and therefore you are still dissatisfied. Or you do not like him, so you feel dissatisfied.

If you think about those three points, then the question will be answered. I do not advise what you shall do. You know we rely on each other for our strength, for our completeness. Husband and wife, brothers and sisters, etc. When that is not supplied, we feel utterly at a loss and we become thoroughly dissatisfied. We look to another for our completion, we look to another for love, for encouragement, because we are lonely. We turn to the other and we increase that loneliness. That loneliness becomes deeper and deeper, only we are trying to run away from it.

So when you realize that, when you really become aware that no one can fulfill you, can give you full completeness, except through your own comprehension, then you put up with minor details as having a husband ill in bed. Then the problem does not arise. The question, choice, of whether to stay or leave does not arise. Please think it over.

Choice arises, as in this case, what you should do, when you feel your husband, your brother, etc. cannot give you that fullness. Therefore you say, "To whom shall I turn? Another man or another woman?" in the hope that another shall give you, instead of the one that you have already. Whereas, if you realize fully, not mentally agree, not intellectually, if you really feel and think that it is utterly impossible for anyone to complete you, then you will act, irrespective of circumstances.

Question: Is impersonal love possible, while sex forces are still driving one into bonds of love which, however highly tuned, are still personal? How far are you in favor of recommending to guide those forces into higher centers by means of occult practices?

KRISHNAMURTI: Life is creative energy. It is the mind that splits it up as mental, emotional and sexual, and because you are caught up in passion, lust, you have divided it, and you want to transmute it somehow or other through practices. Because you do not live a complete life, there is a strong passion which dominates. I say, if you live completely, there will not be this conflict of emotion, sex, mind.

Question: How far are you in favor of recommending to guide those forces to higher centers by means of occult practices?

KRISHNAMURTI: You know, we think by practices, by doing a thing over and over again, we are gaining something. I do not believe in practices. I think they are detrimental. Please do not say, "Must I not practice a piano?" What you call occult practices is to instill in your mind a certain set of ideas, which you repeat, which you practice, so that this thing, against which you are fighting, is gradually submerged, suppressed, and you think you have transmuted sex to a higher plane. Sex is sex, you cannot transmute it. But you can be either caught in that energy, which becomes devastating, or you live in that energy so wholly that your acts are complete. This you have to think over very carefully. Please do not say, "I feel sexual, therefore I am going to live completely in it." Because our minds and hearts are so little awakened, so little ripe, mature, we take delight in passion. That fills our minds and our hearts. The whole of modern civilization is built on it, on sensation, because we are so little, and we hope through practices to conquer that littleness, which exists in our mind and our heart, and thereby transmute our sex to a higher plane.

So long as the mind and the heart are caught up in little things, then you will have all these sexual problems. If mind and heart are rich, full, great, then these things will have secondary importance. If you are truly creative by acting as a complete human being, then this problem does not arise. Then there is no problem. It is only when the mind and heart are divided in action against themselves that there is a problem, and to overcome that division, you want to practice. How absurd. That way you make your mind smaller and smaller, your heart becomes less and less through these continual practices. So, to really understand, and be free, find out if your mind and heart are crippled with conformity. Where there is conformity, there will be no release of life. There is conformity so long as you are seeking a reward, an achievement, the setting-up of authority, and hence the limitation, the curtailment of freedom.

So long as there is limitation of mind and heart, all these other problems will exist, and if you are seeking a solution, when you say "transmuting," that is what you are doing, seeking a solution, a way out, an escape, you are merely limiting that creative energy, which is thought, feeling, and everything, your whole being.

August 4, 1933

Seventh Talk at Ommen

Question: The other day you were speaking of immortality. You said it was neither annihilation nor continuation. You said you would speak further on the subject. Will you please explain further?

KRISHNAMURTI: We are conscious only, at least for the major part of our day, of duality. There is in us a constant conflict of duality. The thing that is going to achieve and the achieved, the actor and the action. So in our mind there is continually the sense of duality, the 'I' and the non 'I'. Now it is only when the mind and the heart are free of this duality, in that completeness, when the mind and heart are free of all sense of duality, in that completeness there is immortality.

Now we look to immortality as a continuance of the 'I'. When we talk about immortality, we want the particular, the 'I' to be continued, through time, indefinitely, enduringly.

We are only conscious, mostly, of the 'I'. We have memory of that 'I' only and nothing else. We occasionally have a glimpse of that permanent thing, of the reality, but most often we are conscious of that 'I', the 'I' of Krishnamurti, of X, Y, Z. So being conscious of that 'I' all the time, we want that 'I' to continue. Otherwise we think there is annihilation.

Now to me, the 'I' is but the result of conflict, is but the result of resistance, and we want to prolong it, this 'I', this conflict. We want to perfect this 'I', whereas if we are free of this conflict altogether, then there is, in that, immortality. In that, it is no longer a question of time, it is no longer 'I' enduring through time continually, without death. When the mind is free of the 'I', which can only happen in action, then in that there is realization of immortality, the timeless existence.

You know, it cannot be pictured, you cannot conceive mentally what immortality is. You cannot philosophize over it. It must be felt and it must be understood. Let me put it another way.

There is immortality, but to realize it, one must start with the transient. Immortality lies in the transient, not away from the transient. Now, we are discarding the transient and trying to find the permanent, whereas I say: Look to the transient and you will find the permanent, because when you discover what the transient values of your action are, born of mind and heart, in that transiency there is the fullness of that which is lasting, is eternal. Inherently in the transient itself is the permanent. We look to immortality as a means of escape or as an end to be arrived at through successive series of experiences. To me immortality is to be free of all sense of conflict, and you can only be free of the sense of conflict, when you have understood right values, and to understand right values, you must know all the transiency about you.

Question: We evade painful or unpleasant experiences. How can we be interested in all experiences?

KRISHNAMURTI: Why does one evade experience? Because one is afraid that one shall not gather the full meaning of that experience. Because one cannot gather the full significance of that experience, one suffers. Therefore one avoids it, and hence you choose experiences which are pleasant and experiences which are unpleasant, out of fear. Therefore the experiences, that you choose, do not yield their full significance. You can only meet experiences without fear, when you are not looking to gather the result from that experience.

Question: Is there a natural control of one's thoughts and emotions, which is not discipline?

KRISHNAMURTI: I went into this pretty thoroughly last week, about discipline and the futility of discipline, so I will go briefly over it, and I hope you will understand. Is not self-discipline born of memory? That is, when one does not understand an experience fully, it leaves a mark, and we call that memory, and that memory is all the time trying to mold us in our action. That is, memory acts as a standard, to which your mind and heart are trying to be consistent all the time. Hence the necessity for self-discipline. Whereas, if you are able to meet every experience with a free mind, with a freshness, then you will understand that experience, and the scratch of memory will not continue to act as a standard.

You see, we discipline ourselves, because in our action there is division. There is the observer and the actor; the mind that looks and the thing that acts. Therefore the mind is acting all the time as a guide.

Most of our thoughts, our mind, is composed of "must," and "must not." It does not act completely. Mind is a guard which watches over and controls, dominates, and therefore when you act, such action is very limited. Whereas if you act with harmony of mind as well as heart, that is with your whole being, then there is not the controller apart from action, and hence the futility of self-discipline.

Question: People who have had a glimpse of truth say that in such moments their 'I' consciousness has disappeared. Why is it not possible for such people to remain in that state permanently? What is the cause of their return to 'I' consciousness?

KRISHNAMURTI: The first part of this question, if I may say so, is wrongly put. The questioner says, "People who have had a glimpse of truth say that in such moments their 'I' consciousness has disappeared."

It is only when you are free from that sense of self-consciousness that you will know the permanent, the eternal. You see, here the questioner implies a coming back from a reality which he has perceived to be self-consciousness. So there is a sense of impermanence and a sense of the permanent. Most of us cling all the time, if we have caught a glimpse of reality, to the permanent; and so we try to make the permanent, through memory, lasting. I say forget the permanent. Don't even think about it, but be only aware of the impermanent.

You know, if you have a pain, you take some kind of medicine and for the moment you forget that pain, and that pain returns again. Likewise, we have an occasional glimpse of the permanent, but more often we are conscious of the impermanent, of the transient, of the conflict, and the mind naturally clings, in the hope to make the permanent lasting, to that glimpse.

If the mind clings to the permanent, it cannot but be a drug, because it is trying to escape from the impermanent, from the conflict, from the transient, so that which it clings to cannot be true, because then that permanent is but an escape. Therefore it is not true. Whereas if you understand the cause of conflict, if you understand the significance of your action, then in that there is permanency, and in that there is not this coming back and forth from the real to the false. So do not look to the permanent, but rather understand the transient, understand the cause of conflict which prevents you from understanding the permanent.

Question: Is there anything which prevents one from being that truth of which you speak, if one attends a ceremony and enjoys that ceremony for its beauty (as another might enjoy a fine picture or jewels or anything) and when one takes part in the ceremony for its own sake and not in order to gain power or degrees or anything of that sort?

KRISHNAMURTI: We go through this regularly. If you enjoy ceremonies, enjoy! Why do you want a reason for it? You never asked this question with regard to music. You never say, "Should I enjoy music?" Or, "Should I enjoy a picture?" So, why do you say, "Should I not enjoy ceremonies?"

My point of view with regard to ceremonies is very simple. I think, where there is unrighteousness, there are ceremonies. Sorry, I am not being dogmatic or harsh. To me, ceremonies have no meaning, no significance. They are created by men through fear. We give all kinds of significance to them, that they help, that they are beautiful, that power pours through them, all those things.

One goes to those ceremonies in order to get sensationally elevated, sensationally gratified, and we all hope we are getting nearer and nearer truth through those ceremonies, somehow or other—that it will help man to coordinate his body, his ideas, etc. To me, ceremonies act as a drug. They help for a moment to make you forget. So do not compare ceremonies with music, with painting, with beautiful pieces of art. The music, art, is born not out of fear; it is a natural spontaneous expression; whereas ceremonies are created through fear in search for divinity and righteous behavior, to urge people in a certain direction.

Please, that is my opinion, and I know that lots of people are feeling uncomfortable. To find out if you are a slave to ceremony—because after all, one is a slave to a thing when one has not found out its true value—to find out if you are really free to act as a complete human being, discover for yourself the true value of ceremonies. To discover, do not say, "It is right," or "It is wrong." Be completely detached from it, and then you will find out whether it has value. But both the ceremonialist and the nonceremonialist are attached, and therefore their discernment is not true. To understand a thing, let it go and then examine it.

Question: Does an action necessarily need to express itself in the physical world to be complete? For example, if a man hates another one to the point of wanting to hurt him, shall his action be complete, only if he hurts or kills him, or can he free himself, and learn in the same way by facing this violent feeling inwardly?

KRISHNAMURTI: Why do you want to hurt another? Either because you want something from him, and he does not give it to you, and therefore you are annoyed, and want to hurt him in return, or he has deprived you of something, or you are jealous. He has taken away something from you or he has not given you what you want. You are awakened to your own insufficiency, to your own littleness, emptiness, and to run away, to escape from that, you get annoyed, you want to hurt. In hurting, would you consider that a complete action, born out of fear, born out of that loneliness?

To me it is not a complete action. Is it not simple? I know, discussions have been taking place here whether you should go out and kill people, because you have heard me talking about acting completely. What a waste of time! Either you do not understand the significance of my words, or you understand merely the superficial meanings. So, wait a minute. You want to hurt another when you are conscious of your own loneliness, when you are forced to face your own emptiness, and you react against the person who forces you to that conscious emptiness, and if you react from that, it is but a reaction. Whereas, if you find out what is the cause of that loneliness and free yourself from that cause and then act, in that there is harmony, in that there is completeness.

Question: The liberation you explain to us, which you have reached yourself, is that all? Or is it the key to the door which leads to still higher conditions of universal life?

KRISHNAMURTI: If you have a pain and someone relieves you of that pain, you don't say, "Is that all?" If you are happy, you don't say, "Is that all?" Why do you put such a question? Because you do not really understand what liberation means! To me it is an eternal becoming, but you can only know it when the mind is free of this continual, ceaseless effort, which is also a transient becoming. That which is growing is not eternal, and we are conscious of this ceaseless growing, expanding of mind and heart and all that, achievement. You say, "If I do not achieve, if I do not grow, what is there?" You will know what is there when your mind and heart have understood the true value, the true worth of this ceaseless growing. Therefore understand that, not what is beyond liberation or whether liberation is a door which opens to greater life. But begin with that thing which is gnawing your mind and heart, that ceaseless growing, wanting to grow.

Liberation to me is an infinite becoming, but one has to understand it, this timeless becoming. Time will exist so long as there is effort, effort in the pursuit of virtue, effort in developing character, effort in regard to the possession of a will, effort with regard to choice. All these indicate a limitation of time and this ceaseless effort of growing with which we identify ourselves as self-consciousness, as the 'I'.

When the mind is free of that, then you will know what liberation is. You cannot picture, you cannot imagine what this timeless becoming is. If you could imagine it, it must of necessity be born of opposites; therefore it cannot be true. Therefore do not begin with that; do not try to picture to yourself what this thing is. Please, do try it, and you will see how simple it is. Begin with something of which you are conscious, of which you know, this conflict, this suffering, this continual battle of choice—and they will exist as long as the mind and heart are craving for achievement, for success, gain, result. And there is that search for a result, gain, achievement, because one is empty. One wants to cover it up, fill it up; we want all the time to accumulate and the very accumulation creates emptiness. The very pursuit of achievement brings emptiness. If you really see this, if you really feel it, then you will not run away, then you will stop up all the avenues of escape, and then you will face that loneliness, and out of that comes pure action.

Question: Should an experience be remembered until it is understood or not remembered at all?

KRISHNAMURTI: You cannot forget an experience which you have not understood. It remains. But if you have understood a thing, it is over. The mind is free to face life afresh, anew. It is experiences which have not been completely understood, that create a barrier, that give the mind a jaded memory, which prevents you from living each day afresh, anew.

So it is not a question of remembering or not remembering a particular experience, but it is meeting all experiences afresh, with open frankness and you can only meet an experience frankly, openly, freshly, when your mind is not seeking a result or when the mind is not shaped, molded, through consistency, born of memory, through limitation. Our minds are caught up in all these things and therefore we cannot meet these experiences frankly. That is why I say: Be fully aware how your mind is acting and how your heart is feeling, whether it is born of the search for a reward, or born of escape from fear. And then, when you are free from all these things, because you understand them, not because you have thrown them away, then you can meet them. Then you can have a mind and heart that are swift to follow wisdom and in that there is ecstacy.

Question: Please explain the difference between awareness and watching.

KRISHNAMURTI: In watchfulness there is always the desire to gain; in awareness there is direct perception.

When do you watch? First of all, why is there a watcher? Who is the watcher? You call it a higher self, who watches the lower. That is, you have established a duality, a division, a distinction in your action, because you do not approach that action fully, completely with both your mind and heart. Therefore there is a distinction, as an observer, a watcher, who looks upon his act. So that watcher is continually guiding, shaping; he is never taking part in the act; he is always aloof, objective. That is not awareness, because that watchfulness creates duality; there is always a distinction. Whereas awareness is complete action in which the mind and heart are one.

When you do anything naturally, with great interest, simply, spontaneously, there is no observer; there is not a thing which watches that act, such as when you love. But there is an observer when your action is born of fear, or when you have incompletely understood an experience, the 'I must' and 'I must not', the mind which is always warning. So I hope you will see the difference between awareness and watchfulness. The two have nothing to do with each other. When you have a natural spontaneous interest, you do that thing harmoniously, wholly, without this division of the watcher, the mind which is looking to analyze it. It is only when your mind and heart are not fully interested, that there is born the watcher, the difficulty, the control, the discipline imposed by the watcher. You may call it the higher self, but it is still a duality.

Question: One begins to untie one knot and finds that there are a dozen others. Where shall one begin and where end?

KRISHNAMURTI: If you untie the knot of one difficulty, because you have found a solution for that knot, then there will be a dozen other knots. If I untie, unravel, a difficulty, a problem, in the search of a solution, then I develop other knots. Most people are seeking a way out of a difficulty; they are seeking a solution. They are not concerned in untying, but they are concerned with a solution, a way out of that difficulty.

If I have a difficulty, I do not want to seek a solution for the difficulty. I know there are solutions, innumerable solutions, but I want to find out what the cause of that problem is, and when I have really understood the cause of that problem, I do not create any other knots, any other problems. If I really understand one problem completely, wholly, then there are no other problems. Please, think it over and you will see.

It is because we do not face one thing completely, we create many others. We go from one thing to another. Life becomes one series of problems, because we have not been able to understand or to tackle one thing only. Therefore it depends on how you untie the knot, not what solution you apply to it, but the manner, with what awareness you do it. You can untie a knot observing it, analyzing it, carefully, mentally, and therefore creating another set of problems, or you can in awareness, in meeting that problem wholly, with your mind and heart, with your whole being, approach that problem and then it dissolves. Therefore everything you meet, you are able to meet wholly, and are therefore free, and therefore the thing that you meet does not leave a scar, which you call a problem.

Question: You spoke of a child who was told of reincarnation when asking about death. The child was weeping at the death of a playmate. What would you have done or what would you have said to it to help it understand?

KRISHNAMURTI: What I am going to say sounds so absurdly simple, that I hope you will understand it. I personally would tell that child: Look at a flower, it withers and dies. I can say it, because I am not afraid of death; it is a natural thing, inevitable. All things must wear out and die. Because one is afraid of death, one is not able to face it simply.

I am not talking of accepting the inevitable. We all do that. That is a foolish way of looking at life. So, if you are not afraid, you do not give complicated reasons, such as reincarnation. What can the child understand about reincarnation? You think it understands it, because you yourself, feel satisfied with that idea. If mommy is satisfied, then I must be satisfied with it. You pass that atmosphere of satisfaction and the child, being very sensitive, takes it on.

So, what causes you to be afraid of death? Because first you say, "I do not know what life is beyond," and you say that because this life has not been full. You are concerned with what lies beyond the grave, and hereafter, only when this life has not given you its richness, its plenitude. If this life is rich, if your single day is immense, complete, then you are not afraid of tomorrow, but you look to tomorrow when today has crumbled.

In reincarnation there is ever death, there is ever a beginning and a death. That idea does not really free you from fear, you momentarily postpone, that is all. You may be united with your friend, your lover, your brother or anyone, but there is still death. You are satisfied with that idea, because it momentarily gives you satisfaction. So as it gives you satisfaction, you pass it on to your child, to your neighbor, to anybody else, because they are all wanting satisfaction. And so they all take up your idea and so you have created a wonderful society, organization, in which all believe in reincarnation and you think you have solved the problem.

I am not sarcastic, but I am just showing you that where there is that idea of reincarnation, there must also be a death at the same time. Therefore you have not really understood, you have but escaped. What creates fear of death is incompleteness, and incompleteness is not overcome by an idea, or by following a pattern or living to a certain set of standards. When the mind is free of all these standards, there is understanding of right values. Then there is a complete act, and in that act, in living completely, which is action in infinity, in that there is no beginning or end and then you are not afraid of death.

You see, you cannot explain all this to a child. If it were a very small child, I would talk to it about the flower, and show it to him or her, and as it grows up, discuss it, awaken its own intelligence, not push down your ideas on it. You see, one must have an exquisitely pliable mind to understand truth, a very subtle mind. For wisdom is very swift and to follow it, you must be unhampered, and all incompleteness which creates memory is hampering, is a limitation, and such a mind cannot understand.

So you will know that deathless becoming without an end or a beginning, when you are living completely. Do not say, "Is that all or will it lead me further?" If you are not completely living, then you will ask, "Is that all or will it lead me further?" Then your day is not rich or simple, then your act is not complete, because you are always looking to further things. Your action is merely then a means to an end. Such an action can only be incomplete. Whereas, if you live completely in action, then you will not be afraid of death, then reincarnation becomes a very small thing.

You know, if you are living without that sense of 'I', which is the discovery of right values, then you are no longer limited by time. Now, we are limited by time. There is yesterday, today, and tomorrow, not a thing which is complete, which has no beginning and no end. That timeless becoming, or that becoming in which there is no time, in which there is not the division of the past, present, and future, you can only understand when your mind is free from all choice, because choice creates opposites. And in true discernment, which is not born of opposites, there is a timeless living reality.

August 5, 1933

Eighth Talk at Ommen

I am going to try to put it differently what I have been saying during the last four days and previously also.

Unconsciously, without our giving deliberate thought to it, we are trying to seek certainty, certainty born from the knowledge which we gather from books, or our experiences, or the experiences of a wise man. So in seeking this certainty, we establish ideals, based on what others have said with conviction, seasoned in tradition. They become, as it were, the touchstone by which we choose, so that as a weight, as a measure, we can use that ideal or that certainty to judge what is false and what is true, what is essential and what is not essential.

You will see that this is so, when you regard all the sacred literature of various countries and what people have made of it. You will see that they have created out of that what they desired truth to be, or God to be, or what they think a perfect spiritual life should be. And having created that certainty, then they use that as a measure by which to judge their conduct, their action, so that they can choose what is essential and what is not essential.

This establishment of certainty creates a constant necessity of choice and thereby increases effort. When once we have established a pattern, then constant choice exists, because according to that pattern we are acting. We decide our conduct, according to that. So, whenever a choice, a decision has to be made, we decide according to that and thereby establish a series of continual choices.

Naturally this constant effort at choice increases, and this continued effort at choice, at decision, differentiating between the essential and the unessential, is called growth, progress, and evolution. This constant effort at choosing the essential because you are seeking a certainty, must necessitate continued effort. And after accumulating through choice, we are afraid to lose what we have accumulated. That is why we are afraid of death. We make all effort to choose and choice is based on certainty, and after accumulating, we are afraid of losing; and when there is death, we are afraid it will put an end to the plan which we have made for accumulating, so we are afraid of death.

Through choice we begin to accumulate, and when there is death, there is a fear of it, because there is a losing of that accumulation. Also there is an end to planning, to further accumulation. Hence there is a constant fear of death, and naturally, when there is a fear of death, we take comfort in the hereafter or in the idea of reincarnation.

After accumulating, we are afraid of loss or of the emptiness which arises in the event of death, which prevents you from further accumulation. We want to be certain that we shall accumulate, that we shall continue that which we have accumulated, and hence we have taken consolation in the hereafter, heaven, hell—no comfort in hell, of course—but in the idea of reincarnation.

Our search is the certainty, not of truth, truth is not a certainty, to me certainty is false. We are seeking certainty and that has become the goal and we call that certainty peace, tranquillity, harmony, silence, light, all the spiritual words you have, higher plane, etc.

So this certainty, please follow this, which you are seeking, prevents you from doubting. Because you are seeking a certainty, you are denying doubt, which has nothing to do with suspicion. If you look at yourself, you will see that you are all the time avoiding being in a condition of doubt, that is, a condition of pliability; you want to be certain, which to me necessitates a choice. In doubt there is no choice; doubt prevents choice.

So when you crave for certainty, when you seek security, you must certainly discard and fear doubt. Now to me, doubt is a continual movement of thought and emotion, not blocked by certainty. When you are seeking certainty, you must have gurus, guides, saviors, and above all, a method of which you constantly ask, "What is the method to get at this truth?" When you say that, you mean, "What is the method by which I can be assured, certain." Truth has nothing whatever to do with certainty, therefore there is no method to it, no technique, no way.

When you are seeking certainty, also there must be discipline, spiritual and religious organization, all of which encourage and give you the support which you want, from which you can act.

To me then, certainty destroys this constant renewing of thought and emotion, this constant pliability, this constant subtlety. A mind that is certain cannot be subtle, swift. To follow wisdom, which is true value, you must be free from this false idea of certainty.

So choice or decision, hence resistance in terms of certainty, which is an illusion, crystallizes and petrifies thought and feeling. That is what you call self-discipline. Please, I am using words here for you to look through. Words for me are like a glass to look through to the real significance of what I am saying.

So this is what is happening to the people who take certainty to their hearts, and to the people who are offering certainty. Where there is this overbalancing of certainty, there is not an even flow of thought and emotion. Where there is certainty, there cannot be understanding. Certainty is an illusion, it is false, inherently, like security. Where a mind is searching for security, it must have discipline, it must have an ideal by which it can guide itself. Then it must have those who will give you those ideals and then it must have many illusions in which it can take shelter and thereby create this stagnation of the mind in which there is choice. Where the mind is certain, crystallized, there exist choice, opposites.

Now if you have understood what I have said, that the illusion of this certainty which everyone is seeking with all its subtleties and deceptions, not only mentally, but if you understand it completely, you will feel the utter valuelessness of certainty. Then your being is not split up, the mind is not trying to control the emotion which wants to be certain. Then your mind does not impose discipline on the emotion which wants to be assured.

But if you want certainty emotionally, then your mind will inflict a discipline, then there is conflict, then there is continual effort. Whereas if you really understand it with all your being, with your mind as well as your heart, wholly, the futility of certainty, which creates time, the fear of death, a beginning and an end, then your action itself is freed from certainty without effort.

Effort exists when your mind and heart are not in full harmonious agreement, when your mind wants certainty and your emotions do not want certainty. To make them come together in perfect union, each must be fully aware of the other, is that not so? What is happening is that you want certainty emotionally, which you keep hidden, and mentally you do not want certainty, which is exposed. So they never meet. Whereas if you are frank and let them meet, you will know then that flame of awareness which destroys false illusions.

You may have understood more or less intellectually, naturally not with all its significance, because you have not had time to think about it. You have understood sufficiently intellectually, but emotionally you may still want certain things and hence the conflict of not wanting and wanting. Do not try to dominate one over the other or do not try to identify one with the other, but let your mind become conscious of your emotional desire for certainty and let your emotion become aware of the mental understanding of the futility of certainty. It is very simple, if you follow it. The difficulty is, you are so full of knowledge, you are so full of certainty, which destroys you. There is not the pliability, the eagerness to find out. When you are eager to find out, there cannot be certainty. There must be a freedom, there must be a movement, there must be swiftness. But a mind that is anchored to a certainty of knowledge, cannot wander, cannot follow, cannot pursue that wisdom.

Question: Why do you say, "Beware of the man who says, 'I know'." Cannot he be truthful, who says, "I know"?

KRISHNAMURTI: He can be truthful, but such a man does not know what truth is. Why do you pay respect to a man who says, "I know that there is God, that there is truth, that there is immortality, that there is a Master"? Why do you pay respect? Because you are seeking certainty.

You can only know that which is static, not that which is dynamic, moving. You cannot say, "I know a thing that is moving." It is truth, that which is alive. You cannot describe it, you cannot put it in a frame and say, "This is it." Because we are seeking this constant certainty, assurance, security, we give all our love, our devotion, our trust, everything to the man who says, "I know." You yourself want to be quiet, you yourself desire this constant assurance, which you think will free you from this conflict. It does not, it only dulls you.

Truth is not to be known, it is not static, it is not an end, a goal. It is a continual renewing, ever-becoming. Therefore beware of the man who says, "I know." Not of the man, but of yourself, because you respect that man, who gives you what you want, comfort. Therein lies exploitation. You are creating that man as your exploiter.

Question: You speak earnestly about understanding, but you depreciate tolerance. Is not a man of true understanding really tolerant?

KRISHNAMURTI: Understanding has nothing to do with tolerance. You do not love anybody, greatly, when you tolerate them, do you? Tolerance is an intellectual thing. You say, "Truth has so many sides, so many paths." All paths lead to truth, whatever the method you have, the mode. So having created a theory, you then proceed to be tolerant to that theory, to the people who follow it, whereas understanding is complete. In that, there is no tolerance, which is such a false thing from my point of view. Either a man is in illusion or he is not in illusion. But because we cannot be friendly, we invent the word *tolerance.* Because you happen to disagree with me, in what I am saying—and I think the majority of you do—don't shake your heads; you do, or otherwise your actions would be different.

I am not tolerant to you. If I were your superior, if I were intellectually saying, "You will also arrive at that truth from your particular illusion," then I would be tolerant. But I say that you cannot know what truth is by any illusion, by the illusion of ceremonies, Masters, discipline, any of these. So there is no tolerance. Not that I am not friendly, not that I want you to come over to my way of understanding. You know when there is real affection, you are not tolerant. You are not tolerant in your love, you are tolerant to the man who thinks differently from you. Because there is no understanding, you have invented intellectually this word *tolerance* or you use a bigger word *brotherhood.*

Don't you see, there are only two things, truth and illusion. And the man who understands truth is not tolerant to an illusion. It is an illusion. He understands it, and he understands it only when he discovers the right value of those illusions. If he does not, then you will have to be tolerant with regard to those illusions. To put it differently, each one of you wants to pursue his own particular narrow little way, either nationalistic, capitalistic, class distinctions or religious or temperamental distinctions. You want to pursue individualistically your own narrow way, and you have to invent the words *tolerance* and *brotherhood,* to keep you within decent bounds. Whereas if you are free of all these limitations, if you are really fighting against that, destroying that, then you would not be tolerant, you would be really friendly because there would be understanding.

Now you want to cling to your own national flag and you feel so elated, when you do it, that when another does the same thing, you have to be tolerant to him. If you have not a flag, if you are perfectly empty, naked, then you would understand true wisdom, which cannot be arrived at through this narrow idea of brotherhood or tolerance.

Question: I do not understand the sentence, "Love not with the mind." Will you explain?

KRISHNAMURTI: Tolerance is loving with the mind, brotherhood is loving with the mind. Because our minds are so acutely developed in cunningness, in subtlety, in selfishness, we are forcing ourselves to be tolerant or love one another, or help another, serve another, all intellectual things. Whereas, if you really love with your mind as well as with your heart, with your whole being, you are not tolerant, you are not helpful, you are not searching out service. You are, and therefore you love, therefore you serve, therefore you help.

Question: You have said that one or two people like yourself would change the face of the world. Would it not be a kindness to us, if you married and brought up a few children, whom you could assist from the very commencement to be free of reactions. At present all my virtues and vices are actually aroused and there seems little hope of getting out of them as an adult. If I could become your child next life, could not you bring me up as a free, liberated man?

KRISHNAMURTI: I think the answer to this question has been given by your laughing about it.

Question: You say that ceremonies are born out of unrighteousness. Is that not a point of view, say, of yours, and of those of a particular temperament, or do you say this as a truth, universal in its application?

KRISHNAMURTI: Did you notice yesterday and the day before, when I talked about sex and ceremonies, what attention there was? I wonder how many of you noticed it. Why was there this attention? Because you were interested. That attention does not exist when I am talking about something real. Not that ceremonies and sex are not real to you. Isn't it extraordinary!

I am not putting them together, but it happens—life is like that. My point is, you are concerned about sex and about ceremonies and yet you are seeking, at least you are attempting to seek truth or God or any of these things. And your natural instincts are these, because by your attention you showed it. I am talking now about what you are really interested in. That struck me so much yesterday and the day before. You want a way out of sex, a way out of ceremonies, whether you should do it or not do it. A complete man, a man who is really rich in himself, self-sufficient, to him this confusion does not exist; there is no choice to be made.

You ask now if where there are ceremonies, there is unrighteousness—is that my particular point of view, representing a particular temperament, or is it universal as a truism? A man who has a temperament, cannot understand truth; a man who is particular cannot understand the whole. I say that I have understood the whole. I say ceremony is an illusion, not as a particular, Krishnamurti, human being, but as a true thing. It has no validity. You may give all kinds of attributes to ceremony in your search for sensation, security. It is longing to grow, which is to accumulate, and therefore not death. I know some of you are ceremonialists, you want to do them and there is nothing more to be said. I am not tolerant with you. I do not feel the distinction. If you feel like it, go ahead and do it. But since you are here and want to understand what I am saying with regard to ceremony, you must have an open mind. You cannot say that is my particular temperament and therefore I feel like that. You say, "Because I have been surrounded by so many ceremonialists, my reaction is to be against ceremonies," or "Because I am so advanced, ceremonies are futile for me, but you say you need them." Or, "We do it because of its intrinsic beauty, like a pianist." A pianist does not talk like that. The people who are insincere, who are not frank, talk like that. I am not harsh, I really do not care, honestly, whether you perform ceremonies. I mean it. Not that I am tolerant, because I understand, at least I think I do, why you perform ceremonies, why ceremonies are so important to you, as your search for the Master and discipleship and all the rest of it, why it is important. I understand it, because it gives you a certain sensation, this idea that you are being looked after, have a personal God, security, certainty, comfort.

So when you see a thing so blatantly, openly, you cannot be tolerant about it. You understand it. So I am not talking out of harshness or hardness of heart, or out of impatience or of a particular temperament, or that I want you to follow what I am saying. I really do not care, because I am not seeking a result. I do not want you to come over to my particular point of view, because I have no point of view at all. I have not a fixed thing which says: This is truth, this is false. I say, in the very illusion, if you understand it with all its significance, lies the flowering of truth, in the very illusion itself. As you are surrounded by illusions, do not cling to them, examine them, go into them profoundly. Do not say, "I like it, therefore I accept it." Because you are so prejudiced, you want to cling to it. I cannot think of all the excuses you give, when you are performing a ceremony. So, do not say, "He did not say that, so therefore I can go on."

To me the whole idea inherently has no true value, because it is born of fear, this search for solution, sensation. And I say, if you really understand it, if you approach it not only intellectually but with your whole being, you ripen your thought with regard to ceremony and ripen your emotion with regard to ceremony; completely let them come together and let them find out without your identifying yourself with one or the other.

Let it flow as you let a kite fly in the sky. Let your thoughts and emotions loose and you will find out. If you feel you should do it, do it, don't discuss about it. It is like people that come to me and ask, "Should I leave a particular society or should I have an attitude to a particular society?" If they want it, they remain. Don't you see life becomes beautifully simple, when you treat it simply. It is only when you are trying to get something out of it, that you have complications.

You can be like the savage who is satisfied with what he has, or a truly consummate man who is free from all sense of want.

Question: How do you look today on your little book: "At the Feet of the Master"?

KRISHNAMURTI: I wonder why you ask me that. Either you want me to censor my book of the past, or ask you not to read it. In other words you want me to act as a censor of what you shall read and what you shall not read. This question implies whether I still believe in Masters, or whether you, who are giving my ideas abroad, should introduce this book, because now I no longer believe in Masters. So you are acting as the censor of what other people should read, and you are asking me to do exactly the same thing with what you should read. Read it, if you are interested in reading it. Don't say, "I should read this book and not this book."

Much more is implied in this question. You are trying to create a sect around me. You have that sectarian mind which is seeking a result, and you ask yourself, "Shall I distribute this or not?" If a man wants it, give it to him, let him find out, for heaven's sake, whether the Master exists, whether you must go through discipleship or all the rest. If you don't give it to him, someone else will. So, why not give it to him?

Now to go further back to this question, this idea of a guru, leading you to truth, a Master, a guide, a leader. You notice, we go through this every year. This whole idea of discipleship, this whole idea of pursuing a Master, who will lead you to truth, is utterly false. Please, I am not talking from a certain temperament, not because I have realized, therefore I looked down on him. Do not think of all these things, but come to it freshly, get your minds fresh, not burdened with all these ideas.

Now what does discipleship and Mastership mean fundamentally, apart from names and people who tell you they exist. We are not discussing that, whether they exist or not; that is a very small thing, but the idea behind it. Why do you want them at all? Why do you seek them at all?

Because you want to be sure that you will come to that truth and so you create exploiters, people who will tell you whether you are disciples or not, priests and all the men who possess you, all the tribe of capitalists or communists or anything.

You want to be assured that you are progressing, that you are growing, that your efforts have an end, and will bring about a result. So when you are seeking that, then people arise naturally who tell you, "There are results, you can be assured, you can be made certain." And so you feel quite happy in your action because you are going to get something at the end of it. That is, if you behave righteously, if you do certain things, you will get something in return, which is the old primitive idea that you butcher the animal to please a God. Only we do it now intellectually, more subtly, we butcher our own individual thinking, freedom, that ecstasy of living, for a reward which we seek.

You cannot realize truth in any action; you cannot know that immortal ecstasy through the search for a reward, nor can you find the thing, realize it or understand it through another. It is only when the mind is absolutely pliable, free from all choices, when action is complete, that you will know what that living ecstasy, that infinite reality is, that ever renewing, becoming, life.

Question: You have said that though one should be free from authority in spiritual life, it was necessary in material work. Is not there a danger that in this statement the authority of those who are in authority and are still "conditioned by fear" is excused, even where this hampers and throttles the developing mentality of spontaneous and pure action in those who work under this authority? What is your opinion on this point?

KRISHNAMURTI: I will put differently the same thing which I put two years ago. Where there is authority, there cannot be understanding. If you are freeing yourself from authority, because you understand it, not because you throw it overboard and say, "I must not obey something"; then you will obey something, then you will obey somebody, because the government will come down and hold you. But if you are freeing yourself, because you understand authority, then authority does not exist for you even in material things.

You do not cooperate because of authority—I know we do because of fear—but if you understand the significance, the meaning, the thing that lies behind authority, and you yourself, because of that understanding, are free of it, then you will cooperate with authority. That is, because you are rich in yourself, nothing can mold you, because you are infinitely pliable, you are not afraid of going into that thing which is holding you, because then, nothing will hold you. It is because we are not free from the exertion of authority or of looking through authority, because we are not rich in ourselves, that we are afraid that external authority will pervert our thought subtly, and feeling.

So when you understand the authority of certainty, when you are really free from this desire to be certain, assured, secure, when your whole being is full as the moon, without anything to lose, then there is no authority, nor its opposite, humility.

Question: By continually looking and searching in oneself, does not one become egotistic?

KRISHNAMURTI: Certainly, you do become egotistic. That is what has happened. Why ask such a question? I have never been advocating that. On the contrary, all these processes of psychoanalysis, dissecting oneself, watching oneself in action, introspection, must necessarily bring about a narrowing down of mind and heart, which we call egotistic. I have been talking of exactly the opposite. I have said that in self-analysis there is destruction and I have explained the reason why. You analyze only when you have not understood, and to understand is not to analyze, to look back, but to meet everything afresh, anew—not to reopen a dead thing and examine that dead thing. From that you will not understand. But if you are fully awakened, alive, alert, and you meet an alive thing, then you will understand that. And in that awakened interest all the hindrances of the past come into being, without your delving into the subconscious to bring it out. You cannot understand a dead thing, you can only understand a live thing.

So naturally, the more and more you think about your actions, the more and more you watch, introspect, and analyze, the narrower, the more irksome, tiresome, struggling becomes your life.

That is what has happened. This is self-discipline, this search for certainty, assurance, all this has led to a deep, subtle egotism. And to me this duality in action, the watcher and the thing that is acting, destroys harmonious action. And it is only in harmonious action which takes place only when there is a crisis, that you discover the true value of things. It is only when you act harmoniously that you discover the right value of things, and that gives you the richness of understanding, and hence all the conflicts of introspection and self-analysis disappear.

August 6, 1933

Ninth Talk at Ommen

As there has been so much confusion as to what I have been talking about, I am going to try and explain it, and put it differently, and I hope I shall make it simpler.

We have an idea that completeness, wholeness, can be understood or realized through a part. You come with your particular problem and you try to seek a solution for that particular problem and try to apply what I have been saying little by little to that particular problem. You hope to understand that wholeness, that completeness, through a particular part, through a particular problem. Now the idea of a series of ideas forming a teaching or of coming to the whole through any one of those single ideas, is to me utterly false. First of all you say I am giving you a certain teaching, then you take a single idea from the whole and try to apply that one idea to your particular problem. So you hope to come to the fullness of the whole through the particular.

Now you come here with the mentality that whatever is troubling you, you want to have solved, and hope that you will find a solution through a particular teaching that I am giving by using one of the ideas of that teaching as a means of solving your problem. That is, by gradually accumulating and understanding a series of problems, you hope you will come to the fullness of the totality—that immensity of life. So you say to yourself, "I shall grow into the whole through understanding, through gathering many particulars."

With all these accumulations, with these methods, you seek to understand what I am saying. Each one has a different problem and you come to listen to me in the hope that applying one idea of which I am talking to your special problem, you will come to the totality, to the wholeness. Most of us are crippled with that idea, that we shall come to the whole through a part.

Now with that idea you come and say, "Please help me to understand my particular problem." Do not look at what I have been saying with that idea of trying to solve a problem, because I want to show that in understanding one experience, the whole is realized. In understanding the cause of one problem, you will understand the whole, if you approach the problem intelligently. As it is now, we make an effort, like a fish caught in a net, to escape from that problem or to seek a solution of that problem, to be rid of it. We say to ourselves, "If I can only be rid of the many hindrances, then I shall realize the whole." So you make a tremendous effort to be rid of these hindrances.

What I want to show is that where there is effort to be rid of something, you create another barrier; whereas in the movement of action in the present, there is awareness of the hindrances which prevent you from action. Now we say, "I must be rid of the hindrances in order to realize that totality of life." So you make an effort to get rid of these hindrances. But in fact, in your desire to conquer truth, you are merely running away from your hindrances when you say you must get rid of them.

Because your longing for truth is so great, you run away from your hindrances. So, in trying to conquer your hindrances, you are like a fish caught in a net; whereas, in the movement of action you will become aware of the hindrances and in that awareness you will be freed of these hindrances, because you will understand their cause. You are trying to get rid of hindrances, because you are wanting truth—while before you wanted a savior, Masters, discipleship, heaven, etc. Now you want liberation in the same way. So you say, "I must get rid of hindrances," and you make a tremendous effort, a desperate effort to get rid of them. Whereas, to understand the totality of life, you cannot come to it or realize it or understand it through effort, because effort is merely an endeavor to overcome something. Where there is conquering, there is an escape. So do not make an effort to be rid of hindrances. In the movement of action—and action is always in the present, not in the dead past—in that movement of action in the present, you will be aware why your actions are not complete, what prevents you from completing that particular action. Then you will know the cause.

But, you will say to me, "The past hindrance is fully alive, it holds me; it is so alive that I cannot act freely in the present." What gives life to past hindrances? The vitality of past hindrances is caused through memory, conscious or unconscious, and we act from that memory. I have a hindrance and my memory is attached to that hindrance, consciously or subconsciously, and I act from that reaction, which I call memory. It is simple, if you think about it a little. We are acting from memory, memory of an idea, a mental picture, a social standard, etc. and so we give life to the hindrances of the past. And we increase and give vitality to that hindrance all the time. Now this memory which exists when there is incomplete action, this series of memories, these layers of memory make up self-consciousness, the 'I', from which all action takes place. This memory, this incompleteness, which is always impressing itself on our minds and hearts, creates the 'I' and this is the source of the 'I'.

To put it differently, the 'I', self-consciousness, that 'I' which is active, is nothing but a bundle of inherited perversions, social virtues and their opposites. Our action, then, which is but a reaction, comes from this memory, which we call the 'I'. So that 'I' is the creator of illusion, and what we are doing now is to try to get rid of illusions one by one. You say, "I am in a particular illusion and I must get rid of it." And so you battle, make a tremendous effort to be free of it. But in that very effort you are creating another illusion, because of the very idea to get free of it, escape from it, conquer it. Whereas to me, when you understand that, your whole series of problems ceases to exist. You cannot approach that wholeness through a series of problems, and that is what we are trying to do, and that is our whole conception of the accumulation of knowledge, virtues, qualities. To understand the whole, which shall dissolve every other conflict and problem, one experience or one problem rightly understood will reveal the cause which creates the problem. Now we are trying to solve the difficulty without understanding who or what created the difficulty. We are trying to solve our particular problem through a desire to be rid of it, by applying a particular idea to it or by submerging it in a mental picture or trying to forget it through sensation. In that very process we are but creating another problem and so we go on creating one problem after another until we die, all the time making a series of efforts to get rid of them. But to understand the whole which shall free the mind of all these particularities, from this accumulation, we must understand who creates the illusions, these bondages, these hindrances. They are all created out of this bundle of memories which is called the 'I', through memory, which is incomplete action.

Now I say, do not examine, consciously or subconsciously, hindrances which lie in the past; do not dig out from the dead past into the present all the dead hindrances, but begin to live in the present and then in that living quality all our hindrances come into activity without your going back. In that there is a joy. Whereas in going back and trying to understand and dig out, through effort, the hindrances of the past, you but create another center of the 'I'. Instead of being in the past, it comes into the present; egotism still remains and therefore it is a hindrance in itself.

It is like a ship. In its movement it knows its hindrances. If it is still it cannot know its hindrances. Now you are still and trying to dig out from the past or trying to get rid of your hindrances. But that is purely a mental picture, a process, a mental effort, which to me is the utter destruction of action, of living. Whereas, if in your movement, if in your action, whatever it is, you are both mentally and emotionally fully awake, then you will know what is impeding you, and in that flame of awareness that impediment is destroyed, because you have understood the cause.

So I hope you see that it is not through the accumulation of ideas, of experience, of knowledge, that you can come to that fullness, that plenitude of life; nor through making an effort to liberate yourself from hindrances, which again is utterly false. But in your action you become aware of your hindrances, and you will, if you act with completeness, with your whole mind and heart, then, in that awareness, you will know what the hindrances are, and therefore the cause.

But then you will tell me, "I am incapable of meeting experience fully. Therefore I go into the subconscious and drag out all the hindrances, so that I can meet fully the present." But you do meet fully, completely, everything in which you are interested. If that action or if that problem is really vital, then you do meet it fully. So what is happening? You do not meet things fully, because you are all the time trying to escape. Do not say I must get rid of escape, but become conscious that you are escaping and then you will cease to escape.

What I want to convey is very difficult to put into words. You cannot understand the whole significance of life through a division, through a part, and all our effort is to go through a part, through individuality, through getting rid of hindrances, through effort, which creates another particularity. Effort exists so long as there is a part, and you cannot come through a part to the whole.

You cannot understand it, you cannot realize the whole loveliness of that completeness through a little thing, though one experience will, if rightly approached, give you the whole. If there is a cessation of the creator of illusions and therefore of the illusions themselves, then you will know the whole, but you cannot destroy that through effort, because the more effort you make against it, the greater the resistance. Please understand this, because to me this is the vital point. Where we make an effort, we but increase and emphasize the part and therefore there is no comprehension of the whole. And we make an effort because we are all the time wanting to gain, to accumulate, to be rid of things, whereas in that flame of awareness which arises when a problem is really acute, when you are really interested with your whole mind and heart, then you will know the creator of illusion, the 'I' with all its hindrances, qualities, virtues, limitations. The moment you know the creator of illusion, there is a cessation of the cause, which creates illusions.

Question: I have thought much about liberation and longed to achieve it. Now I have a new idea. Perhaps it is life that requires to be liberated from me. Perhaps life could flow in its own beautiful way, if I with all my obstacles and hindrances, were out of the way. If this is a true thought, how am I to eliminate and efface myself, so that life may have things all its own way?

KRISHNAMURTI: First of all, that knowledge which you have gathered in search of liberation must totally disappear, because you have gathered it with the idea of gain, with the idea that you should be liberated, that there is liberation, therefore I must seek it. All knowledge must disappear to understand that which is whole, knowledge which you have accumulated through this craving for liberation, and therefore that knowledge is not true. That is the first thing, and is the most difficult.

How do you know what liberation is, to long for it? You say, "I know it because I have had a momentary glimpse of it." So you say, "Are those glimpses true or false?" That is the second point. I say then: Why do you ask whether they are true of false? Because you want to find out whether you have experienced that reality. Whereas to me this is not important. What are you concerned with when you have pain, physical pain, twisted ankle or twisted arm, or tummy ache, or headache, or other ache? When you have no pain, you do not say, "Are those moments real when I had no pain?" You are concerned with the riddance of the pain. Then you will know for yourself whether that which you have experienced is true or false, permanent or transient. Now your chief concern is for liberation, only you have changed the word. You had the same desire before—Masters, saviors, ceremonies, virtues. Now you have changed the word, and you want that equally, you want that either as an escape, or because you are satiated with life, all the incidents of life. You want something more, more sensation. So, you can only be conscious of the struggle, not of liberation. Struggle, conflict, pain, suffering are the only things that we can know and be positive of; all the other things are a negation, imagination, mental pictures that act as drugs.

So, your search for liberation is wholly false; it is a mental desire, stimulation; therefore it cannot have a particle of truth in it. So being conscious of suffering, the next thing you say is, "How shall I get rid of it?" You say, "I must not search for liberation, but I must be rid of suffering." To be rid of suffering you create another idea, and so you go on. Whereas if you are acutely conscious, aware, of your suffering, you will know the cause. If you want to catch anything, you stop its escape. Intellectually, you have created so many holes through which you run away. I say block up all those holes through understanding, and then you will face your problems completely, and then you will find out the creator, the cause of that problem. And in that freedom there is the realization of that fullness. So, do not say, "I must become conscious of hindrances," or "I must get rid of hindrances, barriers, in the hope that I shall realize truth," but begin to live, begin to move, begin to act with full awareness, that is with your mind as well as with your heart. Then you will know what are the impediments. Any other way is a mental picture; any other way demands an effort, creating another set of barriers. Thus, you will discover the true values of your action, not the value that society, inherited prejudices, your own escapes and fears give to that particular action; but in the movement of action, when you are acting, if you are really awake both mentally and emotionally, in that you will discover right values. Therefore you will be free of the false. Hence in that discovery of what is true the totality is realized.

Question: Will you speak further of the relation between understanding and action? For example, in trying to be aware, I find a certain want or craving, but though I have tried to force it, frankly, it still remains.

KRISHNAMURTI: To me action and understanding are the same thing. Understanding is not a mental thing, nor is action apart from your feeling and thought; it is all one. Your action, if it is complete, can only be born out of a harmony of mind and heart, and that is understanding. So you cannot divide action from understanding.

You say, "In trying to be aware, I find a certain want or craving, but though I have tried to force it, frankly, it still remains." You see, you are still trying to be aware—I am not quibbling. Awareness is not natural, so you make an effort to be aware, as you make an effort to achieve liberation, as you are making an effort to be rid of hindrances. So when you say, "I am trying to be aware," you are not aware. When you say, "I must be virtuous," "I must struggle for virtue," then it is no longer a virtue. So, likewise, when you say, "I am trying to be aware," in that there is no value, because awareness is harmony of action in which there is not a duality, as the control and the controller, as the actor and the action. That complete harmony in action happens when you are doing something with your whole being. Now you are not, because you are afraid of society, of your friends, of your neighbors. You are afraid, therefore you act partially, incompletely.

So, when you do anything, do it completely. Do not try to be aware. And in that doing completely, you will find out. And you do that when you are in love, when you are carried away by something immense. But that is merely a stimulation. When you see a beautiful picture, a beautiful painting, you are carried away: momentarily you are all in one, your action is complete, harmonious. That is, an external beauty has completely knocked out of you this idea of 'I', this particular.

The questioner wants to know if he has not gone to the root of the matter in trying to become aware of what causes this craving. "Is it that I have not gone to the root of the matter? Why should the 'I' cease wanting through becoming aware, conscious of this wanting?" I have explained. You know, when you are jealous, mentally, either you are not fully aware that you are jealous or you are. If you are not aware that you are jealous then that is a different question. If you are aware, you realize intellectually the foolishness of it. You say, "How absurd!" "How childish!" "How unreal!" But emotionally you are eaten up with jealousy, because you want to possess, you want to be certain, and all the rest. It is no good fighting against jealousy. You must not say, "I must conquer it, I must get rid of it"—all mental images, superimposing on this emotional thing which wants. Whereas if you really find out if you are jealous both mentally and emotionally, you would be free of jealousy. You know, people like to be jealous because it gives them a sensation, also pain. They revel in it, and at the same time they want to get rid of it. If you want to get rid of it, get rid of it wholly. That is, when jealousy becomes acute, and it is really a problem, then you deal with it completely. Now, we want it and at the same time we don't want it, and hence the mind tries to impose discipline, get rid of it, smother it, suppress it. That is why I say: Live all the time intensely; let everything be a crisis, and if one thing is really in crisis, then you will find out the creator of the illusion which creates that crisis.

Question: You often speak about time and timelessness, but to me it seems that time is an illusion. Though we can't get rid of it, it must be so, for every moment is an illusion.

The very moment it is, it is passed. Something like a knife cutting that divides a thing into two parts (past and future) but it doesn't exist itself. So, mentally time is an illusion to me.

Does the life that you know include the fact that you live in that timeless reality, that you actually see the totality of time? Please will you explain, as everything in the world connected with time seems so futile to me.

KRISHNAMURTI: Why do you ask? If time is an illusion, it is an illusion. But you go further and explain time as an illusion mentally; that we all know. We all say, "Time is an illusion." It is a phrase.

Timelessness is a thing that one has to realize. It is not a mental picture. So do not let us talk about it. Let us find out what creates time, in which mind is caught up. You see the difference? Timelessness, or rather that which has no beginning and no end, is a thing that you cannot talk about, any more than you can talk about truth or God. It is. It must be experienced fully. So to describe it would be false. It can not be mentally realized. Whereas we can find out why mind and heart are caught up in time. You see the difference? You are asking me the same question as when you say, "Tell me what truth is, tell me what God is." So you say, "Tell me what timelessness is." I say: I cannot tell you; you cannot talk about it; you cannot put it into words. Anything which is explained is not true. So we can find out what is the cause, as a past, a present, and a future. When we have understood that, then we enter into a different world, of timelessness.

Now do not ask, "Is there not a tomorrow; are you not going to arrange for a lecture tomorrow; are you not going to be punctual for your talk; must we not have a timetable to catch our trains?" I am not talking about that sort of thing. To me, what creates time is memory, and memory is born out of incomplete action.

What then creates incompleteness in our minds? I say: It is our action, which is but a reaction, born out of this 'I' consciousness, which is the cause of illusion. We act and our action is not a complete action; it is but a reaction born of fear, inherited perversions, social standards, which we have not understood, a search for reward and the escape from punishment, sorrow. From all this we act. Our action is but a reaction on account of this. Such an action is bound to create memory because we do not understand and we do not meet every experience fully, but with these reactions. It is like the sunlight, coming through the plain glass or a colored glass.

So, with this background of false values, we act and hence our action evokes incompleteness, and hence the many layers of memory which divide life into past, present, and future.

How do you act? You say you do not know. That is just it. Nobody is going to reveal it to you. You may be acting from a prejudice, from a fear, from a desire to lay up a store for the future, whether wealth, accumulations, or experiences. So you are unconscious of your action. But you are acting in this way all the time. Therefore you have to become aware of the background from which you act. To become aware of that background, do not go into the past.

So, through our action time exists. Time to me is karma, action limited. Where there is memory, it is born out of the action which is incomplete and that memory creates time.

Don't say then, "Must I be free of memory?" which is again approaching it wrongly. It is the cause that matters, not the effect. The cause of memory is this action born out of reaction, out of a background.

Do not try to imagine what timelessness is or what it is to be without time. To me, all such things have no inherent value. But what has lasting, permanent value is to understand right values, and you cannot understand right values with a mind that is caught up in a background of reaction, or ready-made reaction. Whenever your actions are from that, they must be incomplete. Therefore there is always the incrustation of memory and hence the more and more self-conscious limitation which creates time.

August 10, 1933

Tenth Talk at Ommen

I am not using the word action in any way philosophically; I am using it ordinarily. To the majority of people, when you talk about action, it means physical movement. But to me it is completeness of thinking, feeling, and acting. All that makes an act, not merely to move a thing from here to there or doing a physical act. Even that demands a thought and a feeling which lies behind it.

So to me, when I use the word action, it implies the whole of thought, feeling, and action. When it is harmonious, when a thought is born or there is emotion and hence action, out of that completeness, out of that harmonious thinking, feeling, and acting, then that act is infinite, and to me such action is complete; in it there are no hindrances, no distinction or resistance between thought, emotion, and action.

To me, to think is to act, or to feel is to act; you cannot separate thinking, feeling and acting into three different things—it is all one. To me, to feel is to think, or to act is to think and to feel, so you cannot separate—at least I do not separate. Action, then, is whole. Action is the outcome of a complete unity of mind and heart and action.

Now, to understand action being infinite, not a finality, not an achievement, a goal, or an end, to understand such an action, you must understand what you mean by action, what each one of you means by action. I will try and say what I think one generally means by action.

Action means conformity to the majority of people, imitation, or struggling to reach an end, a result. So action means, generally, self-preservation. You may not mean it in its gross sense, but we have refined it so much, spiritualized it, that self-preservation has become quite spiritual. What you mean by action is conformity and I am going to try and explain that your action is conformity, it is not spontaneous, it is not natural, full, complete. It is always conforming.

You put one action before another in importance. Take the man who says that by having bread first, the whole of life will be understood. That is, solve the economic difficulties and the other things will follow. Or, the man who says, "Understand the spiritual life first, and the bread difficulty will be solved."

We have divided our action as physical, which is economic, social, and religious. Those are our acts, and we think economic acts have nothing to do with our social acts, which in turn have nothing to do with our religious acts.

Now, if you think about your economic act, it is all based on self-preservation; in business, in the acquisition of property, power. There you are acting through a particular idea and therefore your action is always conforming. Economically your idea is to exploit and to be exploited, that is, to lay up for yourself in the future a certain amount of money, so that you will have security. Where there is security, there must be authority and hence power, inheritance etc. So you have established what the end is and you are acting according to that idea, which you call business, but which is self-preservation. So our action is not natural—I am using the word *natural* in what is to me the right sense of the word—that is, that action is independent, it is not complete, not harmonious.

You say, "I must earn, otherwise society will destroy me. I must lay up for the future, otherwise, who will look after me in my old age? There must be inheritance, otherwise I cannot transmit what I have gained to my son." All this is based on the idea of self-preservation, handing down your name, the things you have accumulated, etc.

So your action is always being limited, is independent of what you think and feel, like the man who says, "Bread first." So you say, "Let me act so as to have security, power, and then I will act differently, socially, spiritually."

So what have you established? You have established what you think is the finality of an economic goal, and you are working towards that all the time; so your action is all the time an imitation, a conformity. Therefore, you are not, from my point of view, acting. That is, you are not a complete being in your business.

Again, socially, we are trying to fit into a pattern, and therefore our action is but conformity; or we have certain ideas of class distinction, and we are acting according to that distinction. That is, socially we are making ourselves, by our actions, perfect machines, cogs, that will fit into the social mechanism without the least conflict. So our action is disharmonious. We may think differently, we may earn, do business differently, but we are trying all the time to cover all this up and fit in socially. So again our action is disharmonious, and to me such action is not a true act.

Then, again, religiously, spiritually, or ethically we are all the time afraid. Our actions, that is our thinking and our feeling, are born of fear. All our religious ceremonies, our offerings to gods and our spiritual authority, all that is self-immolation, which we think will bring about right balance—"Because I have been cruel, therefore I am going to be cruel to myself," hoping that will bring about right balance in your thought. Or, having an idea of what God, truth, is, and acting according to that idea.

So when you look to your action, you will see that your business action, your social action and your religious actions have nothing to do with it. They indicate, in a very subtle sense, that you want to preserve yourself as an entity.

We have intellectually said that self-preservation is very selfish, so though we go on earning, exploiting, and being exploited, we are all the time covering that up, and spiritually running away into truth.

So our actions are not harmonious and you will only understand that action which is complete, and therefore infinite, when you do your business, your social activity, your religious idea, as a whole thing. Then you are a complete human being. That means that one has to think quite differently and to feel quite differently from the way in which we are accustomed to.

You will at once say, "What will happen, if I do not lay up money?" You will see. You are looking to security and therefore your actions are always limited through fear, and yet you are trying not to be afraid. So your actions are contradictory. Your actions are not complete in the present, because you are looking to the future, when you lay up and wonder what is going to happen to you when you are sixty.

Again, when you want to fit into society, into the social machine, because that feeling is so strong, you are afraid to go against it, afraid to be yourselves. Or, religiously, it is exactly the same thing. Our actions are not born out of a completeness of thinking and feeling, because we never face these things all together at the same time. We are trying to solve economic difficulties through economic conditions, by altering the economic system. We say we will alter that carefully and we will be perfect along that line; and the same thing socially and spiritually. We do not bring it all together and act completely as a human being. So our actions are broken up, split up, and hence they are conforming all the time and we are unconscious of it.

So to understand that wholeness, that fullness of life, do not try to make the economic system perfect, independent of your social and religious life; and do not make your spiritual life perfect away from your social and economic life.

This is really very simple. You can see for yourself how you are acting. You have a spiritual standard, a social standard, and a business standard, and you are acting according to these standards, and you call that action.

Such action, to me, is purely imitating. It is not action at all; it is just copying. In it, there is no thinking, real individual thinking, questioning.

I said yesterday that you are trying to approach the wholeness through the part. You say, "I will make the economic condition perfect, or the social condition perfect, or the spiritual condition perfect, and I will get the whole." You cannot. You must approach it completely and your actions must be complete.

That means that to think is to act—you cannot separate it—to feel is to act. You cannot divide and say, "I will feel one thing and act another," or "I will think one thing and feel another." In such action there is always a finality, and hence there is fear of death, of unfulfilled opportunities, and therefore a looking to the future.

But when you act completely, that action is infinite, and you will not understand what that is until your business, social, and religious life are completely harmonized. You may not be afraid of what lies in the hereafter or for spiritual authority (you may have given up all your religions and ceremonies) but you are afraid of what will happen when you become old, so you say, "Let me lay up for the future"; or you are afraid unconsciously of what another may say.

Don't you see, when you tackle it as a whole, fear disappears. You do not divide fear into spiritual, economic, and social. It is fear. So, when you tackle and try to understand fear, then your actions will not be separative.

Question: In the very act of thinking and puzzling over what you have said, we are making an effort towards getting rid of hindrances—are we then not creating another barrier by thinking over this thing at all? If not, in what sense do we use the word effort?

KRISHNAMURTI: When we talk about thinking what do we mean? Our thinking is but a reaction, as I have tried to show just now. You're thinking from a background which you have established, and so you are merely reacting. I do not call that thinking. The questioner wants to know if in thinking and puzzling over what I have said we are making an effort to get rid of hindrances. You see, when I use the word *effort* to imply a reaching after, exertion towards an end, straining after, trying to conquer, achieving, changing, molding, imitating, that is what I mean by effort, endeavoring, struggling after, reaching after.

Now our whole mind is made up of it, our whole attitude towards life is that. Isn't it? You want truth, you want to get rid of hindrances, you want self-preservation, you must have money laid up for the future, you are afraid so you must get rid of fear. So our thinking is in terms of achieving, of achievement. We are puzzling in order to arrive at a conclusion, at an end, like a cross-word puzzle. We want to reach an end and so we are making an effort.

Is not one secretively seeking power, which you call self-preservation, or which you call an ideal, or truth? You want to be well-established; you want to know you will exist; so you look after yourself, so that you can lay up your money; when you become old you can be safe, secure. So your whole action is based on that, and naturally you are afraid that security will be destroyed. So you are making constant endeavor, effort, to maintain that security; economically, socially, and spiritually. I am not talking about an effort with regard to when I feel pain I must get rid of it, or when I am deaf I must try to find a way to cure it. I am not talking about such a thing. If you understand this principal thing you will understand where effort is to be used for ordinary things.

Where there is a desire for achievement there must be effort. Where there is understanding there is no effort. Understanding is born out of a complete act. When you want to understand a thing, or when there is a problem which you have to solve, over which you have to decide, you are not trying to conquer it, you are not trying to evade it. You come to it when it is really vital with all your being, don't you? When something is urgent you must decide with your whole being. In that you don't make an effort, because you are not trying to come to the end of that problem. You are trying to find out. Take a flower. It grows naturally. Don't say, "Is not the very growth an effort?" I am not applying that word *effort* to natural growth. Because one is abnormal, unnatural, we think by making tremendous effort we shall come to normality; by going through this effort, by analyzing, by continual watching we think we will come to normality. I say you won't. Whereas, if you are aware what creates abnormality, which you will find out when that abnormality becomes a crisis in your life, and when you are not trying to escape or solve it, then you will find out without effort how to be natural. When you have to decide something vital you sow the seed in your mind as well as in your heart, and you let it grow rightly and then it comes out naturally. You are doing it all the time when you are concerned with something vitally; you are letting your emotions and your thoughts ripen together in the warmth of action, in the movement of action.

But what happens now? We try to decide a thing either intellectually or emotionally, not together. You want a jewel emotionally, it gives you a sensation, value. Intellectually we say "How absurd it is!" Hence there is conflict; hence the effort to overcome. But when you bring them together, let them ripen, find out, experiment, do not identify with one or the other, then you will see. Our action now is the continual sharpening of mind and heart, as you take a stick and sharpen it with a knife. What happens? The more and more you sharpen it, the less and less stick. There is no stick at the end, no piece of wood. That is what you are doing, sharpening your mind and your heart. So gradually as you grow there is less and less of mind and heart, and that is what you call effort, making the mind sharp and the emotions sharp, to run away, to seek a solution, not to understand the fullness of mind, the depth of emotion, but to achieve a pinnacle of sharpness, which is nothing. A mind that is not sharp, but subtle, therefore deep, delicate—such a mind and heart will know that swift movement of action. You think through friction, friction of knowledge, friction of experience, through action, you can make your mind very sharp to find out truth. To find out, to understand, there must be depth of mind, not sharpness, which is but cleverness, superficiality. So, all our endeavor, is like sharpening that stick with a knife, because you think in terms of achievement. Therefore the more and more effort you make, the more you are destroying. A mind and heart that are really harmonious, therefore deep, profound, will understand that wholeness of life. That wholeness of life is not a reward for harmonious action. In harmonious action it is there. But you cannot come to harmonious action through effort, by saying, "I will get rid of hindrances."

I have been over this yesterday, and the day before, and last week. I think either you do not hear or you are here for amusement. I have been trying to put it different ways. Please, I am not disappointed. It does not matter. I will go on. You will go away, all over the world, and I will go somewhere else, but you will emerge out of this with more confusion, I am afraid, because you are not thinking. You have layers of thinking in your mind and you put what I am saying in one of those layers. I say all those layers must disappear. But you are unconscious that you have layers. Become conscious in your movement of action.

I am saying nothing very complicated. When your action is imitative, it is no action at all. Your thinking is but reaction. In that there is not spontaneity because your thinking is born out of false values which you have never questioned. You have never questioned your background; you have never broken away from it and doubted it. You want to conform, and what I am talking about has nothing to do with conformity, with imitative act. You are seeking a method. Method implies an end, the end of achievement, spiritually. So with all this in your mind, choking it, you are trying to understand what I am saying. Naturally the two cannot fit in. Don't try to understand me, but try to understand yourself, not what I am talking about. Now you are making an effort to understand what I am talking about. Don't. Become aware of your own thinking and feeling, that is all, not what I am talking about. Then, when you become aware of your action you will find out that what I am talking about is true. Then you need not make an effort. You are trying to impose and put on top of a mind that is heavy, dull, jaded, dreary, without value, all that I am saying and trying to see through all that rubbish. Please, I am not talking through harshness, because life is far too short. We cannot go on like that every year. Either you want to live harmoniously or not. If you don't, don't come here and spoil your amusement and that of others. Don't you see you have to think anew, think differently, not in your old habitual way, which is reaction, which is not thinking?

As you have collected so many false values and you are acting from that, question those values that you have collected. Don't add more. Question what you have collected. And you can only question that not intellectually but in the movement of action. Surely that is very simple. That does not demand an effort. You make an effort when you are not interested, when you are trying to be spiritual, with haggard faces. But if you are interested, that is, when you are really suffering, or when there is a tremendous problem that you have to decide, then in that movement you will find out what are the hindrances that are holding you. Don't you see your own lives are so miserable, what is the good of taking on my ecstasy? Your own lives are so poor, so shallow, that is why I say become aware of that shallowness, understand, begin anew. Then you will find out. In knowing that you are shallow you will discover riches. In knowing that you are incapable of thinking freely, feeling naturally, in knowing that, when you have really felt it and know it, then you will act differently. Now we are trying to be both, which is compromise.

When there is conformity, authority, effort there cannot be rich living. Now, do not take that and add to your wastepaper basket, but question those things that you have already collected, of which your mind and heart are so full. And to question don't dig into it, don't analyze the past, but begin to act harmoniously with your full being, then all the impediments that you have collected will come into activity, and in that activity they will dissolve, not otherwise. You cannot learn from a dead thing; you can only learn from a living thing. All you have collected are dead things. You know, I could weep over this. I can talk, and you shake your heads, but you don't see the absolute necessity to think wholly anew. And yet sorrow waits round each corner; with each experience, though you get joy out of it there is sorrow because you do not know how to meet it. So we proceed until we die. Then we want a new life, to start it all over again, and we call that hope.

Question: Can you make clearer the difference between the solving of one problem—which you say will not lead us to truth—and the understanding of one experience in the movement of action—which you say will lead us to truth?

KRISHNAMURTI: First of all, no action will lead you to truth. Action itself is truth. You see, because you are looking through action to get something, action has no meaning. You say, "If I am righteous, I shall go to heaven," therefore the importance of heaven. Or you want a title, so you will behave rightly according to the edicts of society. No action is ever going to lead you to truth. If it does, it is not true, nor is it an act. Surely, that is clear. If you love me, because you think I am going to give you truth, of what value is your love? And I am afraid that is what is happening. You want something and therefore you are acting. Your wanting is not real, nor has your action true value. No action of any kind, love, service, work, accumulation of virtues, will bring you that everlasting ecstasy.

Question: What is the difference between the solving of one problem and the understanding of one experience in the movement of action?

KRISHNAMURTI: What are you doing, when you are trying to solve a problem: You are seeking a result, trying to get over that problem, trying to conquer that trouble. When you say, "I have a problem, please tell me the way out," you are not concerned with the cause of the problem, you want to know what is the way out. It is the same thing with the economic problem. We say, "What is the way out of all this," not, "What causes that problem?" Therefore, when I try to solve that problem, whenever I use the word *solve* it means I am trying to run away, trying to replace it by some other thing, by some other action, thought or feeling; so that I immediately create another problem.

Take the problem of sex, or the problem of ceremony. (Now you will all sit up; there is a tension. What a strange world!) Why is it a problem to you and why are you trying to overcome it, saying, "Sex is a tremendous problem" or, "Ceremony is a problem. What am I to do? Tell me the way. Can I do occult practices so as to transmute my feelings into something else?"

That problem exists because you are not in yourself potential; you are not rich in yourself, therefore the less becomes the more. So by trying to solve your problem of sex, or any other problem, you are not getting richer; there is not that richness.

Whereas when there is completeness in action, in yourself, then all these problems will disappear. So in trying to solve a problem, you do not come to the richness of life, because you are only dealing with and trying to solve the part, not trying to understand the whole.

If one experience is understood, you will know the richness, that rich plentitude of life. When you have an experience, if you meet it, not as you do now, partly mentally and partly emotionally, but completely with both your mind and heart, then all the past hindrances come into being. The whole cause of your emptiness is known in one movement of life, whatever that movement is. That means you must be awake, not lazy, not jaded, with your mind and your heart crippled with fear. As it is crippled with fear, with imitation, with thoughtlessness, with false values, you can only find out in the movement of experience, which is in the present. You see that? Well, there it is!

There is a difference, a vast difference between the two. You cannot put them together. The one reveals the creator of illusions. One experience reveals the creator of illusions, and becoming conscious of the illusion, it dissolves; that is, the creator of illusions, when it becomes self-conscious in its own understanding, the illusion is dissolved. The way that you are trying to solve problem after problem, economic, social, religious, sexual, all the rest of it, one by one, that is by trying to solve a part and hoping to understand the whole, you will never do it, because you will but create more illusions, because you don't go to the creator of illusions, which is your own want. Eternal craving is the cause.

You will find out the cause, which is craving, when you meet experience rightly, that is wholly, undividedly. In that undivided movement of action you will discover all the false values you have accumulated for generations, and in that moment of full awareness you will find out, like a fresh breath that destroys all the foul air at one moment, it is all gone. You cannot experiment, because experimentation means action, and you are afraid of action. You are afraid to move out of the old ruts, business, spiritual, social. You want to go along the same way and say what other people are saying. So, naturally, you are confused more and more. But if you question the rut along which you are running and discover that full value, meet everything wholly, then what I am saying will not be confused, will be so simple, you will be astonished that you did not see it yourself.

So, friends, truth is not a thing to be found, attained, or realized. I may have used the words in the past—and I have used them—but I did not mean as an end to be gained, as you have made of them. I might have given the meaning to them, but it was not in my mind or heart, that it is an end to be achieved. Besides, I wish you would scrap all the past and start anew. Nor is that fullness of life to be discovered through an action, but it is known only, that perfume, that richness, that ecstasy, in the fullness of action, not through, but in itself, whatever that action be—your earning money, your ceremony, your sexual problem. It is in that action itself that the whole glory of life lies. It is not through it. Action inherently in itself, when you meet it in the movement of action, of experience, with full awareness, in that lies the glory.

August 11, 1933

Eleventh Talk at Ommen
Questions and Answers

Question: Memory, according to you, gives vitality to the creator of illusion, the ego, the 'I' consciousness, the bundle of hindrances. So, pure action can never spring from this memory.

Is spontaneous recollection of past incidents a hindrance, even though we do not allow our action to spring from that recollection? Freed from this memory, how can we normally adjust our relations with individuals? Is it not almost impossible in life?

KRISHNAMURTI: You have understood the question? I have explained what I mean by memory, i.e. an ill-digested experience or an incident which you do not meet completely, wholly, leaves a scratch in the mind, which we call a memory. Now with that memory we try to meet life and that memory gives vitality, because it creates hindrances. If I had a memory of an experience, which is an experience which I have not completely understood, that memory creates a further hindrance, because that prevents me from meeting experience fully.

Most of us have such memories—many such memories—which you call recollection, with which we try to meet experiences. Naturally, when you meet that recollection with memory, a person, an incident or an experience, you do not meet fully; therefore you are further increasing the burden. Now, if you meet every person, experience, anew, with a free mind, with an awakened full mind, you will meet them with an adaptability, not with a fixation of mind. Memory gives us a rigidity so that when you have many recollections, that rigidity becomes so strong, that when you meet a person, or an experience, you do not fully comprehend it. Therefore that recollection impedes you; whereas if you meet every person or every experience free from that rigidity, which is memory, then in that there is a pliability, there is an adjustment, not a cunningness of mind, which tries to get beyond a person or beyond an experience.

Let us say, someone has deceived me two years ago. That has left a memory, a recollection, and I meet that person again now. I meet him or her with that memory which is still in my mind. So, when I meet him, I am very cunning not to be deceived again, because I am suspicious and I do not want to be deceived, but my mind is so acute, cunning, that it is watching. Now, if you have nothing to give or nothing to receive, if you are not expecting something from that person, you can never be deceived.

Please, I am taking the principle, not the detail. You can apply the detail for yourself, when you think it over. If a person deceives you and you are hurt by that deception, that hurt is a memory, and that memory reacts later, when you meet that person again. Therefore your mind has become more clever, more cunning, not more adaptable, more understanding. It has only become cleverer, more cunning, not to be caught in the same position again, and we think we have understood. We think our mind has become more cunning, and we know how to avoid being deceived the next time and we think experience has taught us that. You have lent someone some money, and he does not return it, and the next time he comes, you think you have learned; your mind has become more cunning and you say, "Shall I give it to him or not?" I feel this is a wrong method of approach, a wrong way of doing things. Either give it to him and forget about it and not have this rigidity of mind or this prejudice, or, when you meet him next time, say, "Sorry, if I could give it to you I would, but I cannot." Be quite open. Do not have a suspicious mind, a cunning mind, a rigid mind, but be frank. A frank mind is adaptable and therefore able to meet everything afresh, anew. Your mind is then so adjustable, so pliable, that when you meet this person again, there is something anew, not the same old suspicion brought forward. But, as long as we do not meet persons or experiences of life completely, with all our mind and heart, there must be conflict, and that conflict creates memory. It is really very simple. When you have no conflict in your mind, there is no memory. You may remember an incident, I am not talking of that, but there is no attachment to that memory, which pursues you through time until you have completed that incident or that experience. We are living constantly in this conflict. That conflict creates memory and the mind is filled with that memory and is identified with it, and so there is in that identification the idea of 'I'—which is conflict. There is a vast difference between the primitive man and the liberated man. The primitive man has no memory, because he acts immediately without thought; whereas the liberated man meets everything completely, because he has understanding. In him there is a richness, a fullness, and therefore through intelligence he is able to meet it. I hope I have answered that question.

Question: Is there a conformity every time that there is craving? Please explain fully.

KRISHNAMURTI: There is a craving for a definite thing and a craving for some indefinable thing. Take for instance when you desire, or crave, or long for happiness, truth, wealth, security, and other such things. In that there is conformity, because you have already pictured in your mind what you want, and you are going after it; you know what the end is and you want it, and your end is but an opposite in which you are again caught. So you are merely conforming to a mental image, which you have created. In that there is imitation. So in one sense, where there is craving, there must be conformity.

But there is the other type of wanting, which is more nebulous. You do not know what you want but there is something missing, something indefinable, impalpable, creating a void. Now, when you seek to fill up, to cover up, to run away from that void, it is also an imitation. First of all, why do we imitate? Please understand what I mean by imitation. There is imitation in art, in poetry, in culture, but I am not talking of that. To me there can only be true action, complete action, when you as an individual are completely individual: when you as an individual have realized full aloneness. When I use that word *aloneness,* I mean by that a solitude (not a running away into a forest) which comes when you discover right values. When you find out what truth is, you are alone, that is, there is only that thing, that true value, and from that action comes. To know that action, that full action, you cannot have imitation; you cannot have any false values. So, where there is false value, there must be imitation, because false value creates want. And with the understanding of right values, there is freedom from want; not the putting away or the destroying of want, which you can never do. You can never destroy desire, because it creates such havoc, and this is what most so-called spiritual people are trying to do. Whereas, if they find out the right values, then they will act from that aloneness, from that solitude, and in that there is no imitation.

You can only discover right values through a complete action. Where there is false value, there must be craving, because it creates an impediment and therefore a want, an incompleteness and therefore an intense desire for completeness, which is also another want. So where there is false value, there must be conflict and that conflict creates a desire to escape, or to solve that particular conflict; and where there is a desire to solve or escape, there must be authority and imitation.

Question: Mentally I am fully convinced of the utter futility of something I want. But it is with me as you pointed out last week: my emotions do not yet reach the same point. Will you be so kind as to tell me once more, how it is possible to have heart and mind fully balanced, harmonious?

KRISHNAMURTI: Why do you want it? What do you want me to tell you? You want to bring your emotions to the level of your mind. You want your emotions to grow or become more refined, more detached, and you want me to help you to grow. Now as I explained the other day, a thing that is growing is not lasting. If your desire does not create such a great conflict in you with regard to something you want, then no amount of balancing will ever produce harmony. If your want does not create havoc in you, great discontent, you cannot artificially bring your heart and mind to a level with each other, to a balance. No amount of discussion or artificial stimulation will ever produce that harmony. But your desire, if it is strong, will create discontent, disharmony, and out of that disharmony comes the ecstasy of harmony.

You are afraid to be disharmonious. You have heard me talking about security, and the falseness of it. If you have listened, as I hope you have listened, for your own delight, it must have struck a deep understanding within you. From that there is a decision on your own part, and that means an act, and from that act you will find out, whether your mind and heart are harmonious or not.

You say now, "Intellectually I do not want security, but emotionally I do want it. How am I to bring them together?" I say both are false. You want security. Do not say, "I understand intellectually the falseness of it, but emotionally I want it." It shows you want security both mentally and emotionally, because, when you really understand a thing, you do not understand intellectually alone, you understand with your heart as well. So when you say, "I understand intellectually, mentally," you mean you are inclined to agree with what I say, but there is no understanding in that. You see the advisability, the niceness of it, to be free of the worry of it, but you are not going to do anything about it. But, when you do do something about it, in that disturbance, you will know how to do it naturally. You do not really see the falseness of security, and therefore you say, "I have heard Krishnamurti and I think he may be right. Therefore I will try to be free from security." That means that you do not understand the significance of freedom from security, the security of money, friends, ideas, authority and imitation. There are infinite possibilities in that freedom, and infinite ecstasy. You do not see that, and yet you agree vaguely, that you must do it because of benefiting society, for kindness, for nonexploitation, and so on. But it has not really awakened a decision, and no one can awaken that decision in you, except your own continual awakened interest in life or if you are thoroughly discontented, intelligently discontented.

So, do not try and bring mind and heart together, as that will be just another discipline. You see how subtle the mind is, how it comes back again and again to the old form of thought. You say, "We must not have discipline," because you have heard me talk about it, but you are trying to do exactly the same thing, when you aim at bringing mind and heart to balance. Do not do such an artificial thing! You only create a further distinction, increasing that observer, all the time dissecting action. But see if you really profoundly understand and agree, first! If you really think that one must be free from all conflict, with all its implications; if you really think about it and really feel about it, and agree, then your action is immediate, then your whole being responds instantaneously and there is discernment. Now, because you do not agree, you do not feel the immense necessity of it, you make this artificial distinction of mind and heart. To me, there is no distinction between mind and heart. If someone talks to me about the stupidity of imitation, and if I agree, there is an intense awareness in my action to see if that action is imitative. Then I shall know, if my mind and heart are balanced. In the full recognition, not repetition or acquiescence, but in the full understanding of the idea or comfort or the freedom from authority, when you agree profoundly, then from that agreement there is action and in that action you will know. If that action is really harmonious, then your mind and heart are in perfect union. So do not seek to bring about a balance, but rather see, if you really understand the falseness of authority, or security or any of these ideas.

It is only in stirring up a muddy pool that you will know what is in that pool. Now, we are only skimming over the surface of the waters, because we are afraid to disturb that superficial tranquillity. And you can only disturb that pool, which is really stagnant water, by action and that action should be born only out of full agreement. If you do not agree, carry on as you are. If you think you need comfort, carry on, but be fully aware that you need comfort, give your whole mind and heart to it, and in that fullness of desire for comfort you will find out its futility.

Question: How can man overcome the sorrow he has when he sees somebody suffering, and not be able to help him? Is compassion a fault, or is it something necessary in social life?

KRISHNAMURTI: When you have compassion you don't suffer. Compassion is like the scent of a flower. We suffer because we want a result; that is when you say, "I am compassionate of the person who is suffering; I want him to get better." In other words you want a result for your compassion. Not that I do not want to see the person better himself, but personally I do everything I can to help him to get better, but there is no suffering in that. You suffer when there is possessive instinct. The many of you who are listening to me, if I am ill tomorrow you would not suffer, because you do not possess me. But if I were your wife or your husband then there would be suffering because I am yours. But compassion is free from sorrow because it is non-possessive.

You ask, "Is compassion a fault, or is it something necessary in social life?"

Why do you think certain things are necessary for social life? If you are a human being, the necessity of behaving in a certain manner disappears. Now we say, "These are necessary for right behavior in society." If my actions, as I have been trying to explain, are complete, if I am truly a human being in its right sense there are no demands or edicts which society can impose on me, because I am not fighting society, because I understand the values of society, with all its falseness and its truth. I am fully cognizant of everything. My point is, if you are truly complete in your action—which is not an impossibility; do not say it is only for the liberated, for the few—if your actions are complete then you do not create a society which is opposed to you. You are not in conflict with society. That does not mean that you do not want to bring about a change and all the rest of it, but society does not impose itself on you with all its false values.

You ask, "Is compassion a fault, or is it something necessary in social life?"

I object to the word *necessary.* That shows you are merely a cog in the social structure. That is what I am trying to say. I have finished about compassion, because there is very little to say about it. You cannot talk about such things. I am talking about this idea that certain actions are necessary for the maintenance of social structure. When you use the word *necessary* you are merely maintaining that instinctive fear to fit into society, and therefore you are not truly individual, which does not mean that you must do the opposite. I have said you will find true individuality only when you have discovered the right values of the social standard. Until then you cannot be true individuals. So when you discover the right values of social standards or any standards— religious, ethical, or political, all the standards that human beings have created— when you really understand then you will not ask, "Are certain actions necessary for the maintenance of society?"

Question: You say that self-analysis is death. I understand your meaning to be that intellectual dissection and examination are destructive. If, however, analysis could be a process whereby energy hitherto absorbed in conflict, released itself emotionally and, to a lesser extent, intellectually, with no ultimate achievement in view, would not such a process come near to an understanding of awareness?

KRISHNAMURTI: You want to release that energy which is now taken up in conflict. I say you cannot free that vital energy through self-analysis, but you can release it only when you are in the movement of action. To me self-analysis implies not that movement but rather the staying back and examining to understand, withholding from that movement in order to examine, and to me it does not release understanding. Whereas if you are fully awake in action, then out of that comes awareness of the many hindrances. Please, this is very simple. Our mind is used to analyze our actions, our emotions. There is always the observer, the controller, the guide watching. Your mind now is nothing but an instrument to warn you of the coming fears, of the coming hopes, always alert, cunning. So our actions are stultified. Whereas if you were to meet the very next thought or emotion or action, with all your being then you will know the hindrances that prevent you from releasing that creative energy. In other words, do not try to solve the problem, but meet the next thought, or next emotion, or next action—all being the same—fully, then you will know the cause of the problem in which you are caught.

Question: Your hint that the new social structure must not be based on selfishness is not possible in practical life. Want is bringing men more and more to selfishness, for themselves and for their families. Self-interest in the work leads people to greater effort, and it develops the faculties. Can't you help us to a deeper insight in the practical possibilities of social construction? After all, one must cooperate in creating, above all, better material circumstances and possibilities of work.

KRISHNAMURTI: First of all, I never give a hint, because it is quite obvious what I say; it is not a hint. I am afraid it was a sledge hammer, but if you like, take it as a hint.

Now if it is not practical, why do you bother about it? Have you tested it, to find out if it is practical? What you call "practical" is a complete system, a complete mold in which you can fit without the least trouble, to carry on as you are without alteration, without thought, without a deepening process of life. So, as you have not experimented with it, how can you possibly say it is not practical? You don't experiment because you are frightened. You know, if you really felt, some of you, the futility of laying up, and experiment with it, not propaganda, converting the other fellow, but really felt and tested and acted from that, you would see how practical it is, how simple life becomes.

We are afraid, with regard to security, what will happen. "I am old," you say to yourself, "What shall I do when I am old?" or, "As I am old I cannot give up security." That is quite right. I am not asking you to give up, but to be free from the idea of security. This needs very careful, frank thinking, otherwise you say, "I am free from security but I can have a good balance in the bank." I am not saying that you must not have money, but it is the idea of security.

So friends, first of all, to make anything practical you have to experiment with it, and I do not think you have experimented, to say it is impractical. You don't feel strongly about it, and hence the impracticality, the vagueness of it all.

With regard to cooperation, which is also implied in the question, I think that there cannot be cooperation until there is true individuality. Please understand what I mean by true individuality—not individualistic action, which is limited action. Now we are too willing to cooperate with a boss, with an authority on top, who tells us exactly what we are to do, spiritually, economically and socially. In all our acts we are quite willing to be guided, to be told what to do. We feel, if only there were a good leader, the world would be perfectly right. So we are looking to leaders and not to the true function of individuality. When you are attempting to understand true individuality, you are bound to cooperate, because that is part of it. In that there is no individuality as against cooperation. Now you place cooperation as against individuality and that is what I feel to be the utter chaos in this world. We are having greater and greater organizations politically to control men, vast legislation to shape men more and more, and I think there will be greater and greater chaos. You may be made all one kind of slave to a particular idea through a legislation and a few years later another slave to another idea through legislation. So we are merely cogs moving from different prisons, moving in different machines, different systems. I do not call that cooperation. It is blindness. In that there is no living, no spontaneity of fullness. Whereas there is, and there will be, there must be cooperation when you as an individual understand the true function of individuality, which is to discover right values. No system, no philosopher, no one on earth is going to tell you what right values are. There are eternal right values. You will find out. I can tell you, but it means nothing, because you will take those in place of the old. That is, you will be a slave to a new kind of order. It may be superficially well arranged, but there will be a rotten core inside.

If we do not cooperate, we cannot do anything in life. There must be cooperation. Everything we do must be done by two, three, four or by a million. To bring about right cooperation there must be right understanding of individuality, and if there is not right understanding, it is not cooperation. It is merely exertion of brutal authority, spiritually, politically or any way you like.

Question: In the life of individuals as well as in groups, there is action, not only individually conditioned, but also conditioned by historical factors which appeal to us from the past: their imminent effect, not only intellectual, and not to be evaded, meets me everywhere, though I personally have totally freed myself from traditions, ceremonies, etc. A human being, ignoring this very source of its being, is like a tree that tries to prevent the growing in the depth of its own roots. I wonder why you do not speak of this aspect of life, though it certainly is no less essential than all that a human being can do and be of itself.

KRISHNAMURTI: My point is discovering in action all right values whereas you bring up all the past whether it is of yesterday or of a century ago. I happen to be a Hindu, a Brahmin, soaked in tradition, older, more rigid than any of yours. I do not sit down and examine the historical tradition which has bound me to inherited centuries of history, or the various little traditions that hold me as a Hindu; but in moving I become aware of all those anchors, historical, religious, national, family, personal prejudices, and in that movement of real creative thinking there is intelligence. That is truly thought, not this mere reaction back and forth of an established background from which you think. We call that "thinking" and therefore "thinking" leaves us more and more empty, more and more shallow.

Question: What is the normal place of sex in the life of the individual—from your point of view?

KRISHNAMURTI: There are sex regulations and legislations for a man who is a slave to sex. There is creative energy, and because we have lost real understanding of that creative energy, we are caught up in sexual problems, not that that is not also creative or that it is something to be looked down on, despised, or reveled in—it is the same, revelling in them or despising them. You may say, "We have lost the true creative power." So long as you do not realize that creative power, you will be a slave to your passions, and there must be legislations to control passionate people, because passionate people like everyone else are promiscuous; they have no sense of proportion and hence for them there must be legislation. So the thing is how to realize that creative power. You will not be bothered, nor will you despise it, nor will you revel in it; it is a part of your whole being. To realize that creative thing, that life itself, that divinity, that infinite becoming, free your mind from all these conformities, this process of your thinking to which you have conformed, your action which is limited. If you really release your mind and heart from imitation, free the mind from the certainty, in that there is a creative ecstasy which is life itself. Then there is not a sexual problem, a moral problem, an intellectual problem. Then you do not distinguish sex from other acts, then you are a complete human being, because such a human being is truly creative and hence spontaneous.

August 12, 1933

Twelfth Talk at Ommen

I am going to try this morning as an experiment to repeat what I have said in ideas, not consecutive ideas, but explain completely each idea. You know we are accustomed to consecutive reasoning and to consecutive ideas, put together as a lecture consequentially leading until we come to a climax. I am not going to do that this morning. I am going to take idea by idea which I have talked about and deal with it completely. So don't look for a sequence. Don't say this arises from this and that comes from that. I don't know that I am going to succeed but I will try.

You know that it is only a thing that is full of tension that can give a right note, like a violin string that is really tuned to its right pitch will give its right tone. So likewise a mind and a heart that are truly in right tension can respond to any experience fully. To understand the full significance of an experience you must give your whole attention to it, undivided. There must be acute sensitiveness. Your whole being must be there when that experience takes place.

Thus there comes, when there is true tension, a decision. Now some of you have heard me over and over again, because there has not been this tension at all. You have not decided. Not the decision of choice but the decision of understanding. For instance I have talked about security. Until you are willing to lose that security there is no decision. When you hear and you really understand the falseness of security, there is out of that tension, a corresponding note which is decision, which is, "I have understood," therefore you act. That is a true decision without effort which cannot take place if you want security and at the same time agree intellectually with me. So you can never have a decision, clear, natural, spontaneous, because there is not the full tension of mind and heart all the time.

Now we are afraid to lose, lose our life, our possessions, our qualities, our virtues, because we say we have accumulated, we have suffered, history has given us culture for so many generations. I have accumulated, my father has left it, how can I get rid of it, how can I leave it, how can I give it away.

So, until you lose everything, until you lose the very thing that you have struggled for through centuries, you will rely on time, because your mind is occupied all the time with gain, and hence suffering. So we say, "I will not lose, but I will accumulate, accumulate experiences." And you will say to yourself, "Intelligence comes through accumulation of experience." To me time does not give intelligence, nor does experience give you intelligence. You can have a dozen experiences but out of that there is not the flower of understanding. You can know that by watching people. And you are the same because you are looking to accumulation, not to complete denudation, loss of everything, of your own life. When you are prepared to do that, then there is true decision.

So, we have accumulated so much (I see this is becoming a regular consequential talk. Sorry, it doesn't matter!) we have made great effort in accumulating, which have become our hindrances. First of all, the idea of choice. That is what we have learned, as we say, "Through accumulation I can learn, therefore let me choose." So you begin to differentiate your action, your choice, between the essential and the unessential. You choose this as opposed to that, and hence the very thing that you have chosen gives vitality to that which you have left. Think it over. You say, "This is evil, and I will go to the good." You have chosen the good, so you have given vitality to the evil from which you have got away. But if you understood the very thing from which you are running away you would be free from both, like the man who is pursuing courage, therefore he gives vitality to fear. To put it differently; where there is choice, and out of that a decision, such decision must create another opposite. And this will exist so long as your mind is looking to accumulation, whether of things or of virtues. Do not say, "I am against virtues," which is the opposite. I say: A man who is pursuing virtue is not virtuous, because he does not know what it is. Now we say a man is of character, as opposed to no character; a man is good as opposed to evil. So he is caught in opposites and trading opposites and giving vitality to that which he has left. But if a man were free from that in which he is caught, whatever it is, through understanding, he would be free from all of them. He is neither good nor bad. It is something more exquisite, something much more vital, dynamic, free like the wind.

So, where action is born of choice there must be a hindrance, and life cannot flow through it naturally, spontaneously. Which does not mean that you shall do the opposite. I am sorry to all the time emphasize this, but this is what has been understood by people who want to have time. It is the same thing with regard to knowledge.

Then there is the other hindrance of consistency. Your minds are trained to be consistent; your whole life, your conduct, is to be consistent. I am going to explain what I mean, which again, please bear in mind, is not that you must not be consistent. Consistency is memory. Which means that when you have partially understood a thing, that has given you a principle or an idea, to which you are being consistent. For instance, you have an idea of what right conduct is, which you have learned, and you are being consistent throughout your life to that particular idea. Your memory is pushing you back to a principle which you have established, and to which you consistently behave. Now to me that is a hindrance because it involves time, whereas if you meet that experience or that incident or that person completely each time, you will no longer be consistent, consistent to a principle. Out of this consistency there is born self-discipline which twists the 'now', the present. That is the whole process of what we call self-discipline. We want to twist the 'now', the present, to a certain formula which you have learned through experience, and that twisting process we call self-discipline. You establish an idea from an incident, from an experience, which has become a memory to which you will try to be consistent, and whatever you meet in the present you twist according to that consistency. This is what you call discipline, or following a system, finding a method. You have a mental picture, an idea or a method, invented by another, and because you want to gain, search out a reward for your action which is born of fear. You are being consistent to that memory, not to understanding. In understanding there is never consistency, there is pliability; which does not mean the opposite.

Then there is the hindrance of security. Please follow this. I am leading up to something, not as a lecture. I want to show awareness without effort. We search out security because in security, in things, in money, in possession, in lands, in houses, in virtues, in this idea of being safe, in one word, security, we hope to derive happiness, strength from that security because we are insecure in ourselves. We are empty, therefore we say, "If I have money," or "If I have land," or "If I have power, there is sustenance, so let me accumulate." You are merely looking to power, to virtue, to possessions, to comfort, to give you vitality to battle with life. Being aware of your own littleness, of your own empty shallowness, you accumulate these things around you in the hope that you can smother, dry out that shallow stream of loneliness. To me this is false.

The more and more you look to security, the greater and greater that emptiness becomes. The more and more you accumulate wealth, power, possessions, lands, virtues, the more shallow your thoughts and emotions. So all these hindrances, conformity, authority— which is included in security— give vitality to that consciousness which you call 'I'-consciousness. These various bundles of hindrances go to create that 'I', and having created that 'I', we think by expanding it more and more that that is progress. Now you come to listen to me and you hear quite the opposite, so you say, "Now I have made the effort to accumulate," which you have done. You have sought out virtues; you have sought out standards; you have sought out methods; you have sought out, carefully developed, choice, which is merely cunningness; you have sought out possessions, whether earthly things or super-earthly things, such as virtues. So you have made tremendous efforts to accumulate, and when I say these are hindrances you begin to use the same effort to get rid of them. So what have you done? You are merely vitalizing those things which you think you ought to get rid of: security, conformity, consistency, and so on. Please follow this. You have, by trying to get rid of it, given vitality to the very thing you are trying to get rid of. That is, you are acting in choice. You say, "I have accumulated through effort; through effort I must get rid of it.'' So, like the man who is eschewing evil and becoming good, he only increases evil. Therefore a man who says, ''These are hindrances, therefore let me fight them, get rid of them,'' only increases them, the very same hindrances, only he will give them different names, more sweet-sounding, but in relation it is exactly the same thing from which he is trying to run away.

Now there is a decision which is choiceless. We have made a tremendous effort through centuries. I feel there is for me no effort in this, and I want to help you to find out for yourself how to live without effort. To understand it you must have followed all that I have said. You have accumulated through centuries and stored in your granaries of mind and heart all kinds of things which to me are rubbish. So don't go to the opposite and say, ''They are rubbish; I am going to get rid of them.'' That is what you are doing. You are making an effort to get rid of them and hence your action is instantly caught up in choice and effort. Therefore there is not a decision without choice. When I talk about security, if you really agree with your mind and heart, then there is no choice about it; a decision is made. But choice exists, which is conflict, when you agree intellectually and your emotions are the other, say, that is, when you are no longer tense.

The majority of you, almost all of you, are in that position. You agree that there cannot be security, with all its implications. You are with me intellectually; but emotionally you are quite the opposite. Don't say, ''I don't know how to do it.'' Don't say, ''I don't know how I shall live without money.'' You will find out. That is the point. The point is, the idea of security, or the falseness of security must, if you are tense, have given you the right response, intention.

So when you are decided, and in that decision there is intense awareness, once you decide wholly the falseness of conformity, then your actions become fully active, then your actions will reveal if they are conforming. Do you see what I mean? When once you have decided with your whole being the futility of being consistent, because you understand, not because you have heard me, but because you understand what it means; when you have decided your next action will show if you are conforming, and in that flame of awareness there is not an effort.

Action then can be free of its limitation by individuality alone. Now we look to action being freed, that is, mind and heart being freed by something, by a virtue, by a security, by knowledge, by an idea. Action, to be complete, can only exist when you as an individual can discover true values. I don't know if you are getting all the implications. We have false values and from that we act; we act from the false values that we have accumulated, and we hope through that action to free the mind from false values. I say that mind and heart, which is action, can be freed only when you are truly individual, when you stand alone in right value. That means you must question every standard that you have, not do the opposite. Until you are truly individual, which is to discover right value, which is eternal, you can only do it—it is not an idea, not self-discipline, not choice, not time—you can only discover right value when there is absolute decision, when you meet everything wholly. Then in you there is a corresponding decision which is not an effort.

You know I have done this myself, that is why I am talking about it. I have heard people talk about security differently. I have heard people talk about virtue. ''Because,'' you say, ''you have suffered, you are tormented, there is so much suffering in the world, choose the essential, which will liberate you.'' For myself, I have experimented. I have known what suffering is, like everybody else. There is so much suffering, and because I feel and I know, I have found out, I have freed myself from that suffering without effort. I want to tell you how to do it; it is not a method. Because I have freed myself from that suffering which everyone goes through, there is a way of acting without effort. This is what I mean. We make an effort to gain, and after gaining we make an effort not to lose. So we are caught up in this wheel of effort, struggle, conflict, pain, suffering. Realize that effort of any kind is only destructive, like sharpening a pencil; the more and more you sharpen the less and less pencil with which to write. That is what we have done through generations, with mind and heart, sharpening until we find we have nothing. We say that after having nothing we must accumulate, so we begin again. The effort shows again that there is a craving, because you want to accumulate, to possess. You hear me talk about all this and say, "I must get rid of effort, I must get rid of possession" and you make an effort. So the whole process is wrong. You must think anew and act intuitively, spontaneously. To act intuitively is to act completely, harmoniously, with the whole of your being, mind and heart.

There is an effortless existence, as the flower lives. There is an eternal thing which cannot be found or come out of effort. But do not say, "I must not make an effort," which is the opposite. But understand the cause of effort and all opposites will disappear. Some of you have heard, and some of you have understood. Some of you have heard with attention and therefore you have decided, and hence your actions will reveal themselves, whether they are hindered or spontaneous in action. Your own actions will reveal the depth of your own understanding, not born out of effort, choice, and all the rest. Because there is tremendous tension, and because of that tenseness there is a corresponding reply in your action. That is true awareness. After decision is action, with full significance, with full awareness, in which all your hindrances are revealed. You know, when you see a hindrance ahead, barbed wire, you don't fight it, you go round it. When you see an ordinary physical hindrance you pass it by because you understand it is a hindrance. Now you don't understand it is a hindrance, this craving, this desire to possess power; it is not obvious, you don't understand it. Therefore you want, and hence the whole gamut of suffering. I say there is a way out of this, and because I have gone through it I tell you how to do it. That is, meet everything fully, meet all persons, meet all experiences afresh. In that movement of action you will awaken all the past hindrances and thereby be free, and then you will know what immortality is, and then there is that eternal becoming, which is life itself.

Question: Are you immortal? In what sense?—as an item in the memory of humanity, or in yourself as a being, perfect, eternal. You speak of immortality as eternal timeless being, yet, within the illusion of time the illusions of death and reincarnation continue. What is the real, vital attitude toward them, as one has to deal with them, even though they be essentially illusions?

KRISHNAMURTI: As I was trying to explain the other day, as long as the mind is occupied with the idea of continuity and noncontinuity, with duality, it cannot understand this timeless becoming, which to me is immortality. Now our minds are occupied with time, that is yesterday, today and tomorrow, and we want to know if as an individual we shall continue. Our chief concern when we talk about immortality is whether we shall continue as individuals. The very question, whether you as an individual will continue, arises from this sense of duality. When you say, "Shall I continue?" you imply a distinction and therefore a resistance. So then you ask me, "Is it total annihilation? If the individual does not continue, there must be total annihilation." I say it is neither of these and you will never understand what immortality is, so long as your mind is occupied with the duality; does the individual continue or is he annihilated? Does he disappear totally?

I say there comes into being a new element, which you cannot understand, if your action is divided into a yesterday, today and tomorrow. And as most of our action is divided in that manner, the question arises, "Shall I be immortal, are you immortal, are you an incident in history, or do you as an individual continue through eternity?" To me all these questions cannot be answered, because when I answer you will not understand. I can answer it, but it will have no value.

To me, immortality is an infinite becoming, not a growing. That which grows is self-limited consciousness, therefore it has no inherent endurance. But that timeless eternal life, becoming, that is immortal, and to realize that, there cannot be this sense of duality in action.

Now with regard to the question of reincarnation. As I have tried to explain, the 'I' is the result of effort, conflict and choice, and that 'I' has no inherent value, has no permanent existence. So to me, whether that lives in time, through reincarnation, through a set period, is irrelevant. Whether an illusion can be carried in time, is not the question. When you say, "Is there reincarnation?" that is what you mean, at least that is what I mean. To you it has a very definite meaning—that you as an individual shall go through time. To me, that is not reincarnation, it is the illusion of the 'I'. And you want to know if that illusion can be carried through time until it becomes perfect by growing, by expanding, by accumulating. The very question as to whether you can carry the 'I' through time, indicates a duality and hence your very thought regarding it is an illusion. I am not saying whether it is true or not. We are not concerned with that. I am not dodging or trying to avoid the question. You cannot answer categorically "yes" or "no," because it has no value. You are concerned, if the 'I' will be continued. Now I say, that very 'I' of which you are conscious, is an illusion. You want to carry that illusion through time, which is opportunity, experience, and we think that by understanding that we shall have understood the whole process of injustice in the world, illness, lack of opportunity, and so on. I say: You will not understand the injustice, lack of opportunity and all the other things through understanding an illusion. So when you ask if there is reincarnation, you are concerning your mind with time, whereas I say that if you free the mind of time, you will know immortality. Not through time or through reincarnation will you find immortality, but in the idea of timelessness you will know it. I hope you see the difference. The one emphasizes time and the other is the absolute understanding of that timelessness.

Now I will tell you a story briefly. A Hindu, a Brahmin, in ancient days was giving away things in sacrifice to the priests and the gods. And his son came often and asked him to whom he was giving away these things. A little later the son asked, "To whom are you going to give me?" And the father in annoyance, because the boy had been pestering him, told him that he was going to send him to Death. Now a Brahmin, in ancient days, had to fulfill what he said, even though he said it in anger. So he sent him to Death, and while he was sending him, he asked him to visit many shrines, many teachers. At last he arrives at the house of Death, but Death is absent. So he waits until at last Death arrives and apologizes for keeping the Brahmin waiting, because it was the custom that when the host is absent the guest could not eat. So the son did not eat for three days, because the host was absent. So Death apologizes and says that in return for his discourtesy the son can accept three gifts. So the son chooses first to return to his father and that his father will not be angry with him; secondly he chooses a certain fire ritual which is not important, and lastly he says, "I have listened to many wise men. Some say there is continuance after death and some say there is total annihilation. What do you, Death, who must know, say?" And Death replies, "Do not ask me that question! I will give you power, palaces, riches, amusements, sensation, anything you like, but do not ask me that!" But the boy insists, and so Death says, "I wish all the pupils who come to me, were like you." And Death teaches him what immortality is, never once replying, whether there is continuity or annihilation.

Now you are all concerned with that question—whether you will exist or not after death. And hence the whole conflict of time, and the whole preoccupation with the division of opportunity, of experience. You will not find immortality through time, which is experience, nor through the multiplication of experiences will you find immortality. There is immortality only when there is this understanding of the cessation of time in action.

Question: What is really the root cause of our sympathy, pity, compassion for the suffering and pain and sorrow in life in all its forms? Is this normal to one free of the ego illusion?

KRISHNAMURTI: I tried to explain this yesterday. I said, "Where there is compassion, there is no suffering." Do not ask me whether if you see a dog or a horse hurt you should not feel suffering or hurt. There are two ways of looking at it. Either you are hurt because you want or you possess; or else because it is a beautiful thing, because it is life itself and therefore you are not hurt, but awakened to the cruelty. When you see a beautiful thing spoiled, you are not hurt, you are shocked. That created thing is a natural thing of life itself, and when that is despoiled, then your natural sympathies are awakened instantaneously, spontaneously. In that there is no ego-consciousness, at least from my point of view. But when we possess, and in that object which we possess there is pain, we also suffer. That is, if my friend is ill, or my wife or child, I suffer; because there is an emptiness in us. So, where there is reliance on another, in that there is ever suffering, and we mistake that for compassion. To me, it is not compassion. We have a peculiar idea of compassion. We think that God, who is all-compassionate, will save us from our suffering. Our suffering is created from our own illusion, and no one is going to save you except yourself. So, where there is true compassion, there is no suffering. Compassion is spontaneous, natural; but where there is possession of any kind, there arises that consciousness of emptiness and we try to run away from that emptiness. So when that person whom we possess is taken away or is hurt or is suffering, then we ourselves suffer.

Question: If love of power is the fundamental craving in us, do you know the way by which we can become utterly free of it?

KRISHNAMURTI: I am going to talk about that presently. And there is the other question which was asked, "Why do we fear death and what is the way of freeing ourselves from that fear of death?"

Someone dies, your brother, wife, child or husband, and you suffer. This is a common event of life, and why do we suffer so intensely? Because we have been relying on that person to complement us. When that person dies, we come to a full consciousness of loneliness; we become fully aware of our emptiness. Before, we have tried to hide it, to compensate, to run away, through the possession of another. Becoming conscious of that emptiness which we call death or the losing of another, then to escape from that suffering, what is it we do? We want happiness, to escape from that sorrow, or to have the return of the loved one. Please follow this, because that is what we are doing. When we suffer there is an immediate desire to appease that suffering. Where there is want there is no discernment, because the moment you want to satisfy that sorrow you accept any gift that is offered you in order to cover up your sorrow. You accept the gift of consolation, the gift of reincarnation, the gift of a hereafter or a heaven or of unity in the One Life. You accept, in your sorrow, the gifts of others, and therefore diminish your sorrow, hide it, put it away, and hence what you have accepted, creates blindness. When you are really in acute sorrow then you are questioning, then, in that acuteness, in that alertness, instead of subjugating it, dulling it, or hiding it away, you no longer try to escape from it. When you are no longer wanting more happiness or consolation, then the acuteness of your sorrow will show you the true cause of suffering or the true cause of the fear of death.

Someone dies and you suffer, and you want that person back. And so you turn to the idea of reincarnation, of seances. What has happened? You are merely dulling the mind which has awakened to loneliness, in which there is sorrow; you are merely running away from it. But if you inquire what is the cause of suffering, you will come to it, when you really examine, when you are really awake to all the gifts which people offer, and therefore discern their true value. Then you will find out the true cause which is loneliness. Where there is want there is loneliness. Wanting creates loneliness, and wanting is the cause. But to you it is not the cause, it is only intellectual theory. You will find out the cause and therefore be free of this fear of death, when in the moment of acute suffering you become fully conscious of everything that is offered as consolation. Then you will know whether you are escaping, whether you are seeking consolation or comfort, and so in the very offering of that gift you will know its full significance, and then your mind is forced to face the cause naturally.

Question: In your talk of the 11th August you said that the fullness and ecstasy of life is discovered "not through action, but in the action itself, whatever it be—your earning of money, your ceremonies, your sexual problems." As this has led to much confusion in the minds of some of us who attended the discussion meeting, will you kindly further clarify your statement? What do you mean by the discovery of ecstasy of life in the sexual action or in the ceremony itself?

KRISHNAMURTI: Look here, my friends, those of you who want to do ceremonies, why discuss it? A person who wants to play the piano does not discuss about it. It is only the hypocritical mind which wants to find a loophole in what I am saying to justify his actions. He puts out this question constantly. Please do not look round at your ceremonialist friends; we are all doing it in a different way in ourselves. It may not be with regard to ceremonies, it may be with regard to earning money, or to sex, or to the accumulation of things which give us power. I have said what I mean with regard to ceremonies quite clearly. I think they are an illusion; that inherently they have no value. But to find out for yourself, do not discuss about it. Find out if your reason and your heart are really in harmony in what you are doing. To find out if they are in harmony, they must both be ripe. That is the difficulty. To find out if they are in harmony, do not hold on to things. If you are performing ceremonies, let it go for a day, or a week, or a year. I am not asking you to do this, but if you want to find out and experiment as to whether you are acting truly in harmony, let it go; and at the end of the year see if you really need it. But do not say, "Other people need it and for their sake I must do it." That shows a hypocritical mind. What is a poison to you is also poison to another; what is valueless to you is valueless to another. Why pass on that which is useless for you to another? We do it because it gives us assurance, power, vanity, like a person who has decorations from the government. I assure you there is not much difference between these ceremonies and the ceremonies of courts and kings. I am awfully sorry but this is my opinion. Where unrighteousness is rampant all these things exist. Where there is unnaturalness, which is fear, all these things exist.

Please, I have said my last say with regard to ceremonies. We go over and over and over again every year and I am not going to answer it any more. I may answer it to those who hear it for the first time, but not to the accustomed ear, to the man who has already made up his mind to do what he wants to do, and who wants my confirmation. Why ask me? If you want to do something, if you think it is right, do it! You will find out. But to find out, be open about it, be frank, not hypocritical. Do not base your actions on authority. Do not perform ceremonies, because someone has said, "There is power in ceremonies," or because you yourself get a certain stimulation and think it is spiritual, divine. To me, there is no external spiritual power, nor that subjective thing which we call the 'I' or the higher self from which we derive power. Both are sensation. And when the mind is free from both the object and the subject, then you will know *what is;* then you will know that ecstasy of living in which there is no fear.

August 13, 1933

Camp Fire Address at Ommen

Please, sit with your faces to the fire, as I shall not talk very long. There will be no music after I have talked and the camp fire will be over soon as I have talked.

You know, we all want to take what we have understood, to help another to bring a change into the world. I feel we cannot change the world with that attitude. If you have understood what I have been talking about during the last three weeks, by your action born of understanding you will bring about a change. Not when you desire to change the world, will you bring a change in the world. But if we act out of understanding, that action will bring about its own change. There is a vast difference between the desire to change, and action born of understanding which brings about change.

Some of you have listened with great earnestness and others have merely heard, and those of you who have really understood and therefore will act, will bring about a change; they will carry the flame. However little it is, it will be the vital flame that will give sustenance, that will be understanding. And you can only carry that flame, if you have really searched out and you have really pondered over what has been said during these three weeks. From that, natural action comes. And that action won't be the action of patchwork, changing little things here and little things over there. It will be a fundamental change.

I hope you all will have a happy journey and that we shall meet again in two years.

August 13, 1933

Oslo, Norway, 1933

Talk in University Hall, Oslo

Friends,

I have been given some questions which I shall answer after my talk.

Wherever you go throughout the world you find suffering. There seems to be no limit to suffering, no end to the innumerable problems that concern man, no way out of his continual conflict with himself and his neighbors. Suffering seems to be ever the common lot of man, and he tries to overcome that suffering through the search for comfort; he thinks that by searching for consolation, by seeking comfort, he will free himself from this continual battle, from his problems of conflict and suffering. And he sets out to discover what will give him the most satisfaction, what will give him the greatest consolation in this continual battle of suffering, and goes from one consolation to another, from one sensation to another, from one satisfaction to another. Thus, through the process of time, he gradually sets up innumerable securities, shelters, to which he runs when he experiences intense suffering.

Now there are many kinds of securities, many kinds of shelters. There are those that give temporary emotional satisfaction, such as drugs or drinking; there are amusements and all that pertains to transient pleasure. Again, there are the innumerable beliefs in which man seeks shelter from his suffering; he clings to beliefs or ideals in the hope that they will shape his life and that by conformity he will gradually overcome suffering. Or he takes refuge in systems of thought which he calls philosophies, but which are merely theories handed down through the centuries, or theories that may have been true for those who thought them out, but are not necessarily true for others. Or again, man turns to religion, that is, to a system of thought that tries to shape him, to mold him to a particular pattern, to lead him toward an end; for religion, instead of giving man understanding, gives him merely consolation. There is no such thing as comfort in life, no such thing as security. But in his search for comfort, man has built up through the centuries the securities of religion, ideals, beliefs, and the idea of God.

To me there is God, a living, eternal reality. But this reality cannot be described; each one must realize it for himself. Anyone who tries to imagine what God is, what truth is, is but seeking an escape, a shelter from the daily routine of conflict.

When man has set up a security—the security of public opinion or of the happiness that he derives from possessions or from the practice of virtue, which is but an escape—he meets every incident of life, every one of the innumerable experiences of life, with the background of that security; that is, he never meets life as it really is. He comes to it with a prejudice, with a background already developed through fear; with his mind fully clothed, burdened with ideas, he approaches life.

To put it differently, man in general sees life only through the tradition of time which he bears in his mind and his heart; whereas to me life is fresh, renewing, moving, never static. Man's mind and heart are burdened with the unquestioned desire for comfort, which must necessarily bring about authority. Through authority he meets life, and hence he is incapable of understanding the full significance of experience, which alone can release him from suffering. He consoles himself with the false values of life and becomes merely a machine, a cog in the social structure or the religious system.

One cannot find out what is true value as long as one's mind is seeking consolation; and since most minds are seeking consolation, comfort, security, they cannot find out what truth it. Thus, most people are not individuals; they are merely cogs in a system. To me, an individual is a person who, through questioning, discovers right values; and one can truly question only when one is suffering. You know, when you suffer, your mind is made acute, alive; then you are not theoretical; and only in that state of mind can you question what is the true value of the standards that society, religion, and politics have set about us. Only in that state can we question, and when we question, when we discover true values, then we are true individuals—not until then. That is, we are not individuals as long as we are unconscious of the values to which we have become accustomed through securities, through religions, through the pursuit of beliefs and ideals. We are merely machines, slaves to public opinion, slaves to the innumerable ideals that religions have placed about us, slaves to economic and political systems that we accept. And since everyone is a cog in this machine, we can never find out true values, lasting values, in which alone there is eternal happiness, eternal realization of truth.

The first thing to realize, then, is that we have these barriers, these values, given to us. To find out their living significance we must question, and we can question only when our minds and hearts are burning with intense suffering. And everyone does suffer; suffering is not the gift of a few. But when we suffer we seek immediate consolation, comfort, and therefore there is no longer questioning; there is no longer doubt, but mere acceptance. Hence, where there is want, there cannot be the understanding of right values which alone sets man free, which alone gives him the capacity of existing as a complete human being. And as I was saying, when we meet life partially, with all this traditional background of unquestioned and dead values, naturally there is conflict with life, and this conflict creates in each one of us the idea of ego-consciousness. That is, when our minds are prejudiced by an idea or by a belief or by unquestioned values, there is limitation, and that limitation creates the self-consciousness which in turn brings about suffering.

To put it differently, as long as mind and heart are caught up in the false values that religions and philosophies have set about us, as long as the mind has not discovered true, living values for itself, there is limitation of consciousness, limitation of understanding, which creates the idea of 'I'. And from this idea of 'I', from the fact that consciousness knows the limitation of time as a beginning and an end, springs sorrow. Such consciousness, such a mind and heart are caught up in the fear of death, and hence the inquiry into the hereafter.

When you understand that truth, life, can be realized only when you discover for yourself, without any authority or imitation, the true significance of suffering, the living value of every action, then your mind frees itself from ego-consciousness.

Since most of us are unconsciously seeking a shelter, a place of safety in which we shall not be hurt, since most of us are seeking in false values an escape from continual conflict, therefore I say, become conscious that the whole process of thought, at the present time, is a continual search for shelter, for authority, for patterns to conform to, for systems to follow, for methods to imitate. When you realize that there is no such thing as comfort, no such thing as security, either in possession of things or of ideas, then you face life as it is, not with the background of intense longing for comfort. Then you become aware, but without the constant struggle to become aware—a struggle that goes on as long as your mind and your heart are seeking a continual escape from life through ideals, through conformity, through imitation, through authority. When you realize that, you give up seeking an escape; you are then able to meet life completely, nakedly, wholly, and in that there is understanding, which alone gives you that ecstasy of life.

To put it in another way, since our minds and hearts have through ages been crippled by false values, we are incapable of meeting experience wholly. If you are a Christian you meet it in one way, as dictated by all your prejudices of Christianity and your religious training. If you are a conservative or a communist, you meet it in another way. If you hold any particular belief, you meet life in that particular way, and hope to understand its full significance through a prejudiced mind. Only when you realize that life, that free, eternal movement, cannot be met partially and with prejudice, only then are you free, without effort. Then you are unhampered by all the things you possess—by inherited tradition or acquired knowledge. I say knowledge, not wisdom, for wisdom does not enter here. Wisdom is natural, spontaneous; it comes only when one meets life openly and without any barrier. To meet life openly man must free himself of all knowledge; he must not seek an explanation of suffering, for when he seeks such an explanation he is being caught by fear.

So I repeat, there is a way of living without effort, without the constant strain of achievement and struggle for success, without the constant fear of loss or gain; I say there is a harmonious way of living life that comes when you meet every experience, every action completely, when your mind is not divided against itself, when your heart is not in conflict with your mind, when you do all things wholly, with complete unity of mind and heart. Then in that richness, in that plenitude, there is the ecstasy of life, and that to me is everlasting, that to me is eternal.

Question: You say that your teachings are for all, not for any select few. If that is so, why do we find it difficult to understand you?

KRISHNAMURTI: It is not a question of understanding me. Why should you understand me? Truth is not mine, that you should understand me. You find my words difficult to understand because your minds are suffocated with ideas. What I say is very simple. It is not for the select few; it is for anyone who is willing to try. I say that if you would free yourselves from ideas, from beliefs, from all the securities that people have built up through centuries, then you would understand life. You can free yourselves only by questioning, and you can question only when you are in revolt—not when you are stagnant with satisfying ideas. When your minds are suffocated with beliefs, when they are heavy with knowledge acquired from books, then it is impossible to understand life. So it is not a question of understanding me.

Please—and I am not saying this with any conceit—I have found a way; not a method that you can practice, a system that becomes a cage, a prison. I have realized truth, God, or whatever name you like to give it. I say there is that eternal living reality, but it cannot be realized while the mind and heart are burdened, crippled with the idea of 'I'. As long as that self-consciousness, that limitation exists, there can be no realization of the whole, the totality of life. That 'I' exists as long as there are false values—false values that we have inherited or that we have sedulously created in our search for security, or that we have established as our authority in our search for comfort. But right values, living values—these you can discover only when you really suffer, when you are greatly discontented. If you are willing to become free from the pursuit of gain, then you will find them. But most of us do not want to be free; we want to keep what we have gained, either in virtue or in knowledge or in possessions; we want to keep all these. Thus burdened we try to meet life, and hence the utter impossibility of understanding it completely.

So the difficulty lies not in understanding me, but in understanding life itself; and that difficulty will exist as long as your minds are burdened with this consciousness that we call 'I'. I cannot give you right values. If I were to tell you, you would make of that a system and imitate it, thus setting up but another series of false values. But you can discover right values for yourself, when you become truly an individual, when you cease to be a machine. And you can free yourself from this murderous machine of false values only when you are in great revolt.

Question: It has been claimed by some that you are the Christ come again. We should like to know quite definitely what you have to say about this. Do you accept or reject the claim?

KRISHNAMURTI: I do neither. It does not interest me. Of what value, my friends, is it to you to ask me this? I am asked this question wherever I go. People want to know if I am, or if I am not. If I say I am, they either take my words as authority or laugh at them; if I say I am not, they are delighted. I neither assert nor deny. To me the claim is of very little importance because I feel that what I have to say is inherently right in itself. It does not depend on titles or degrees, revelation or authority. What is of importance is your understanding of it, your intelligence and your own awakened desire to find out, your own love of life—not the assertion that I am or that I am not the Christ.

Question: Is your realization of truth permanent and present all the time, or are there dark times when you again face the bondage of fear and desire?

KRISHNAMURTI: The bondage of fear exists as long as there remains the limitation of consciousness that you call the 'I'. When you become rich within yourself, then you will no longer feel want. It is in this continual battle of want, in this seeking of advantage from circumstances, that fear and darkness exist. I think I am free from that. How can you know it? You can't. I might be deceiving you. So do not bother about it. But I have this to say: One can live effortlessly, in a way that cannot be arrived at through effort; one can live without this incessant struggle for spiritual achievement; one can live harmoniously, completely in action—not in theory, but in daily life, in daily contact with human beings. I say that there is a way to free the mind from all suffering, a way to live completely, wholly, eternally. But to do that, one must be completely open towards life; one must allow no shelter or reserve to remain in which mind can dwell, to which heart can withdraw in times of conflict.

Question: You say that truth is simple. To us, what you say seems very abstract. What is the practical relation, according to you, between truth and actual life?

KRISHNAMURTI: What is it that we call actual life? Earning money, exploiting others and being exploited ourselves, marriage, children, seeking friends, experiencing jealousies, quarrels, fear of death, the inquiry into the hereafter, laying up money for old age—all these we call daily life. Now to me, truth or the eternal becoming of life cannot be found apart from these. In the transient lies the eternal—not apart from the transient. Please, why do we exploit, either in physical things or in spiritual things? Why are we exploited by religions that we have set up? Why are we exploited by priests to whom we look for comfort? Because we have thought of life as a series of achievements, not as a complete action. When we look to life as a means to acquisition, whether of things or of ideas, when we look to life as a school in which to learn, in which to grow, then we are dependent upon that self-consciousness, upon that limitation: we create the exploiter, and we become the exploited. But if we become utterly individual, completely self-sufficient, alone in our understanding, then we do not differentiate between actual living and truth, or God. You know, because we find life difficult, because we do not understand all the intricacies of daily action, because we want to escape from that confusion, we turn to the idea of an objective principle; and so we differentiate, we distinguish truth as being impractical, as having nothing to do with daily life. Thus truth, or God, becomes an escape to which we turn in days of conflict and trouble. But if, in our daily life, we would find out why we act, if we would meet the incidents, the experiences, the sufferings of life wholly, then we would not differentiate practical life from impractical truth. Because we do not meet experiences with our whole being, mentally and emotionally, because we are not capable of doing that, we separate daily life and practical action from the idea of truth.

Question: Don't you think that the support from religions and religious teachers is a great help to man in his effort to free himself from all that binds him?

KRISHNAMURTI: No teacher can give us right values. You may read all the books in the world, but you cannot gather wisdom from them. You may follow all the religious systems of the world and yet remain a slave to them. Only when you stand alone can you find wisdom and be wholly free, liberated. By aloneness I do not mean living apart from humanity. I mean that aloneness which comes from understanding, not from withdrawal. It exists, in other words, when one is utterly individual, not individualistic. You know, we think that by continually practicing the piano under the direction of an instructor we shall become great pianists, creative musicians; and similarly we look to religious teachers for guidance. We say to ourselves, "If I practice daily what they have laid down, I shall have the flame of creative understanding." I say, you can practice it without end, and you will still not have that creative flame. I know many who daily practice certain ideals, but they become only more and more withered in their understanding, because they are merely imitating, they are merely living up to a standard. They have freed themselves from one teacher and have gone to another; they have merely transferred themselves from one cage to another. But if you do not seek comfort, if you continually question—and you can question only when you are in revolt—then you establish freedom from all teachers and all religions; then you are supremely human, belonging neither to a party nor to a religion nor to a cage.

Question: Do you mean to say that there is no help for men when life grows difficult? Are they left entirely to help themselves?

KRISHNAMURTI: I think, if I am not mistaken—if I am, please correct me—I think the questioner wants to know if there is not a source, a person or an idea, to which one can turn in time of trouble, in time of grief, in time of suffering.

I say there is no permanent source that can give one understanding. You know, to me the glory of man is that no one can save him except himself. Please, as you look at man throughout the world, you see that he has always turned to another for help. In India we look to theories, to teachers, for help. Here also you do the same. All over the world man turns to somebody to lift him out of his own ignorance. I say no one can lift you out of your own ignorance. You have created it through fear, through imitation, through the search for security, and hence you have established authorities. You have created it for yourselves, this ignorance that holds each one of you, and no one can free you except you yourselves through your own understanding. Others may free you momentarily, but as long as the root cause of ignorance exists, you merely create another set of illusions.

To me, the root cause of ignorance is the consciousness of 'I', from which arise conflict and sorrow. As long as that 'I' consciousness exists, there must be suffering from which no one can free you. In your devotion to a person or to an idea you may momentarily sever yourselves from that consciousness, but while that consciousness remains it is like a wound that is always festering. The mind can free itself from that ignorance only when it meets life wholly, when it experiences completely, without prejudice, without preconceived ideas, when it is no longer crippled by a belief or an idea. It is one of the illusions that we cherish, that someone else can save us, that we cannot lift ourselves out of this mire of suffering. For centuries we have looked for help from without, and we are still held by the belief.

Question: What is the real cause of the present chaos in the world, and how can this painful state of things be remedied?

KRISHNAMURTI: First of all, I feel, by not looking to a system as a remedy. You know, through centuries we have built up a system, the possessive system based on security. We have built it up; each one of us is responsible for this system wherein acquisition, gain, power, authority, and imitation play the most important part. We have made laws to preserve that system, laws based on our selfishness, and we have become slaves to these laws. Now we want to introduce a new set of laws, to which we shall again become slaves, laws by which possession becomes a crime.

But if we understood the true function of individuality, then we would tackle the root cause of all this chaos in the world, this chaos that exists because we are not truly individual. Please understand what I mean by being individual; I do not mean individualistic. We have for centuries been individualistic, seeking security for ourselves, comfort for ourselves. We have looked to the physical things of life to give us inward shelter, happiness, spiritual ease. We have been dead and have not known it. Because we have imitated and followed, we have blindly exploited beliefs. And being spiritually dead, naturally we have tried to realize our creative powers in the world of acquisition—hence the present chaos wherein each man seeks only his own advantage. But if each one individually begins to free himself from all imitation, and thus begins to realize that creative life, that creative energy which is free, spiritual, then, I feel, he will not look for or give emphasis to either possession or nonpossession. Isn't that so?

Our entire lives are a process of imitation. Public opinion says this, so we must do it. I am not saying, please, that you must go against all convention, that you must impetuously do whatever you like: that would be equally stupid. What I am saying is this: Since we are merely machines, since we are ruthlessly individualistic in the world of acquisition, I say, free yourselves from all imitation, become individuals; question every standard, everything that is about you, not just intellectually, not when you feel at ease with life, but in the moment of suffering when your mind and heart are acute and awake. Then, in that realization which comes from the discovery of living values, you will not divide life into sections—economic, domestic, spiritual; you will meet it as a complete unit; you will meet it as a complete human being.

To put an end to the chaos in the world, the ruthless aggression and exploitation, you cannot look to any system. Only you yourselves can do it, when you become responsible, and you can be responsible only when you are really creating, when you are no longer imitating. In that freedom there will be true cooperation, not the individualism that now exists.

September 5, 1933

First Talk at Frognerseteren

Friends,

Our very search for the understanding of life, for the meaning of life, our struggle to comprehend the whole substance of life or to find out what truth is, destroys our understanding. In this talk I am going to try to explain that where there is a search to understand life, or to find out the significance of life, that very search perverts our judgment.

If we suffer, we want an explanation of that suffering; we feel that if we don't search, if we don't try to find out the meaning of existence, then we are not progressing or gaining wisdom. So we are constantly making an effort to understand, and in that search for understanding we consciously or unconsciously set up a goal towards which we are driven. We establish a goal, the ideal of a perfect life, and we try to be true to that goal, to that end.

As I have said, consciously or unconsciously we set up a goal, a purpose, a principle or belief, and having established that we try to be true to it; we try to be true to an experience which we have but partly understood. By that process we establish a duality. Because we do not understand the immediate with its problems, with its conventions, because we do not understand the present, we establish an idea, a goal, an end, towards which we try to advance. Because we are not prepared to be alert in meeting suffering wholly as it comes, because we have not the capacity to face experience, we try to establish a goal and be consistent. Thereby we develop a duality in action, in thought, and in feeling, and from this duality there arises a problem. In that development of duality lies the cause of the problem.

All ideals must ever be of the future. A mind that is divided, a mind that is striving after the future, cannot understand the present, and thus it develops a duality in action.

Now, having created a problem, having created a conflict, because we cannot meet the present wholly, we try to find a solution for the problem. That is what we are constantly doing, isn't it? All of us have problems. Most of you are here because you think that I am going to help you solve your many problems, and you will be disappointed when I say that I cannot solve them. What I am going to do is try to show the cause of the problem, and then you, by understanding, can solve your problem for yourself. The problem exists as long as mind and heart are divided in action. That is, when we have established an idea in the future and are trying to be consistent, we are incapable of meeting the present fully; so, having created a problem, we try to seek a solution, which is but an escape.

We imagine that we find solutions for various problems, but in finding solutions we have not really solved, we have not understood the cause of the problem. The moment we have solved one problem, another arises, and so we continue to the end of our lives seeking solutions to an endless series of problems. In this talk I want to explain the cause of the problem and the manner of dissolving it.

As I have said, a problem exists as long as there is reaction—either a reaction to external standards, or a reaction to an inner standard, as when you say, "I must be true to this idea," or, "I must be true to this belief." Most educated, thoughtful people have discarded external standards, but they have developed inner standards. We discard an external standard because we have created an inner standard to which we are trying to be true, a standard which is continually guiding us and shaping us, a standard which creates duality in our action. As long as there are standards to which we are trying to be true, there will be problems, and hence the continual search for the solution of these problems.

These inner standards exist as long as we do not meet the experiences and incidents of life wholly. As long as there is a guiding principle in our lives to which we are trying to be true, there must be duality in action, and therefore a problem. That duality will exist as long as there is conflict, and conflict exists wherever there is the limitation of self-consciousness, the 'I'. Though we have discarded external standards and have found for ourselves an inner principle, an inner law, to which we are trying to be true, there is still distinction in action, and hence an incompleteness in understanding. It is only when we understand, when we no longer search for understanding, then there is an effortless existence.

So when I say, do not seek a solution, do not search for an end, I do not mean that you must turn to the opposite and become stagnant. My point is: Why do you seek a solution? Why are you incapable of meeting life openly, nakedly, simply, fully? Because you are continually trying to be consistent. Therefore there is the exertion of will to conquer the immediate obstacle; there is conflict, and you do not try to find out the cause of the conflict. To me this continual search for truth, for understanding, for the solution of various problems, is not progress; this going from one problem to another is not evolution. Only when the mind and heart meet every idea, every incident, every experience, every expression of life, fully—only then can there be a continual becoming which is not stagnation. But the search for a solution, which we mistakenly call progress, is merely stagnation.

Question: Do you mean to say that sooner or later all human beings will inevitably, in the course of existence, attain perfection, complete liberation from all that binds them? If so, why make any effort now?

KRISHNAMURTI: You know, I am not talking of the mass. To me there is not this division of the individual and the mass. I am talking to you as individuals. After all, the mass is but yourself multiplied. If you understand, you will give understanding. Understanding is like the light that dispels darkness. But if you do not understand, if you apply what I am saying only to the other man, the man outside, then you are but increasing darkness.

So you want to know if you—not this imaginary man from the mass—if you will inevitably attain perfection. If that is so, you think, why make any effort in the present? I quite agree. If you think that you will inevitably realize the ecstasy of living, why trouble yourself? But nevertheless, because you are caught up in conflict, you are making an effort.

I will put it differently: it is like saying to a hungry man that he will inevitably find some means of satisfying his hunger. How does it help him today if you tell him that he will be fed ten days hence? By that time he may be dead. So the question is not, "Is there inevitably perfection for me as an individual?" Rather, it is, "Why do I make this ceaseless effort?"

To me, a man who is pursuing virtue is no longer virtuous. Yet that is what we are doing all the time. We are trying to be perfect; we are engaging in the incessant effort to be something. But if we make an effort because we are really suffering and because we want to be free from that suffering, then our chief concern is not perfection—we do not know what perfection is. We can only imagine it or read of it in books. Therefore, it must be illusory. Our chief concern is not with perfection, but with the question, "What creates this conflict that demands effort?"

Question: Is not the spiritual man always perfect?

KRISHNAMURTI: A spiritual man may be, but we are not. That is, we have a sense of duality; we think of a higher man who is perfect and a lower man who is not, and we think of the higher man as trying to dominate the lower. Please try to follow this for a moment, whether you agree or disagree.

You can know only the present conflict; you cannot know perfection so long as you are in conflict. So you need not be concerned with what perfection is, with the question of whether or not man is perfect, whether or not spirit is perfect, whether or not soul is perfect; you are not concerned with that. But surely you are concerned with what causes suffering.

You know, a man confined in a prison is concerned with the destruction of that prison in order to be free; he is not concerned with freedom as an abstract idea. Now you are not concerned with what causes suffering, but you are concerned with the way of escaping from that suffering into perfection. So you want to know if you as an individual will ever realize perfection.

I say that that is not the point. The point is, are you conscious in the present, are you fully aware in the present of the limitations that create suffering? If you know the cause of suffering, from that you will know what perfection is. But you cannot know perfection before you are free of suffering. That is the cause of limitation. So do not question whether you will ever attain perfection, whether the soul is perfect, or whether the God in you is perfect, but become fully conscious of the limitations of your mind and heart in action. And these limitations you can discover only when you act, when you are not trying to imitate an idea or a guiding principle.

You know, our minds are clogged with national and international standards, with standards that we have received from our parents and standards that we have evolved for ourselves. Guided by these standards we meet life. Therefore we are incapable of understanding. We can understand only when our minds are really fresh, simple, eager—not when they are burdened with ideas.

Now each of us has many limitations, limitations of which we are wholly unconscious. The very question, "Is there perfection?" implies the consciousness of limitation. But you cannot discover these limitations by analyzing the past. The attempt to analyze oneself is destructive, but that is what you are trying to do. You say, "I know that I have many limitations; so I shall examine. I shall search and discover what my barriers and limitations are, and then I shall be free." When you do that you are but creating a new set of barriers, hindrances. To really discover the false standards and barriers of the past you must act with full awareness in the present, and in that activity you become aware of all the undiscovered hindrances. Experiment, and you will see. Begin to move with full awareness, with fully awakened consciousness in action, and you will see that you have innumerable barriers, beliefs, limitations, that prevent your acting freely.

Therefore I say, self-analysis, analysis to discover the cause in the past, is false. You can never find out from that which is dead, but only from that which is living; and what is living is ever in the present and not in the past. What you must do is to meet the present with full awareness.

Question: Who is the savior of souls?

KRISHNAMURTI: If one thinks about it for a moment, one sees that that phrase, "the savior of souls," has no meaning. What is it that we mean when we say a soul? An individual entity? Please correct me if I am wrong. What do we mean when we talk about a soul? We mean a limited consciousness. To me there is only that eternal life—contrasted with that limited consciousness which we call the 'I'. When that 'I' exists, there is duality—the soul and the savior of souls, the lower and the higher. You can understand that complete unity of life only with the cessation of self-consciousness or 'I'-ness, which creates the duality. To me immortality, that eternal becoming, has nothing in common with individuality. If man can free himself of his many limitations, then that freedom is eternal life; then mind and heart know eternity. But man cannot discover eternity so long as there is limitation.

So the question, "Who is the savior of souls?" ceases to have any meaning. It arises because we are looking at life from the point of view of self-limited consciousness which we call the 'I'. Therefore we say, "Who will save me? Who will save my soul?" No one can save you. You have held that belief for centuries, and yet you are suffering; there is still utter chaos in the world. You yourself must understand; nothing can give you wisdom except your own action in the present, which must create harmony out of conflict. Only from that can wisdom arise.

Question: Some say that your teaching is only for the learned and the intellectual and not for the masses, who are doomed to constant struggle and suffering in daily life. Do you agree?

KRISHNAMURTI: What do you say? Why should I agree or disagree? I have something to say, and I say it. I am afraid that it is not the learned who will understand. Perhaps this little story will make clear what I mean: Once a merchant, who had some time on his hands, went to an Indian sage and said, "I have an hour to spare; please tell me what truth is." The sage replied, "You have read and studied many books. The first thing that you must do is to suppress all that you have learned."

What I am saying is not only applicable to the leisured class, to the people who are supposed to be intelligent, well-educated—and I am purposely using the word *supposed*—but also to the so-called masses. Who are keeping the masses in daily toil? The intelligent, those who are supposedly learned; isn't that so? But if they were really intelligent they would find a way to free the masses from daily toil. What I am saying is applicable not only to the learned, but to all human beings.

You have leisure to listen to me. Now you may say, "Well, I have understood a little, and therefore I am going to use that little understanding to change the world." But you will never change or alter the world that way. You may listen for a while and you may think that you have understood something, and say to yourself, "I am going to use this knowledge to reform the world." Such reform would be merely patchwork. But if you really understood what I am saying, you would create disturbance in the world—that emotional and mental disquiet from which there comes about the betterment of conditions. That is, if you understand you will try to create a state of discontent about you, and that you can do only if you change yourself; you cannot do this if you think that what I say is applicable to the learned only rather than to yourself. The man in the street is you. So the question is: Do you understand what I am saying?

If you are intensely caught up in conflict, you want to find out the cause of that conflict. Now if you are fully aware of that conflict, you will find that your mind is trying to escape, trying to avoid facing that conflict completely. It is not a question of whether or not you understand me, but whether you as an individual are completely aware, alive to confront life wholly. What prevents you from meeting life wholly? That is the point. What prevents you from meeting life wholly is the continual action of memory, of a standard from which arises fear.

Question: According to you, there appears to be no connection between intellect and intelligence. But you speak of awakened intelligence as one might of trained intellect. What is intelligence, and how can it be awakened?

KRISHNAMURTI: Training the intellect does not result in intelligence. Rather, intelligence comes into being when one acts in perfect harmony, both intellectually and emotionally. There is a vast distinction between intellect and intelligence. Intellect is merely thought functioning independently of emotion. When intellect, irrespective of emotion, is trained in any particular direction, one may have great intellect, but one does not have intelligence, because in intelligence there is the inherent capacity to feel as well as to reason; in intelligence both capacities are equally present, intensely and harmoniously.

Now modern education is developing the intellect, offering more and more explanations of life, more and more theories, without the harmonious quality of affection. Therefore we have developed cunning minds to escape from conflict; hence we are satisfied with explanations that scientists and philosophers give us. The mind—the intellect—is satisfied with these innumerable explanations, but intelligence is not, for to understand there must be complete unity of mind and heart in action.

That is, now you have a business mind, a religious mind, a sentimental mind. Your passions have nothing to do with business; your daily earning mind has nothing to do with your emotions, and you say that this condition cannot be altered. If you bring your emotions into business, you say, business cannot be well managed or be honest. So you divide your mind into compartments: in one compartment you keep your religious interest, in another your emotions, in a third your business interest which has nothing to do with your intellectual and emotional life. Your business mind treats life merely as a means of getting money in order to live. So this chaotic existence, this division of your life continues.

If you really used your intelligence in business, that is, if your emotions and your thought were acting harmoniously, your business might fail. It probably would. And you will probably let it fail when you really feel the absurdity, the cruelty, and the exploitation that is involved in this way of living. Until you really approach all of life with your intelligence, instead of merely with your intellect, no system in the world will save man from the ceaseless toil for bread.

Question: You often talk of the necessity of understanding our experiences. Will you please explain what you mean by understanding an experience in the right way?

KRISHNAMURTI: To understand an experience fully you must come to it freshly each time it confronts you. To understand experience you must have an open, simple clarity of mind and heart. But we do not approach the experiences of life with that attitude. Memory prevents us from approaching experience openly, nakedly. Isn't that so? Memory prevents us from meeting experience wholly, and therefore it prevents us from understanding experience completely.

Now what causes memory? To me, memory is but the sign of incomplete understanding. When you meet an experience wholly, when you live fully, that experience or that incident does not leave the scar of memory. Only when you live partially, when you do not meet experience wholly, there is memory; only in incompleteness is there memory. Isn't that so? Take, for instance, your being consistent to a principle. Why are you consistent? You are consistent because you cannot meet life openly, freely; therefore you say, "I must have a principle that will guide me." Hence the constant struggle to be consistent, and with that memory as a background you meet every incident of life. Thus there is incompleteness in your understanding because you approach experience with a mind that is already burdened. Only when you meet all things, whatever they are, with an unburdened mind, only then will you have true understanding.

"But," you say, "what am I to do with all the memories that I have?" You cannot discard them. But what you can do is meet your next experience wholly; then you will see those past memories come into action, and then is the time to meet them and to dissolve them.

So what gives right understanding is not the residue of many experiences. You cannot meet new experiences wholly when the remainder of past experiences is burdening your mind. Yet that is how you are continually meeting them. That is, your mind has learned to be careful, to be cunning, to act as a signal, to give a warning; therefore, you cannot meet any incident fully. To free your mind of memory, to free it from this burden of experience, you must meet life fully; in that action your past memories come into activity, and in the flame of awareness they are dissolved. Try it and you will see.

As you go away from here you will meet friends; you will see the sunset, the long shadows. Be fully aware in these experiences, and you will find that all kinds of memories surge forward; in your acute awareness you will understand the falseness and the strength of these memories, and you will be able to dissolve them; you will then meet with full awareness every experience of life.

September 6, 1933

Second Talk at Frognerseteren

Friends,

Today I want to explain that there is a way of living naturally, spontaneously, without the constant friction of self-discipline, the constant battle of adjustment. But to understand what I am going to say, please consider it not only intellectually, but also emotionally. You must feel it; for you can bring about fulfillment of life only when your emotions as well as your thoughts are acting harmoniously. When you live completely in the harmony of your mind and heart, then your action is natural, spontaneous, effortless.

Most minds are seeking security. We want to be sure. We set up in authority those who offer us that security, and we worship them as our authority because we ourselves are seeking a certainty to which the mind can cling, in which the mind can feel safe, secure.

If you consider the matter, you will find that most of you come to listen to me because you are seeking certainty—certainty of knowledge, certainty of an end, certainty of truth, certainty of an idea—in order that you may act with that certainty, choose through that certainty. Your minds and hearts desire to act with the background of that certainty. Your choice and your actions do not awaken true discernment or true perception because you are constantly engaged in the gathering in of knowledge, in the accumulation of experiences, in searching out various kinds of gain, in seeking authorities that give you security and comfort, in striving for the development of character. Through all these attempts at accumulation you hope to have the assurance of certainty; certainty that takes away all doubt and anxiety; certainty that gives you—at least you hope that it will give you—surety of choice. With the thought of certainty, you choose in the hope of gaining further understanding. Thus, in the search for certainty there is born fear of gain and fear of loss.

So you make life into a school where you learn to be certain. Isn't that what your life is? A school where you learn, not to live, but how to be sure. To you life is a process of accumulation, not a matter of living.

Now I differentiate between living and accumulation. A man who is really living has no sense of accumulation. But the man who is seeking certainty and security, who is seeking a shelter from which he can act—the shelter of character, of virtue—that man thinks of life as accumulation, and hence to him life becomes a process of learning, of gain, of struggle.

Where there is the idea of accumulation and of gain, there must be a sense of time, and hence incompleteness in action. If we are constantly looking to a future gain, to a future from which we shall derive advantage, development, greater strength for acquisition, then our action in the present must be incomplete. If our minds and hearts are continually seeking gain, achievement, success, then our action, whatever it be, has no true significance; our eyes are fixed on the future, our minds are concerned only with the future. Hence, all action in the present creates incompleteness.

From this incompleteness there arises conflict, which we hope to overcome through self-discipline. We make a distinction in our minds between the things that we wish to gain, which we call the essential, and the things that we do not wish to acquire, which we call the unessential. Thus, there is a constant battle, a constant struggle; conflict and suffering result from this distinction.

I shall explain this point in another way, because unless you see and really understand it, you will not fully comprehend what I shall have to say later.

We have made life into a school of continual learning. But to me life is not a school; it is not a process of gathering in. Life is to be lived naturally, fully, without this constant battle of conflicts, this distinction between the essential and the unessential. From this idea of life as a school, there arises the constant desire for achievement, success, and therefore the search for an end, the desire to find the ultimate truth, God, the final perfection which will give us—at least, we hope it will give us—certainty, and hence our attempts at the continual adjustment to certain social conditions, to ethical and moral demands, to the development of character and the cultivation of virtues. These standards and demands, if you really think about them, are but shelters from which we act, shelters developed through resistance.

This is the life that most people are living—a life of constant search for gain, for accumulation, and therefore a life of incompleteness in action. The idea of gain, which divides action into past, present, and future, is always in our minds; therefore there is never complete understanding in action itself. The mind is continually thinking of gain, and hence it finds no meaning in the action with which it is occupied.

So this is the state in which you are living. Now to me that state is utterly false. Life is not a process of gathering in, a school in which you must learn, in which you must discipline yourself, in which there is constant resistance and struggle. Where there is this constant gathering in, this desire for accumulation, there must exist incompleteness which creates want; if you do not want, you do not gather. And where there is want there is no discernment, even though you may go through the process of choice.

Now you say to me, "How am I to get rid of this want? How am I to free my mind from this process of gathering in? How am I to conquer these hindrances? You say that life is not a school in which to learn, but how am I to live naturally? Tell me the path on which I must walk, the method that I must practice every day to live fully."

To me, this is not the way to look at the problem. The question is not how you are to live fully, but rather, what urges you to this constant accumulation; the question is not how you shall get rid of the idea of gathering, of accumulation, but rather, what creates in you this desire to accumulate. I hope you see the distinction.

Now you look at the problem from the point of view of getting rid of something, of acquiring nonacquisition, which is essentially the same thing as desiring to acquire something, since all opposites are the same. So, what prevents you from living naturally, harmoniously? I say that it is this process of gathering, this searching for certainty.

Then you want to know how to be free from the search for certainty. I say, do not approach the problem in this way. The futility of gain will have a meaning for you only when you are really in conflict, only when you are fully conscious of the disharmony of your actions. If you are not caught up in conflict, then continue in your present way; if you are absolutely unconscious of struggle and suffering, if you are unaware of your own disharmony, then go on living as you are. Then do not try to be spiritual, for you do not know what that signifies at all. The ecstasy of understanding comes only when there is great discontent, when all false values about you are destroyed. If you are not discontented, if you are not aware of intense disharmony in and about you, then what I tell you of the futility of accumulation can have no meaning to you.

But if there is this divine revolt in you, then you will understand when I say that life is not a school in which to learn; life is not a process of constant accumulation, a process in which there is continual want which is blinding. Then that very revolt in which you are caught up, that very suffering, gives you understanding, because it awakens in you the flame of awareness. And when you are fully aware that want is blinding, then you will see its full significance, which dissipates want. Then you will have freedom from want, from gathering in. But if you are unconscious of such a struggle, of such a revolt, you can but continue your life as you are living it, in a half-awakened state. When people suffer, when they are caught up in conflict, that very suffering and conflict should keep them intensely aware; but most of them only ask how to get rid of want. When you understand the full significance of not desiring to gain, to accumulate, then there is no longer the struggle to get rid of something.

To put it differently, why do you go through the process of self-discipline? You do it because of fear. Why are you afraid? Because you want surety, the surety that a social standard, a religious belief, or the idea of acquiring virtue gives you. So you set about disciplining yourself. That is, when the mind is enslaved by the idea of gain or conformity, there is self-discipline. That you are awakened to suffering is but the indication that mind is trying to free itself from all standards; but when you suffer you immediately try to quieten that suffering by drugging the mind with what you call comfort, security, certainty. So you continue this process of seeking certainty, which is but an opiate. But if you understand the illusion of certainty—and you can understand it only in the intensity of conflict from which alone all inquiry can truly begin—then want, which creates certainty, disappears.

So the question isn't how to get rid of want; it is rather this: are you fully aware when there is suffering? Are you fully conscious of conflict, of the disharmonious life about you and within you? If you are, then in that flame of awareness there is true perception, without this constant battle of adjustment, of self-discipline. However, seeing the falsity of self-discipline does not mean that one can indulge in rash, impetuous action. On the contrary, then action is born out of completeness.

Question: Can there be happiness when there is no longer any 'I' consciousness? Is one able to feel anything at all if the 'I' consciousness is extinguished?

KRISHNAMURTI: First of all, what does one mean by the 'I' consciousness? When are you aware of this 'I'? When are you conscious of yourself? You are conscious of yourself as 'I', as an entity, when you are in pain, when you experience discomfiture, conflict, struggle.

You say, "If that 'I' does not exist, what is there?" I say you will find out only when your mind is free of that 'I'; so do not inquire now. When your mind and heart are harmonious, when they are no longer caught up in conflict, then you will know. Then you will not ask what it is that feels, that thinks. As long as this 'I' consciousness exists there must be the conflict of choice, from which arises the sensation of happiness and unhappiness. That is, this conflict gives you the sense of limited consciousness, the 'I', with which the mind becomes identified. I say that you will find out that life which is not identified with the 'you' or the 'me', that life which is eternal, infinite, only when this limited consciousness dissolves itself. You do not dissolve that limited consciousness; it dissolves itself.

Question: The other day you spoke of memory as a hindrance to true understanding. I have recently had the misfortune of losing my brother. Should I try to forget that loss?

KRISHNAMURTI: I explained the other day what I mean by memory. I shall try to explain it again.

After you have seen a beautiful sunset, you return to your home or office and begin again to live in that sunset, as your home or office is not as you would have it, it is not beautiful; so to escape from that ugliness you return in memory to that sunset. Thus you create in your mind a distinction between your home, which does not give you joy, and the thing that gives you great delight, the sunset. So, when you are confronted by circumstances which are not pleasant, you turn to the memory of that which is joyous. But if, instead of turning to a dead memory, you would try to alter the circumstances that are unpleasant, then you would be living intensely in the present and not in the dead past.

So when one loses someone whom one loves greatly, why is there this constant looking back, this constant holding on to that which gave us pleasure, this longing to have that person back again? This is what everyone goes through when he experiences such a loss. He escapes from the sorrow of that loss by turning to the remembrance of the person who is gone, by living in a future, or by belief in the hereafter—which is also a kind of memory. It is because our minds are perverted through escape, because they are incapable of meeting suffering openly, freshly, that we have to revert to memory, and thus the past encroaches upon the present.

So the question is not whether you should or should not remember your brother or your husband, your wife or your children; rather, it is a matter of living completely, wholly, in the present, though that does not imply that you are indifferent to those who are about you. When you live completely, wholly, there is in that intensity, the flame of living, which is not the mere imprint of an incident.

How is one to live completely in the present, so that the mind is not perverted with past memories and future longings—which are also memory? Again, the question is not how you should live completely, but what prevents you from living completely. For when you ask how, you are looking for a method, a means, and to me, a method destroys understanding. If you know what prevents you from living completely, then out of yourself, out of your own awareness and understanding, you will free yourself from that hindrance. What prevents you from freeing yourself is your search for certainty, your continual longing for gain, for accumulation, for achievement. But do not ask, "How am I to conquer these hindrances?" for all conquering is but a process of further gain, further accumulation. If this loss is really creating suffering in you, if it is really giving you intense—not superficial—sorrow, then you will not ask how; then you will see immediately the futility of looking back or forward for consolation.

When most people say that they suffer, their suffering is but superficial. They suffer, but at the same time they want other things: they want comfort, they are afraid, they search out ways and means of escape. Superficial sorrow is always accompanied by the desire for comfort. Superficial suffering is like shallow plowing of the soil; it achieves nothing. Only when you till the soil deeply, to the full depth of the plowshare, is there richness. In the state of complete suffering there is complete understanding, in which hindrances as memories both of the present and of the future cease to exist. Then you are living in the eternal present.

You know, to understand a thought or an idea does not mean merely to agree with it intellectually.

There are various kinds of memories: there is the memory that forces itself upon you in the present, the memory to which you turn actively, and the memory of looking forward to the future. All these prevent your living completely. But do not begin to analyze your memories. Do not ask, "Which memory is preventing my complete living?" When you question in that way, you do not act; you merely examine memory intellectually, and such an examination has no value because it deals with a dead thing. From a dead thing there is no understanding. But if you are truly aware in the present, in the moment of action, then all these memories come into activity. Then you need not go through the process of analyzing them.

Question: Do you think it is right to bring up children with religious training?

KRISHNAMURTI: I shall answer this question indirectly, for when you understand what I am going to say, you can answer it specifically for yourselves.

You know, we are influenced not only by external conditions, but also by an inner condition which we develop. In bringing up a child, parents subject him to many influences and limiting circumstances, one of which is religious training. Now, if they let the child grow up without such hindering, limiting influences, either from within or from without, then the child will begin to question as he grows older, and he will intelligently find out for himself. Then, if he wants religion, he will have it, whether you prohibit or encourage the religious attitude. In other words, if his mind and heart are not influenced, not hindered, either by external or by inner standards, then he will truly discover what is true. This requires great perception, great understanding.

Now parents want to influence the child one way or another. If you are very religious, you want to influence the child toward religion; if you are not, you try to turn him away from religion. Help the child to be intelligent, then he will find out for himself the true significance of life.

Question: You spoke of harmony of mind and heart in action. What is this action? Does this action imply physical movement, or can action take place when one is quite still and alone?

KRISHNAMURTI: Does not action imply thought? Is not action thought itself? You cannot act without thinking. I know that most people do, but their action is not intelligent, not harmonious. Thought is action, which is also movement. Again, we think apart from our feeling, thus setting up another entity separate from our action. So we divide our lives into three distinct parts, thinking, feeling, acting. Therefore you ask, "Is action purely physical? Is action purely mental or emotional?"

To me the three are one: to think, to feel, to act, there is no distinction. Therefore you may be alone and quiet for a while, or you may be working, moving, acting: both states can be action. When you understand this, you will not make a separation between thinking, feeling and acting.

To most people, thinking is but a reaction. If it is merely a reaction, it is no longer thinking, for then it is uncreative. Most people who say that they think are but blindly following their reactions; they have certain standards, certain ideas, according to which they act. These they have memorized, and when they say that they think, they are but following these memories. Such imitation is not thinking; it is but a reaction, a reflection. True thinking exists only when you discover the true significance of these standards, these preconceptions, these securities.

To put it differently, what is the mind? Mind is speech, thought, consideration, understanding; it is all these, and it is also feeling. You cannot separate feeling from thinking; the mind and heart are in themselves complete. But because we have created innumerable escapes through conflict, there arises the idea of thought as apart from feeling, as apart from action, and hence our life is broken up, incomplete.

Question: Among your listeners are people old and feeble in mind and body. Also, there may be those who are addicts to drugs, drink, or smoking. What can they do to change themselves, when they find that they cannot change even when they long to?

KRISHNAMURTI: Remain as you are. If you really long to change, you will change. You see, that is just it: intellectually you want to change, but emotionally you are still enticed by the pleasure of smoking or the comfort of a drug. So you ask, "What am I to do? I want to give this up, but at the same time I don't want to give it up. Please tell me how I can do both." That sounds amusing, but that is really what you are asking.

Now if you approach the problem wholly, not with the idea of wanting or nonwanting, giving up or not giving up, you will find out whether or not you really want to smoke. If you find that you do want to, then smoke. In that way you will find out the worth of that habit without constantly calling it futile and yet continuing it. If you approach the act completely, wholly, then you will not say, "Shall I give up smoking or not?" But now you want to smoke because it gives you a pleasant sensation, and at the same time you don't want to because mentally you see the absurdity of it. So you begin to discipline yourself, saying, "I must sacrifice myself; I must give this up."

Question: Do you not agree that man shall gain the kingdom of heaven through a life, like that of Jesus, wholly dedicated to service?

KRISHNAMURTI: I hope you will not be shocked when I say that man will not gain the kingdom of heaven in this way.

Now see what you are saying: "Through service I shall obtain something that I want." Your statement implies that you do not serve completely; you are looking for a reward through service. You say, "Through righteous behavior I shall know God." That is, you are really interested, not in righteous behavior but in knowing God, thus divorcing righteous from God. But neither through service, nor love, nor worship, nor prayer, but only in the very action of these, is there truth, God. Do you understand? When you ask, "Shall I gain the kingdom of heaven through service?" your service has no meaning because you are primarily interested in the kingdom of heaven; you are interested in getting something in return; it is a kind of barter, as much of your life is.

So when you say, "Through righteousness, through love, I shall attain, I shall realize," you are interested in the realization, which is but an escape, a form of imitation. Therefore your love or your righteous act has no meaning. If you are kind to me because I can give you something in return, what significance has your kindness?

That is the whole process of our life. We are afraid to live. Only when someone dangles a reward before our eyes do we act, and then we act not for the sake of action itself, but in order to obtain that reward. In other words, we act for what we can get out of action. It is the same in your prayers. That is, because for us action has no significance in itself, because we think that we need encouragement in order to act rightly, we have placed before us a reward, something we desire, and we hope that enticement, that toy, will give us satisfaction. But when we act with that hope of reward, then action itself has no significance.

That is why I say that you are caught up in this process of reward and gain, this hindrance born of fear, which results in conflict. When you see this, when you become aware of this, then you will understand that life, behavior, service, everything, has significance in itself; then you do not go through life with the purpose of getting something else, because you know that action itself has intrinsic value. Then you are not merely a reformer; you are a human being; you know that life which is pliable and therefore eternal.

September 8, 1933

Third Talk at Frognerseteren

This morning I am going to answer questions only.

Question: Do you believe in the efficacy of prayer, and the value of prayer that is directed out of wholehearted sympathy to the misfortune and suffering of others? Cannot prayer, in the right sense, ever bring about the freedom of which you speak?

KRISHNAMURTI: When we use the word *prayer,* I think we use it with a very definite meaning. As it is generally understood, it means praying to someone outside of ourselves to give us strength, understanding, and so on. That is, we are looking for help from an external source. When you are suffering and you look to another to relieve you from that suffering, you are but creating in your mind, and therefore in your action, incompleteness, duality. So from my point of view, prayer, as it is commonly understood, has no value. You may forget your suffering in your prayer, but you have not understood the cause of suffering. You have merely lost yourself in prayer; you have suggested to yourself certain modes of living. So prayer in the ordinary sense of the word, that is, looking to another for relief from suffering, has to me no value.

But if I may use the word with a different meaning, I think there is prayer which is not a looking to another for help; it is a continued alertness of mind, an awakened state in which you understand for yourself. In that state of prayer you know the cause of suffering, the cause of confusion, the cause of a problem. Most of us, when we have a problem, immediately seek a solution. When we find a solution we think that we have solved the problem, but we have not. We have only escaped from it. Prayer, in the conventional meaning of the word, is thus an escape. But real prayer, I feel, is action with awakened interest in life.

Question: Do you think that the prayer of a mother for her children may be good for them?

KRISHNAMURTI: What do you think?

Comment: I hope it will be good for them.

KRISHNAMURTI: What do you mean by its being good for them? Is there not something else one can do to help? What can one do for another when that person is suffering? One can give sympathy and affection. Suppose that I am suffering because I love someone who does not love me in return, and that I happen to be your son. Your prayer will not relieve my suffering. What happens? You discuss the matter with me, but the pain still remains because I want that love. What do you want to do when you see someone suffer whom you love? You want to help; you want to take away the suffering from him. But you cannot, because that suffering is his prison. It is the prison that he himself has created, a prison that you cannot take away—but that does not mean that your attitude should be one of indifference.

Now when one whom you love is suffering, and you can do nothing for him, you turn to prayer, hoping that some miracle will happen to alleviate his sorrow; but if you once understand that the suffering is caused by the ignorance created by that person himself, then you will realize that you can give him sympathy and affection, but you cannot remove his suffering.

Comment: But we want to relieve our own suffering.

KRISHNAMURTI: That is different.

Question: You say, "Meet all experiences as they come." What about such terrible misfortunes as being condemned to lifelong imprisonment, or being burned alive for holding certain political or religious opinions—misfortunes that have actually been the lot of human beings? Would you ask such people to submit themselves to their misfortunes and not try to overcome them?

KRISHNAMURTI: Suppose that I commit murder; then society puts me in prison because I have done something that is inherently wrong. Or suppose that some force from the outside impels me to do something of which you disapprove, and you in return do me harm. What am I to do? Suppose that some years hence you, in this country, decide that you do not want me here because of what I say. What can I do? I cannot come here. Now, isn't it after all the mind that gives value to these terms *fortune* and *misfortune?*

If I hold a certain belief and am imprisoned for holding it, I do not consider that imprisonment as suffering, because the belief is really mine. Suppose I believe in something—something not external, something that is real to me; if I am punished for holding that belief, I will not consider that punishment as suffering, for the belief I am being punished for is to me not merely a belief, but a reality.

Question: You have spoken against the spirit of acquisition, both spiritual and material. Does not contemplation help us to understand and meet life completely?

KRISHNAMURTI: Is not contemplation the very essence of action? In India there are people who withdraw from life, from daily contact with others, and retire into the woods to contemplate, to find God. Do you call that contemplation? I wouldn't call it contemplation—it is but an escape from life. Out of meeting life fully comes contemplation. Contemplation is action.

Thought, when it is complete, is action. The man who, in order to think, withdraws from the daily contact with life, makes his life unnatural; for him life is confusion. Our very seeking for God or truth is an escape. We seek because we find that the life we live is ugly, monstrous. You say, "If I can understand who created this thing, I shall understand the creation; I shall withdraw from this and go to that." But if, instead of withdrawing, you tried to understand the cause of confusion in the very confusion itself, then your finding out, your discovery, would destroy the thing that is false.

Unless you have experienced truth, you cannot know what it is. Not pages of description nor the clever wit of man can tell you what it is. You can only know truth for yourself, and you can know it only when you have freed your mind from illusion. If the mind is not free, you but create opposites, and these opposites become your ideals, as God or truth.

If I am caught in suffering, in pain, I create the idea of peace, the idea of tranquillity.

I create the idea of truth according to my like and dislike, and therefore that idea cannot be true. Yet that is what we are constantly doing. When we contemplate as we generally do, we are merely trying to escape from confusion. "But," you say, "When I am caught in confusion I cannot understand; I must escape from it in order to understand." That is, you are trying to learn from suffering.

But as I see it, you can learn nothing from suffering, though you should not withdraw from it. The function of suffering is to give you a tremendous shock; the awakening caused by that shock gives you pain, and then you say, "Let me find out what I can learn from it." Now if, instead of saying this, you keep awake during the shock of suffering, then that experience will yield understanding. Understanding lies in suffering itself, not away from it; suffering itself gives freedom from suffering.

Comment: You said the other day that self-analysis is destructive, but I think that analyzing the cause of suffering gives one wisdom.

KRISHNAMURTI: Wisdom is not in analysis. You suffer, and by analysis you try to find the cause; that is, you are analyzing a dead event, the cause that is already in the past. What you must do is find the cause of suffering in the very moment of suffering. By analyzing suffering you do not find the cause; you analyze only the cause of a particular act. Then you say, "I have understood the cause of that suffering." But in reality you have only learned to avoid the suffering; you have not freed your mind from it. This process of accumulation, of learning through the analysis of a particular act, does not give wisdom. Wisdom arises only when the 'I' consciousness, which is the creator, the cause of suffering, is dissolved. Am I making this difficult?

What happens when we suffer? We want immediate relief, and so we take anything that is offered. We examine it superficially for the moment, and we say that we have learned. When that drug proves insufficient in providing relief, we take another, but the suffering continues. Isn't that so? But when you suffer completely, wholly, not superficially, then something happens; when all the avenues of escape which the mind has invented have been understood and blocked, there remains only suffering, and then you will understand it. There is no cessation through an intellectual drug. As I said the other day, life to me is not a process of learning; yet we treat life as though it were merely a school for learning things, merely a suffering in order to learn; as though everything served only as a means to something else. You say that if you can learn to contemplate you will meet life fully, whereas I say that if your action is complete, that is, if your mind and heart are in full harmony, then that very action is contemplation, effortlessness.

Question: Can a minister who has freed himself from the doctrines still be a minister in the Lutheran church?

KRISHNAMURTI: I think that he will not remain in the ministry. What do you mean by a minister? One who gives you what you want spiritually, that is, comfort? Surely the question has been already answered. You are looking to mediators to help you. You are making me also into a minister—a minister without doctrines, but still you think of me as a minister. But I am afraid I am not. I can give you nothing. One of the conventionally accepted doctrines is that others can lead you to truth, that through the suffering of another you can understand it; but I say that no one can lead you to truth.

Question: Suppose that the minister is married and dependent upon his position for his living?

KRISHNAMURTI: You say that if the minister gave up his work, his wife and children would suffer, which is real suffering for him, as well as for his wife and children. Should he give it up? Suppose that I am a minister; that I no longer believe in churches, and feel the necessity of freeing myself from them. Do I consider my wife and children? No. That decision needs great understanding.

Question: You have said that memory represents an experience that has not been understood. Does that mean that our experiences are of no value to us? And why does a fully understood experience leave no memory?

KRISHNAMURTI: I am afraid that most of the experiences that one has are of no value. You are repeating the same thing over and over again, whereas to me an experience really understood frees the mind from all search for experience. You confront an incident from which you hope to learn, from which you hope to profit, and you multiply experiences, one after another. With that idea of sensation, of learning, of gaining, you meet various experiences; you meet them with a prejudiced mind. Thus you are using the experiences that confront you merely as a means to get something else—to get rich emotionally or mentally, to enjoy. You think that these experiences have no inherent value; you look to them only to get something else through them.

Where there is want there must be memory, which creates time. And most minds, being caught in time, meet life with that limitation. That is, bound by this limitation they try to understand something that has no limit. Therefore there is conflict. In other words, the experiences from which we try to learn are born of reaction. There is no such thing as learning from experience or through experience.

The questioner wants to know why a fully understood experience leaves no memory. We are lonely, empty; being conscious of that emptiness, that loneliness, we turn to experience to fill it. We say, "I shall learn from experience; let me fill my mind with experience which destroys loneliness." Experience does destroy loneliness, but it makes us very superficial. That is what we are always doing; but if we realize that this very want creates loneliness, then loneliness will disappear.

Question: I feel the entanglement and confusion of attachment in the thoughts and feelings that make up the richness and variety of my life. How can I learn to be detached from experience from which I seem unable to escape?

KRISHNAMURTI: Why do you want to be detached?—because attachment gives you pain. Possession is a conflict in which there is jealousy, continual watchfulness, never-ending struggle. Attachment gives you pain; therefore you say, "Let me be detached." That is, your detachment is merely a running away from pain. You say, "Let me find a way, a means, by which I shall not suffer." In attachment there is conflict which awakens you, stirs you, and in order not to be awakened, you long for detachment. You go through life wanting the exact opposite of that which gives you pain, and that very wanting is but an escape from the thing in which you are caught.

It is not a matter of learning detachment, but of keeping awake. Attachment gives you pain. But if, instead of trying to escape, you try to keep awake, you will meet openly and understand every experience. If you are attached and are satisfied with your state, you experience no disturbance. Only in time of pain and suffering do you want the opposite, which you think will give you relief. If you are attached to a person, and there is peace and quiet, everything moves smoothly for a while; then something happens that gives you pain. Take, for example, a husband and wife; in their possession, in their love, there is complete blindness, happiness. Life goes smoothly until something happens—he may leave, or she may fall in love with another. Then there is pain. In such a situation you say to yourself, "I must learn detachment." But if you love again you repeat the same thing. Again, when you experience pain in attachment, you desire the opposite. That is human nature; that is what every human being wants.

So it is not a matter of acquiring detachment. It is a matter of seeing the foolishness of attachment when you suffer in attachment; then you do not go to the opposite. Now, what happens? You want to be attached and at the same time you want to be detached, and in this conflict there is pain. If in pain itself you realize the finality of pain, if you do not try to escape to the opposite, then that very pain will free you from both attachment and detachment.

September 9, 1933

Talk in the Colosseum, Oslo

Friends,

You know, we go from belief to belief, from experience to experience, hoping and searching for some permanent understanding that will give us enlightenment, wisdom; and thereby we also hope to discover for ourselves what truth is. So we begin to search for truth, God, or life. Now to me, this very search for truth is a denial of it, for that everlasting life, that truth, can be understood only when mind and heart are free from all ideas, from all doctrines, from all beliefs, and when we understand the true function of individuality.

I say that there is an everlasting life of which I know and of which I speak, but one cannot understand it by searching for it. What is our search now? It is but an escape from our daily sufferings, confusions, conflicts; an escape from our confusion of love in which there is a constant battle of possession, of jealousy; an escape from the continual striving for existence. So we say to ourselves, "If I can understand what truth is, if I can find out what God is, then I will understand and conquer the confusion, the struggle, the pain, the innumerable battles of choice. Let me therefore find out *what is,* and in understanding that, I shall understand the everyday life in which there is so much suffering." To me, the understanding of truth lies not in the search for it; it lies in understanding the right significance of all things; the whole significance of truth is in the transient, and not apart from it.

So our search for truth is but an escape. Our search and our inquiry, our study of philosophies, our imitation of ethical systems and our continual groping for that reality which I say exists, are but ways of escape. To understand that reality is to understand the cause of our various conflicts, struggles, sufferings; but through the desire to escape from these conflicts, we have built up many subtle ways to avoid conflict, and in these we take shelter. Thus, truth becomes but another shelter in which mind and heart can take comfort.

Now that very idea of comfort is a hindrance; that very conception from which we derive consolation is but a flight from the conflict of everyday life. For centuries we have been building avenues of escape, such as authority; it may be the authority of social standards, or of public opinion, or of religious doctrines; it may be an external standard, such as the more educated people today are discarding, or an inner standard, such as one creates after discarding the external. But a mind that has regard for authority, that is, a mind that accepts without question, a mind that imitates, cannot understand the freedom of life. So, though we have built up through past centuries this authority that gives us a momentary pacification, a momentary consolation, a transient comfort, that authority has but become our escape. Likewise, imitation—the imitation of standards, the imitation of a system or a method of living; to me, this also is a hindrance. And our searching for certainty is but a way of escape; we want to be sure, our minds desire to cling to certainties, so that from that background we can look at life, from that shelter we can go forth.

Now to me, all these are hindrances which prevent that natural, spontaneous action which alone frees the mind and heart so that man can live harmoniously, so that man can understand the true function of individuality.

When we suffer we seek certainty, we want to turn to values that will give us comfort—and that comfort is but memory. Then again we come into contact with life, and again we experience suffering. So we think that we learn from suffering, that we gather understanding from suffering. A belief or an idea or a theory gives us momentary satisfaction when we suffer, and from this satisfaction we think that we have understood or gathered understanding from that experience. Thus we go on from suffering to suffering, learning how to adjust ourselves to outward conditions. That is, we do not understand the real movement of suffering; we merely become more and more cunning and subtle in our dealings with suffering. This is the superficiality of modern civilization and culture: many theories, many explanations of our suffering are put forward, and in these explanations and theories we take shelter, going from experience to experience, suffering, learning, and hoping through all this to find wisdom.

I say that wisdom is not to be bought. Wisdom does not lie in the process of accumulation; it is not the result of innumerable experiences; it is not acquired through learning. Wisdom, life itself, can be understood only when the mind is free from this sense of search, this search for comfort, this imitation, for these are but the ways of escape that we have been cultivating for centuries.

If you examine our structure of thought, of emotion, our whole civilization, you will see that it is but a process of escape, a process of conformity. When we suffer, our immediate reaction is a desire for relief, for consolation, and we accept the theories offered without finding out the cause of our suffering; that is, we are momentarily satisfied, we live superficially, and so we do not find out profoundly for ourselves what the cause of our suffering is.

Let me put this in another way: though we have experiences, these experiences do not keep us awake, but rather put us to sleep, because our minds and hearts have been trained for generations merely to imitate, to conform. After all, when there is any kind of suffering, we should not look to that suffering to teach us, but rather to keep us fully awake, so that we can meet life with complete awareness—not in that semiconscious state in which almost every human being meets life.

I shall explain this again, so as to make myself clear; for if you understand this you will naturally understand what I am going to say.

I say that life is not a process of learning, accumulating. Life is not a school in which you pass examinations in learning, in learning from experiences, learning from actions, from suffering. Life is meant to be lived, not to be learned from. If you regard life as something from which you have to learn, you act but superficially. That is, if action, if daily living, is but a means towards a reward, towards an end, then action itself has no value. Now when you have experiences, you say that you must learn from them, understand them. Therefore experience itself has no value to you because you are looking for a gain through suffering, through action, through experience. But to understand action completely, which to me is the ecstasy of life, the ecstasy which is immortality, the mind must be free of the idea of acquisition, the idea of learning through experience, through action. Now both mind and heart are caught in this idea of acquisition, this idea that life is a means to something else. But when you see the falseness of that conception, you will no longer treat suffering as a means to an end. Then you no longer take comfort in ideas, in beliefs; you no longer take shelter in standards of thought or feeling; you then begin to be fully aware, not for the purpose of seeing what you can gain from it, but in order intelligently to release action from imitation and from the search for a reward. That is, you see the significance of action, and not merely what profit it will bring you.

Now most minds are caught in the idea of acquisition, the search for reward. Suffering comes to awaken them to this illusion, to awaken them from their state of semiconsciousness, but not to teach them a lesson. When mind and heart act with a sense of duality, thus creating opposites, there must be conflict and suffering. What happens when you suffer? You seek immediate relief, whether it be in drink or in amusement or in the idea of God. To me, these are all the same, for they are merely avenues of escape that the subtle mind has devised, making of suffering a superficial thing. Therefore I say, become fully aware of your actions, whatever they may be; then you will perceive how your mind is continually finding an escape; you will see that you are not confronting experiences completely, with all your being, but only partially, semiconsciously.

We have built up many hindrances that have become shelters in which we take refuge in the moment of pain. These shelters are but escapes and therefore in themselves of no inherent worth. But to find out these shelters, these false values that we have created about us, which hold and imprison us, one must not try to analyze the actions which spring from these shelters. To me, analysis is the very negation of complete action. One cannot understand a hindrance by examining it. There is no understanding in the analysis of a past experience, for it is dead; there is understanding only in the living action of the present. Therefore self-analysis is destructive. But to discover the innumerable barriers that surround you is to become fully conscious, to become fully aware in whatever action is taking place about you, or in whatever you are doing. Then all the past hindrances, such as tradition, imitation, fear, defensive reactions, the desire for security, for certainty—all these come into activity; and only in that which is active is there understanding. In this flame of awareness, mind and heart free themselves from all hindrances, all false values; then there is liberation in action, and that liberation is the freedom of life which is immortality.

Question: Is it only from sorrow and suffering that one awakens to the reality of life?

KRISHNAMURTI: Suffering is the thing with which we are most familiar, with which we are constantly living. We know love and its joy, but in their wake there follow many conflicts. Whatever gives us the greatest shock which we call suffering, will keep us awake to meet life fully, will help us to discard the many illusions which we have created upon and about us. It is not only suffering or conflict that keeps us awake, but anything that gives us a shock, that makes us question all the false standards and values which we have created about us in our search for security. When you suffer greatly, you become wholly aware, and in that intensity of awareness you discover true values. This liberates the mind from creating further illusions.

Question: Why am I afraid of death? And what is beyond death?

KRISHNAMURTI: I think that one is afraid of death because one feels that one has not lived. If you are an artist, you may be afraid that death will take you away before you have finished your work; you are afraid because you have not fulfilled. Or if you are a man in ordinary life, without special capacities, you are afraid because you also have not fulfilled. You say, "If I am cut off from my fulfillment, what is there? As I do not understand this confusion, this toil, this incessant choice and conflict, is there further opportunity for me?" You have a fear of death when you have not fulfilled in action; that is, you are afraid of death when you do not meet life wholly, completely, with a fullness of mind and heart. Therefore, the question is not why you are afraid of death, but rather, what prevents you from meeting life fully. Everything must die, must wear out. But if you have the understanding that enables you to meet life fully, then in that there is eternal life, immortality, neither beginning nor end, and there is no fear of death. Again, the question is not how to free the mind from the fear of death, but how to meet life fully, how to meet life so that there shall be fulfillment.

To meet life fully, one must be free of all defensive values. But our minds and hearts are suffocated with such values, which make our action incomplete, and hence there is fear of death. To find true value, to be free of this continual fear of death, and of the problem of the hereafter, you must know the true function of the individual, both in the creative as well as in the collective.

Now as to the second part of the question: "What is beyond death?" Is there a hereafter? Do you know why a person usually asks such questions, why he wants to know what is on the other side? He asks because be does not know how to live in the present; he is more dead than alive. He says, "Let me find out what comes after death," because he has not the capacity to understand this eternal present. To me, the present is eternity; eternity lies in the present, not in the future. But to such a questioner life has been a whole series of experiences without fulfillment, without understanding, without wisdom. Therefore to him the hereafter is more enticing than the present, and hence the innumerable questions concerning what lies beyond. The man who inquires into the hereafter is already dead. If you live in the eternal present, the hereafter does not exist; then life is not divided into the past, present, and future. Then there is only completeness, and in that there is the ecstasy of life.

Question: Do you think that communication with the spirits of the dead is a help to the understanding of life in its totality?

KRISHNAMURTI: Why should you think the dead more helpful than the living? Because the dead cannot contradict you, cannot oppose you, whereas the living can. In communication with the dead you can be fanciful; therefore you look to the dead rather than to the living to give you help. To me, the question is not whether there is a life beyond what we call death; it is not whether we can communicate with the spirits of the dead; to me, all that is irrelevant. Some people say that one can communicate with the spirits of the dead; others, that one cannot. To me, the discussion seems of very little value; for to understand life with its swift wanderings, with its wisdom, you cannot look to another to free you from the illusions that you have created. Neither the dead nor the living can free you from your illusions. Only in the awakened interest in life, in the constant alertness of mind and heart, is there harmonious living, is there fulfillment, the richness of life.

Question: What is your opinion regarding the problem of sex and of asceticism in the light of the present social crisis?

KRISHNAMURTI: Let us not look at this problem, if I may suggest, from the point of view of the present condition, because conditions are constantly changing. Let us rather consider the problem itself; for if you understand the problem, then the present crisis can also be understood.

The problem of sex, which seems to trouble so many people, has arisen because we have lost the flame of creativeness, of harmonious living. We have but become imitative machines; we have closed the doors to creative thought and emotion; we are constantly conforming; we are bound by authority, by public opinion, by fear, and thus we are confronted by this problem of sex. But if the mind and heart free themselves from the sense of imitation, from false values, from the exaggeration of the intellect, and so release their own creative function, then the problem does not exist. It has become great because we like to feel secure, because we think that happiness lies in the sense of possession. But if we understand the true significance of possession, and its illusory nature, then the mind and heart are freed from both possession and nonpossession.

So also with regard to the second part of the question, which concerns asceticism. You know, we think that when confronted by a problem—in this case, the problem of possession—we can solve it and understand it by going to its opposite. I come from a country where asceticism is in our blood. The climate encourages the custom. India is hot, and there it is much better to have very few things, to sit in the shade of a tree and discuss philosophy, or to withdraw entirely from harrowing, conflicting life, to take oneself into the woods to meditate. The question of asceticism also arises when one is a slave to possession.

Asceticism has no inherent value. When you practice it, you are merely escaping from possession to its opposite, which is asceticism. It is like a man who seeks detachment because he experiences pain in attachment. "Let me be detached," he says. Likewise, you say, "I will become an ascetic," because possession creates suffering. What you are really doing is merely going from possession to nonpossession, which is another form of possession. But in that move also there is conflict, because you do not understand the full significance of possession. That is, you look to possession for comfort; you think that happiness, security, the flattery of public opinion, lies in having many things, whether they be ideas, virtues, land, or titles. Because we think that security and happiness and power lie in possession, we accumulate, we strive to possess, we struggle and compete with each other, we stifle and exploit each other. That is what is happening throughout the world, and a cunning mind says, "Let us become ascetic; let us not possess; let us become slaves to asceticism; let us make laws so that man shall not possess." In other words, you are but leaving one prison for another, merely calling the new one by a different name. But if you really understand the transient value of possession, then you become neither an ascetic nor a person burdened by the desire for possession; then you are truly a human being.

Question: I have received the impression that you have a certain disdain for acquiring knowledge. Do you mean that education or the study of books—for instance, the study of history or science—has no value? Do you mean that you yourself have learned nothing from your teachers?

KRISHNAMURTI: I am talking of living a complete life, a human life, and no amount of explanation, whether of science or of history, will free the mind and heart from suffering. You may study, you may learn the encyclopedia by heart, but you are a human being, active; your actions are voluntary, your mind is pliable, and you cannot suffocate it by knowledge. Knowledge is necessary, science is necessary. But if your mind is caught up in explanations, and the cause of suffering is intellectually explained away, then you lead a superficial life, a life without depth. And that is what is happening to us. Our education is making us more and more shallow; it is teaching us neither depth of feeling nor freedom of thought, and our lives are disharmonious.

The questioner wants to know if I have not learned from teachers. I am afraid that I have not, because there is nothing to learn. Someone can teach you how to play the piano, to work out problems in mathematics; you can be taught the principles of engineering or the technique of painting; but no one can teach you creative fulfillment, which is life itself. And yet you are constantly asking to be taught. You say, "Teach me the technique of living, and I shall know what life is." I say that this very desire for a method, this very idea, destroys your freedom of action, which is the very freedom of life itself.

Question: You say that nobody can help us but ourselves. Do you not believe that the life of Christ was an atonement for our sins? Do you not believe in the grace of God?

KRISHNAMURTI: These are words that I am afraid I do not understand. If you mean that another can save you, then I say that no one can save you. This idea that another can save you is a comfortable illusion. The greatness of man is that no one can help him or save him but man himself. You have the idea that an external God can show us the way through this conflicting labyrinth of life; that a teacher, a savior of man, can show us the way, can take us out, can lead us away from the prisons that we have created for ourselves. If anyone gives you freedom, beware of that person, for you will but create other prisons through your own lack of understanding. But if you question, if you are awake, alert, constantly aware of your action, then your life is harmonious; then your action is complete for it is born out of creative harmony, and this is true fulfillment.

Question: Whatever activity a person takes up, how can he do anything else but patchwork as long as he has not fully attained the realization of truth?

KRISHNAMURTI: You think that work and assistance can help those who are suffering. To me such an attempt to do social good for the welfare of man is patchwork. I am not saying that it is wrong; it is undoubtedly necessary, because society is in a state which demands that there be those who work to bring about social change, those who work to better social conditions. But there must also be workers of the other type, those who work to prevent the new structures of society from being based on false ideas.

To put it differently, suppose that some of you are interested in education; you have listened to what I have been saying, and suppose you start a school or teach in a school. First of all, find out if you are interested merely in ameliorating conditions in education, or whether you are interested in sowing the seed of real understanding, in awakening people to creative living; find out if you are interested merely in showing them a way out of troubles, in giving them consolation, panaceas, or if you are really eager to awaken them to an understanding of their own limitations, so that they can destroy the barriers which now hold them.

Question: Please explain what you mean by immortality. Is immortality as real to you as the ground on which you stand, or is it just a sublime idea?

KRISHNAMURTI: What I am going to tell you about immortality will be difficult to understand, because to me immortality is not a belief: it is. This is a very different thing. There is immortality—and not that I know or believe in it. I hope that you see the distinction. The moment I say "I know," immortality becomes an objective, static thing. But when there is no 'I', there is immortality. Beware of the person who says, "I know immortality," because to him immortality is a static thing, which means that there is duality: there is the 'I', and there is that which is immortal, two different things. I say that there is immortality, and that it is because there is no 'I' consciousness.

Now please don't say that I don't believe in immortality. To me belief has nothing to do with it. Immortality is not external. But where there is a belief in a thing there must be an object and a subject. For example, you don't believe in sunshine: it is. Only a blind man who has never seen what sunshine is has to believe in it.

To me there is an eternal life, an everbecoming life; it is ever-becoming, not ever-growing, for that which grows is transient. Now to understand that immortality which I say exists, the mind must be free of this idea of continuity and noncontinuity. When a person asks, "Is there immortality?" he wants to know if he, as an individual, will continue, or if he, as an individual, will be destroyed. That is, he thinks only in terms of opposites, in terms of duality: either you exist or you do not. If you try to understand my answer from the point of view of duality, then you will utterly fail. I say that immortality is. But to realize that immortality, which is the ecstasy of life, mind and heart must be free from the identification with conflict from which arises the consciousness of the 'I'; and free also from the idea of annihilation of the ego-consciousness.

Let me put it in a different way. You know only opposites—courage and fear, possession and nonpossession, detachment and attachment. Your whole life is divided into opposites—virtue and nonvirtue, right and wrong—because you never meet life completely but always with this reaction, with this background of division. You have created this background; you have crippled your mind with these ideas, and then you ask, "Is there immortality?" I say there is, but to understand it, mind must be free from this division. That is, if you are afraid, do not seek courage, but let the mind free itself from fear; see the futility of what you call courage; understand that it is but an escape from fear, and that fear will exist as long as there is the idea of gain and loss. Instead of always reaching out for the opposite, instead of struggling to develop the opposite quality, let mind and heart free themselves from that in which they are caught. Do not try to develop its opposite. Then you will know for yourself, without anyone's telling you or leading you, what immortality is; immortality which is neither the 'I' nor the 'you', but which is life.

September 10, 1933

Fourth Talk at Frognerseteren

Friends,

Today am going to make a résumé of what I have been saying here.

We have the idea that wisdom is a process of acquisition through constant multiplication of experience. We think that by multiplying experiences we shall learn, and that learning will give us wisdom, and through that wisdom in action we hope to find richness, self-sufficiency, happiness, truth. That is, to us experience is but a constant change of sensation, because we look to time to give us wisdom. When we think in this manner, that through time we shall acquire wisdom, we have the idea of getting somewhere. That is, we say that time will gradually reveal wisdom. But time does not reveal wisdom, because we use time only as a means of getting somewhere. When we have the idea of acquiring wisdom through the constant change of experience, we are looking for acquisition, and so there is no immediate perception, which is wisdom.

Let us take an example; perhaps it will clarify what I mean. This change of desire, this change of sensation, this multiplication of experiences which that change of sensation brings about, we call progress. Suppose we see a hat in a shop, and we desire to possess it; having obtained that hat, we want something else—a car, and so on. Then we turn to emotional wants, and we think that in thus changing our desire from a hat to an emotional sensation we have grown. From emotional sensation we turn to intellectual sensations, to ideas, to God, to truth. That is, we think that we have progressed through constant change of experiences, from the state of wanting a hat to the state of wanting and searching for God. So we believe that through experiences, through choice, we have made progress.

Now to me that is not progress; it is merely a change in sensation, sensation more and more subtle, more and more refined, but still sensation, and therefore superficial. We have merely changed the object of our desire; at first it was a hat, now it has become God, and therein we think we have made tremendous progress. That is, we think that through this gradual process of refining sensation we shall find out what truth, God, eternity is. I say you will never find truth through the gradual change of the object of desire. But if you understand that only through immediate perception, immediate discernment, lies the whole of wisdom, then this idea of the gradual change of desire will disappear.

Now what are we doing? We think, "I was different yesterday, I am different today, and I shall be different tomorrow"; so we look to difference, to change—not to discernment. Take, for instance, the idea of detachment. We say to ourselves, "Two years ago I was very much attached, today I am less attached, and in a few years I shall be still less, eventually coming to a state in which I shall be quite detached." So we think that we have grown from attachment to detachment through the constant shock of experience, which we call progress, development of character.

To me this is not progress. If you perceive with your entire being the whole significance of attachment, then you do not progress towards detachment. The mere pursuit of detachment does not reveal the shallowness of attachment, which can be understood only when the mind and heart are not escaping through the idea of detachment. This understanding is not brought about through time, but only in the realization that in attachment itself there is pain as well as transient joy. Then you ask me, "Won't time help me to perceive that?" Time will not. What will make you perceive is either the transiency of joy or the intensity of pain in attachment. If you are fully aware of this, then you are no longer held by the idea of being different now from what you were a few years ago, and later on being different again. The idea of progressive time becomes illusory.

To put it differently, we think that through choice we shall advance, we shall learn, through choice we shall change. We choose mostly through want. There is no satisfaction in comparative choice. That which does not satisfy us we call the unessential, and that which does, the essential. Thus we are constantly being caught in this conflict of choice from which we hope to learn. Choice, then, is merely opposites in action; it is calculation between the opposites, and not enduring discernment. Hence, we grow from what we call the unessential to what we call the essential, and that, in turn, becomes the unessential. That is, we grow from the desire for the hat, which we thought was the essential and which has now become the unessential, to what we think is the essential, only to discover that also to be the unessential. So through choice we think that we shall come to the fullness of action, to the completeness of life.

As I have said, to me perception or discernment is timeless. Time does not give you discernment of experiences; it makes you only more clever, more cunning, in meeting experiences. But if you perceive and live completely in the very thing that you are experiencing, then this idea of change from the unessential to the essential disappears, and so mind frees itself from the idea of progressive time.

You look to time to change you. You say to yourself, "Through the multiplication of experiences, as in changing from the desire for the hat to the desire for God, I shall learn wisdom, I shall learn understanding." In action born of choice there is no discernment, choice being calculation, a remembrance of incomplete action. That is, you now meet an experience partially, with a religious bias, with the prejudices of social or class distinctions, and this perverted mind, when it meets life, creates choice; it does not give you the fullness of understanding. But if you meet life with freedom, with openness, with simplicity, then choice disappears, for you live completely, without creating the conflict of opposites.

Question: What do you mean by living fully, openly, freely? Please give a practical example. Please also explain, with a practical example, how in the attempt to live fully, openly, and freely one becomes conscious of one's hindrances which prevent freedom, and how by becoming fully conscious of them one can be liberated from them.

KRISHNAMURTI: Suppose I am a snob and am unconscious that I am a snob; that is, I have class prejudice, and I meet life, unconscious of this prejudice. Naturally, having my mind distorted by this idea of class distinction, I cannot understand, I cannot meet life openly, freely, simply. Or again, if I have been brought up with strong religious doctrines or with some particular training, my thoughts and emotions are perverted; with this background of prejudice I go forth to meet life, and this prejudice naturally prevents my complete understanding of life. In such a background of tradition and false values, of class distinction and religious bias, of fear and prejudice, we are caught. With that background, with those established standards, either inner or outer, we go forth trying to meet life and trying to understand. From these prejudices there arises conflict, transient joys and suffering. But we are unconscious of this, unconscious that we are slaves to certain forms of tradition, to social and political environment, to false values.

Now to free yourself from this slavery, I say, do not try to analyze the past, the background of tradition to which you are a slave and of which you are unconscious. If you are a snob, do not try to find out after your action is over whether you are a snob. Be fully aware, and through what you say and through what you do, the snobbery that you are unconscious of will come into activity; then you can be free of it, for this flame of awareness creates an intense conflict, which dissolves snobbery.

As I said the other day, self-analysis is destructive, because the more you analyze yourself the less there is of action. Self-analysis takes place only when the incident is over, when it has passed away; then you return to that incident intellectually and try intellectually to dissect it, to understand it. There is no understanding in a dead thing. Rather, if you are fully conscious in your action, not as a watcher who only observes, but as an actor who is wholly consumed in that action—if you are fully aware of it and not apart from it, then the process of self-analysis does not exist. It does not exist because you are then meeting life wholly, you are then not separate from experience, and in that flame of awareness you bring into activity all your prejudices, all the false standards that have crippled your mind; and by bringing them into your full consciousness you free yourself from them, because they create trouble and conflict, and through that very conflict you are liberated.

We hold to the idea that time will give us understanding. To me this is but a prejudice, a hindrance. Now suppose you think about this idea for a moment—not accept it, but think it over and desire to find out if it is true. You will find then that you can test it only in action, not by theorizing about it. Then you will not ask if what I say is true—you will test it in action. I say that time does not bring you understanding; when you look to time as a gradual process of unfoldment you are creating a hindrance. You can test this only through action; only in experience can you perceive whether this idea has any value in itself. But you will miss its deep significance if you try to use it as a means to something else.

The idea of time as a process of unfoldment is but a cultivated method of postponement. You do not meet the thing that confronts you because you are afraid; you do not want to meet experience wholly, either because of your prejudices or because of the desire to postpone.

When you have a twisted ankle, you cannot gradually untwist it. This idea that we learn through many and increasing experiences, through the multiplication of joy and suffering, is one of our prejudices, one of our hindrances. To find out if this is true, you have to act; you will never find out merely by sitting down and discussing about it. You can find out only in the movement of action, by seeing how your mind and heart react, not by shaping them, pushing them towards a particular end; then you will see that they are reacting according to the prejudice of accumulation. You say, "Ten years ago I was different; today I am different, and ten years hence I shall be still more different"; but the meeting of experiences with the idea that you will be different, that you will gradually learn, prevents you from understanding them, from discerning instantaneously, fully.

Question: Would you also give a practical example of how self-analysis is destructive? Does your teaching on this point spring from your own experience?

KRISHNAMURTI: First of all, I have not studied philosophies or the sacred books. I am giving you of my own experiences. I am often asked if I have studied the sacred books, philosophies, and other such writings. I have not. I am telling you what to me is truth, wisdom, and it is for you to find out, you who are learned. I think that in that very process of accumulation which we call learning lies our misfortune. When it is burdened with knowledge, with learning, mind is crippled—not that we must not read. But wisdom is not to be bought; it must be experienced in action. I think that answers the second part of the question.

I shall answer the question differently, and I hope that I shall explain it more clearly. Why do you think that you must analyze yourself? Because you have not lived fully in experiences, and that experience has created a disturbance in you. Therefore you say to yourself, "The next time I meet it I must be prepared, so let me look at that incident which is past, and I shall learn from it; then I shall meet the next experience fully, and it will not then trouble me." So you begin to analyze, which is an intellectual process, and therefore not wholly true; as you have not understood it completely, you say: "I have learned something from that past experience; now, with that little knowledge, let me meet the next experience from which I shall learn a little more." Thus you never live completely in the experience itself; this intellectual process of learning, accumulating, is always going on.

This is what you do every day, only unconsciously. You have not the desire to meet life harmoniously, completely; rather you think that you will learn to meet it harmoniously through analysis; that is, by adding little by little to the granary in the mind, you hope to become full, and to be able to meet life fully, wholly. But your mind will never become free through this process; full it may become—but never free, open, simple. And what prevents your being simple, open, is this constant process of analyzing an incident of the past, which must of necessity be incomplete. There can be complete understanding only in the very movement of experience itself. When you are in a great crisis, when there must be action, then you do not analyze, you do not calculate: you put all that aside, for in that moment your mind and heart are in creative harmony and there is true action.

Question: What is your view concerning religious, ceremonial, and occult practices—to mention only some activities that help mankind? Is your attitude to them merely one of complete indifference, or is it one of antagonism?

KRISHNAMURTI: To take up such practices seems to me a waste of effort. When you say "practice," you mean following a method, a discipline, which you hope will give you the understanding of truth. I have said a great deal about this, and I have not the time to go into it fully again. The whole idea of following a discipline makes the mind and heart rigid and consistent. Having already laid down a plan of conduct and desiring to be consistent, you say to yourself, "I must do this and I must not do that," and your memory of that discipline is guiding you through life. That is, because of the fear of religious dogmas and the economic situation, you meet experiences partially, through the veil of these methods and disciplines. You meet life with fear, which creates prejudices; so there is incomplete understanding, and from this arise conflicts. And in order to overcome these conflicts you find a method, a discipline, according to which you judge, "I must" and "I must not." So, having established a consistency, a standard, you discipline yourself according to it through constant memory, and this you call self-discipline, occult practices. I say that such self-discipline, practice, this continual adjustment to a pattern or not adjusting to a standard, does not free the mind. What liberates the mind is meeting life fully, being fully aware, which does not demand practice. You cannot say to yourself, "I must be aware, I must be aware." Awareness comes in complete intensity of action. When you suffer greatly, when you enjoy greatly, at that moment you meet life with full awareness, and not with a divided consciousness; then you meet all things completely, and in this there is freedom.

With regard to religious ceremonies, the matter is very simple from my point of view. A ceremony is merely a glorified sensation. Some of you probably do not agree with this opinion. You know, it is with religious ceremonials as it is with worldly pomp: when a king holds court, the spectators are tremendously impressed and greatly exploited. The reason the majority of people go to church is to find comfort, to escape, to exploit and to be exploited; and if some of you have listened to what I have been saying during the last five or six days, you will have understood my attitude and action towards ceremonies.

"Is your attitude to them merely one of complete indifference, or is it one of antagonism?" My attitude is neither indifferent nor antagonistic. I say that they must ever hold the seed of exploitation, and therefore they are unintelligent and unrighteous.

Question: Since you do not seek followers, why then do you ask people to leave their religions and follow your advice? Are you prepared to take the consequences of such advice? Or do you mean that people need guidance? If not, why do you preach at all?

KRISHNAMURTI: Sorry, I have never created such a thing as a follower. I have said to no one, "Leave your church and follow me." That would be but asking you to come to another church, into another prison. I say that by following another you become but a slave, unintelligent; you become a machine, an imitative automaton. In following another you can never find out what life is, what eternity is. I say that all following of another is destructive, cruel, leading to exploitation. I am concerned with the sowing of the seed. I am not asking you to follow. I say that the very following of another is the destruction of that life, that eternal becoming.

To put it differently, by following another you destroy the possibility of discovering truth, eternity. Why do you follow? Because you want to be guided, you want to be helped. You think that you cannot understand; therefore you go to another and learn his technique, and to his method you become a slave. You become the exploiter and the exploited, and yet you hope that by continually practicing that method you will release creative thinking. You can never release creative thinking by following. It is only when you begin to question the very idea of following, of setting up authorities and worshipping them, that you can find out what is true; and truth shall free your mind and heart.

"Do you mean that people need guidance?" I say that people do not need guidance; they need awakening. If you are guided to certain righteous actions, those actions are no longer righteous; they are merely imitative, compelled. But if you yourself, through questioning, through continual awareness, discover true values—and you can only do this for yourself and none other—then the whole question of following, guidance, loses its significance. Wisdom is not a thing that comes through guidance, through following, through the reading of books. You cannot learn wisdom second-hand, yet that is what you are trying to do. So you say, "Guide me, help me, liberate me." But I say, beware of the man who helps you, who liberates you.

"Why do you preach at all?" That is very simple: because I cannot help it, and also because there is so much suffering, so much joy that fades. For me there is an eternal becoming which is an ecstasy; and I want to show that this chaotic existence can be changed to orderly and intelligent cooperation in which the individual is not exploited. And this is not through an oriental philosophy, through sitting under a tree, drawing away from life, but quite the contrary; it is through the action which you find when you are fully awake, completely aware in great sorrow or joy. This flame of awareness consumes all the self-created hindrances that destroy and pervert the creative intelligence of man. But most people, when they experience suffering, seek immediate relief or try, through memory, to catch a fleeting joy. Thus their minds are constantly escaping. But I say, become aware, and you yourselves will free your minds from fear; and this freedom is the understanding of truth.

Question: Is your experience of reality something peculiar to this time? If not, why has it not been possible in the past?

KRISHNAMURTI: Surely reality, eternity, cannot be conditioned by time. You mean to ask whether people have not searched and struggled after reality throughout the centuries. To me, that very struggle after truth has prevented them from understanding.

Question: You say that suffering cannot give us understanding, but can only awaken us. If that is so, why does not suffering cease when we have been fully awakened?

KRISHNAMURTI: That is just it. We are not fully awakened through suffering. Suppose that someone dies. What happens? You want an immediate relief from that sorrow; so you accept an idea, a belief, or you seek amusements. Now what has happened? There has been true suffering, an awakened struggle, a shock, and to overcome the shock, that suffering, you have accepted an idea such as reincarnation, or faith in the hereafter, or belief in communication with the dead. These are all ways of escape. That is, when you are awakened there is conflict, struggle, which you call suffering; but immediately you want to put away that struggle, that awakening; you long for forgetfulness through an idea, a theory, or through an explanation, which is but a process of being put to sleep again.

So this is the everyday process of existence: you are awakened through the impact with life, experience, which causes suffering, and you want to be comforted; so you seek out people, ideas, explanations, to give you comfort, satisfaction, and this creates the exploiter and the exploited. But if in that state of acute questioning, which is suffering, if in that state of awakened interest, you meet experiences completely, then you will find out the true value and significance of all the human shelters and illusions which you have created; and the understanding of them alone will free you from suffering.

Question: What is the shortest way to get rid of our worries and troubles and our hard feelings and reach happiness and freedom?

KRISHNAMURTI: There is no shortest way; but hard feelings, worries, and troubles themselves liberate you if you are not trying to escape from them through the desire for freedom and happiness. You say that you want freedom and happiness, because hard feelings and troubles are difficult to bear. So you are merely running away from them, you don't understand why they exist; you don't understand why you have worries, why you have troubles, hard feelings, bitterness, suffering, and passing joy. And since you don't understand, you want to know the shortest way out of the confusion. I say, beware of the man who shows you the shortest way out. There is no way out of suffering and trouble except through that suffering and trouble itself. This is not a hard saying; you will understand it if you think it over. The moment you stop trying to escape you will understand; you cannot but understand, for then you are no longer entangled in explanations. When all explanations have ceased, when they no longer have any meaning, then truth is. Now you are seeking explanations; you are seeking the shortest way, the quickest method; you are looking to practices, to ceremonials, to the newest theory of science. These are all escapes. But when you really understand the illusion of escape, when you are wholly confronting the thing that creates conflict within you, then that very thing will release you.

Now life creates great disturbance in you, problems of possession, sex, hatred. So you say, "Let me find a higher life, a divine life, a life of nonpossession, a life of love." But your very striving for such a life is but an escape from these disturbances. If you become aware of the falseness of escape, which you can understand only when there is conflict, then you will see how your mind is accustomed to escape. And when you have ceased to escape, when your mind is no longer seeking an explanation, which is but a drug, then that very thing from which you have been trying to escape reveals its full significance. This understanding frees the mind and heart from sorrow.

Question: Have you no faith whatever in the power of Divinity that shapes the destiny of man? If not, are you then an atheist?

KRISHNAMURTI: The belief that there is a Divinity that can shape man is one of the hindrances of man; but when I say that, it does not mean that I am an atheist. I think the people who say they believe in God are atheists, not only those who do not believe in God, because both are slaves to a belief.

You cannot believe in God; you have to believe in God only when there is no understanding, and you cannot have understanding by searching for it. Rather, when your mind is really free from all values, which have become the very center of ego-consciousness, then there is God. We have an idea that some miracle will change us; we think that some divine or external influence will bring about changes in ourselves and in the world. We have lived in that hope for centuries, and that is what is the matter with the world—complete chaos, irresponsibility in action, because we think someone else is going to do everything for us. To discard this false idea does not mean that we must turn to its opposite. When we free the mind from opposites, when we see the falseness of the belief that someone else is looking after us, then a new intelligence is awakened in us.

You want to know what God is, what truth is, what eternal life is; so you ask me, "Are you an atheist or a theist? If you are a believer in God, then tell me what God is." I say the man who describes what truth or God is, to him truth does not exist. When it is put in the cage of words, then truth is no longer a living reality. But if you understand the false values in which you are held, if you free yourself from them, then there is an ever-living reality.

Question: When we know that our way of living will inevitably disgust others and produce complete misunderstanding in their minds, how should we act, if we are to respect their feelings and their points of view?

KRISHNAMURTI: This question seems so simple that I do not see where the difficulty is. "How should we act in order not to trouble others?" Is that what you want to know? I am afraid then we should not be acting at all. If you live completely, your actions may cause trouble; but what is more important: finding out what is true, or not disturbing others? This seems so simple that it hardly needs to be answered. Why do you want to respect other people's feelings and points of view? Are you afraid of having your own feelings hurt, your point of view being changed? If people have opinions that differ from yours, you can find out if they are true only by questioning them, by coming into active contact with them. And if you find that those opinions and feelings are not true, your discovery may cause disturbance to those who cherish them. Then what should you do? Should you comply with them, or compromise with them in order not to hurt your friends?

Question: Do you think that pure food has anything to do with the fulfillment of your ideas of life? Are you a vegetarian? (Laughter)

KRISHNAMURTI: You know, humor is impersonal. I hope that the questioner is not hurt when people laugh. If I am a vegetarian, what of it? It is not what goes into your mouth that will free you, but the finding out of true values, from which arises complete action.

Question: Your message of disinterested remoteness, detachment, has been preached in all ages and in many faiths to a few chosen disciples. What makes you think that this message is now fit for everyone in a human society where there is of necessity interdependence in all social actions?

KRISHNAMURTI: I am very sorry, but I have never said that one should be remotely disinterested, that one should be detached; quite the contrary. So first please understand what I say, and then see if it has any value.

Let us take the question of detachment. You know, for centuries we have been gathering, accumulating, making ourselves secure. Intellectually you may see the foolishness of possessiveness, and say to yourself, "Let me be detached." Or rather, you don't see the foolishness of it; so you begin to practice detachment, which is but another way of gathering in, laying up. For if you really perceive the foolishness of possessiveness, then you are free from both detachment and its opposite. The result is not a remote inactivity, but rather, complete action.

You know, we are slaves to legislation. If a law were passed tomorrow decreeing that we should not possess property, we should be forced to comply with it, with a good deal of kicking. In that also there would be security, security in nonpossession. So I say, do not be the plaything of legislation, but find out the very thing to which you are a slave—that is, acquisitiveness. Find out its true significance, without escaping into detachment; how it gives you social distinctions, power, leading to an empty, superficial life. If you relinquish possessions without understanding them, you will have the same emptiness in nonpossession—the sensation of security in asceticism, in detachment, which will become the shelter to which you will withdraw in times of conflict. As long as there is fear there must be the pursuit of opposites; but if the mind frees itself from the very cause of fear, which is self-consciousness, the 'I', the limited consciousness, then there is fulfillment, completeness of action.

September 12, 1933

Adyar, India, 1933

First Talk at Adyar

Mr. Warrington, the acting president of the Theosophical Society, kindly invited me to come to Adyar and to give some talks here. I am very glad to have accepted his invitation and I appreciate his friendliness, which I hope will continue, even though we may differ completely in our ideas and opinions.

I hope that you will all listen to my talks without prejudice, and will not think that I am trying to attack your society. I want to do quite another thing. I want to arouse the desire for true search, and this, I think, is all that a teacher can do. That is all I want to do. If I can awaken that desire in you, I have completed my task, for out of that desire comes intelligence, that intelligence which is free from any system and organized belief. This intelligence is beyond all thought of compromise and false adjustment. So during these talks, those of you who belong to various societies or groups will please bear in mind that I am very grateful to the Theosophical Society and its acting president for having asked me to come here to speak, and that I am not attacking the Theosophical Society. I am not interested in attacking. But I hold that while organizations for the social welfare of man are necessary, societies based on religious hopes and beliefs are pernicious. So though I may appear to speak harshly, please bear in mind that I am not attacking any particular society, but that I am against all these false organizations which, though they profess to help man, are in reality a great hindrance and are the means of constant exploitation.

When mind is filled with beliefs, ideas, and definite conclusions which it calls knowledge and which become sacred, then the infinite movement of thought ceases. That is what is happening to most minds. What we call knowledge is merely accumulation; it prevents the free movement of thought, yet we cling to it and worship this so-called knowledge. So mind becomes enmeshed, entangled in it. It is only when mind is freed from all this accumulation, from beliefs, ideals, principles, memories, that there is creative thinking. You cannot blindly put away accumulation; you can be free from it only when you understand it. Then there is creative thought; then there is an eternal movement. Then mind is no longer separated from action.

Now, the beliefs, ideals, virtues, and sanctified ideas which you are pursuing, and which you call knowledge, prevent creative thinking and thereby put an end to the continual ripening of thought. For thought does not mean the following of a particular groove of established ideas, habits, traditions. Thought is critical; it is a thing apart from inherited or acquired knowledge. When you merely accept certain ideas, traditions, you are not thinking, and there is slow stagnation. You say to me, "We have beliefs, we have traditions, we have principles; are they not right? Must we get rid of them?" I am not going to say that you must get rid of them or that you must not. Indeed, your very readiness to accept the idea that you must or must not get rid of these beliefs and traditions prevents you from thinking; you are already in a state of acceptance, and therefore you have not the capacity to be critical.

I am talking to individuals, not to organizations or groups of individuals. I am talking to you as an individual, not to a group of people holding certain beliefs. If my talk is to be of any value to you, try to think for yourself, not with the group consciousness. Don't think along the lines to which you have already committed yourself, for they are merely subtle forms of comfort. You say, "I belong to a certain society, to a certain group. I have given that group certain promises and accepted from it certain benefits. How can I think apart from these conditions and promises? What am I to do?" I say: Do not think in terms of commitments, for they prevent you from thinking creatively. Where there is mere acceptance there cannot be free, flowing, creative thought which alone is supreme intelligence, which alone is happiness. The so-called knowledge that we worship, that we strive to attain by reading books, prevents creative thought.

But because I say that such knowledge and such reading prevent creative thinking, don't immediately turn to the opposite. Don't say, "Must we not read at all?" I am talking of these things because I want to show you their inherent significance; I do not want to urge you to the opposite.

Now, if your attitude is one of acceptance, you live in fear of criticism, and when doubt arises, as it must arise, you carefully and sedulously destroy it. Yet it is only through doubt, through criticism, that you can fulfill; and the purpose of life is to fulfill, not to accumulate, not to achieve, as I shall explain presently. Life is a process of search, search not for any particular end, but to release the creative energy, the creative intelligence in man; it is a process of eternal movement, untrammelled by beliefs, by sets of ideas, by dogmas, or by so-called knowledge.

So when I talk of criticism, please do not be partisans. I don't belong to your societies; I don't hold your opinions and ideals. We are here to examine, not to take sides. Therefore please follow open-mindedly what I shall say, and take sides—if you must take sides—after these talks are concluded. Why do you take sides? Belonging to a particular group gives you a feeling of comfort, of security. You think that because many of you hold certain ideas or principles, thereby you shall grow. But for the present, try not to take sides. Try not to be biased by the particular group to which you now belong, and don't try to take my side either. All that you have to do during these talks is to examine, to be critical, to doubt, to find out, to search, to fathom the problems before you.

You are accustomed to opposition, not to criticism. When I say "you," please do not think that I am talking with an attitude of superiority. I say that you are not accustomed to criticism, and through this lack of criticism you hope to develop spiritually. You think that through this destruction of doubt, by getting rid of doubt, you will advance, for it has been put before you as one of the necessary qualities for spiritual progress; and you are thereby exploited. But in your careful destruction of doubt, in your putting away of criticism, you have merely developed opposition. You say, "The scriptures are my authority for this," or, "The teachers have said that," or, "I have read this." In other words, you hold certain beliefs, certain dogmas, certain principles with which you oppose any new and conflicting situation, and you imagine that you are thinking, that you are critical, creative. Your position is like that of a political party which acts merely in opposition. If you are truly critical, creative, you will never merely oppose; then you will be concerned with realities. But if your attitude is merely one of opposition, then your mind will not meet mine; then you will not understand what I am trying to convey.

So when the mind is accustomed to opposition, when it has been carefully trained, through so-called education, through tradition and belief, through religious and philosophical systems, to acquire this attitude of opposition, it naturally does not have the capacity to criticize and to doubt truly. But if you are going to understand me, this is the first thing you should have. Please don't shut your minds against what I am saying. True criticism is the desire to find out. The faculty to criticize exists only when you want to discover the inherent worth of a thing. But you are not accustomed to that. Your minds are cleverly trained to give values, but by that process you will never understand the inherent significance of a thing, of an experience, or of an idea.

To me, then, true criticism consists in trying to find out the intrinsic worth of the thing itself, and not in attributing a quality to that thing. You attribute a quality to an environment, to an experience, only when you want to derive something from it, when you want to gain or to have power or happiness. Now this destroys true criticism. Your desire is perverted through attributing values, and therefore you cannot see clearly. Instead of trying to see the flower in its original and entire beauty, you look at it through colored glasses, and therefore you can never see it as it is.

If you want to live, to enjoy, to appreciate the immensity of life, if you really want to understand it, not merely to repeat, parrotlike, what has been taught you, what has been dinned into you, then your first task is to remove the perversions that entangle you. And I assure you that this is one of the most difficult tasks, for these perversions are part of your training, part of your upbringing, and it is very difficult to detach yourself from them.

The critical attitude demands freedom from the idea of opposition. For example, you say to me, "We believe in Masters; you do not. What have you to say to this?" Now that is not a critical attitude; it is, but please do not think I am speaking harshly, a childish attitude. We are discussing whether certain ideas are fundamentally true in themselves, not whether you have gained something from these ideas; for what you have gained may be merely perversions, prejudices.

My purpose during this series of talks is to awaken your own true critical capacity, so that teachers will become unnecessary to you, so that you will not feel the necessity for lectures, for sermons, so that you will realize for yourself what is true and live completely. The world will be a happier place when there are no more teachers, when a man no longer feels that he must preach to his neighbor. But that state can come about only when you, as individuals, are really awakened, when you greatly doubt, when you have truly begun to question in the midst of sorrow. Now you have ceased to suffer. You have suffocated your minds with explanations, with knowledge; you have hardened your hearts. You are not concerned with feeling, but with beliefs, ideas, with the sanctity of so-called knowledge, and therefore you are starved; you are no longer human beings, but mere machines.

I see you shake your heads. If you do not agree with me, ask me questions tomorrow. Write down your questions and hand them to me, and I will answer them. But this morning

I am going to talk, and I hope you will follow what I have to say.

There is no resting place in life. Thought can have no resting place. But you are seeking such a place of rest. In your various beliefs, religions, you have sought such a resting place, and in this seeking you have ceased to be critical, to flow with life, to enjoy, to live richly.

As I have said, true search—which is different from the search for an end, or the search for help, or the pursuit of gain—true search results in understanding the intrinsic worth of experience. True search is as a swift-moving river, and in this movement there is understanding, an eternal becoming. But the search for guidance results merely in temporary relief, which means a multiplication of problems and an increase of their solutions. Now what are you seeking? Which of these do you want? Do you want to search, to discover, or do you want to find help, guidance? Most of you want help, temporary relief from suffering; you want to cure the symptoms rather than to find the cause of suffering. "I am suffering," you say, "Give me a method which will free me from it." Or you say, "The world is in a chaotic condition. Give us a system that will solve its problems, that will bring about order."

Thus, most of you are seeking temporary relief, temporary shelter, and yet you call that the search for truth. When you talk of service, of understanding, of wisdom, you are thinking merely in terms of comfort. As long as you merely want to relieve conflict, struggle, misunderstanding, chaos, suffering, you are like a doctor who deals only with the symptoms of a disease. As long as you are merely concerned with finding comfort, you are not really seeking.

Now let us be quite frank. We can go far if we are really frank. Let us admit that all that you are seeking is security, relief; you are seeking security from constant change, relief from pain. Because you are insufficient you say, "Please give me sufficiency." So what you call search for truth is really an attempt to find relief from pain, which has nothing to do with reality. In such things we are like children. In time of danger we run to our mother, that mother being belief, guru, religion, tradition, habit. Here we take refuge, and hence our lives are lives of constant imitation, with never a moment of rich understanding.

Now, you may agree with my words, saying, "You are quite right: we are not seeking truth, but relief, and that relief is satisfactory for the moment." If you are satisfied with this, there is nothing more to be said. If you hold that attitude, I may as well say no more. But, thank heaven! not all human beings hold that attitude. Not all have reached the state of being satisfied with their own little experiences which they call knowledge, which is stagnation.

Now when you say, "I am seeking," you imply that you are seeking the unknown. You desire the unknown, and that is the object of your search. Because the known is to you appalling, unsatisfactory, futile, sorrow-laden, you want to discover the unknown, and hence the inquiry, "What is truth? What is God?" From this arises the question, "Who will help me to attain truth?" In that very attempt to find truth or God you create gurus, teachers, who become your exploiters.

Please don't take offense at my words, don't become prejudiced against what I am saying, and don't think that I am riding my favorite hobby. I am merely showing you the cause of your being exploited, which is your seeking for a goal, an end; and when you understand the falseness of the cause, that understanding shall free you. I am not asking you to follow my teachings, for if you desire to understand truth you cannot follow anyone; if you desire to understand truth you must stand entirely alone.

What is one of the most important things in which you are interested in your search for the unknown? "Tell me what is on the other side"; you say, "Tell me what happens to a person after death." The answer to such questions you call knowledge. So when you inquire into the unknown, you find a person who offers you a satisfactory explanation of it, and you take shelter in that person or in that idea that he gives you. Therefore that person or that idea becomes your exploiter, and you yourself are responsible for that exploitation, not the man or the idea that exploits you. From such inquiry into the unknown is born the idea of a guru who will lead you to truth. From such inquiry comes the confusion as to what truth is, because, in your search for the unknown, each teacher, each guide, offers you an explanation of what truth is, and that explanation naturally depends on his own prejudices and ideas; but through that teaching you hope to learn what truth is. Your search for the unknown is merely an escape. When you know the real cause, when you understand the known, then you will not inquire into the unknown.

The pursuit of the variety and diversity of ideas about truth will not yield understanding. You say to yourself, "I am going to listen to this teacher, then I shall listen to someone else, then to another; and I shall learn from each the various aspects of truth." But by this process you will never understand. All that you do is to escape; you try to find that which will give you the greatest satisfaction, and he who gives you most you cherish as your guru, your ideal, your goal. So your search for truth has ceased.

Now, don't think that my showing you the futility of this search is mere cleverness on my part: I am explaining the reason for the exploitation that is taking place all over the world in the name of religion, in the name of government, in the name of truth.

The unknown is not your concern. Beware of the man who describes to you the unknown, truth, or God. Such a description of the unknown offers you a means of escape; and besides, truth defies all description. In that escape there is no understanding, there is no fulfillment. In escape there is only routine and decay. Truth cannot be explained or described. It is. I say that there is a loveliness which cannot be put into words; if it were, it would be destroyed; it would then no longer be truth. But you cannot know this loveliness, this truth, by asking about it; you can know it only when you have understood the known, when you have grasped the full significance of that which is before you.

So you are constantly seeking escape, and these attempts at escape you dignify with various spiritual names, with grand-sounding words; these escapes satisfy you temporarily, that is, until the next storm of suffering comes and blows away your shelter.

Now, let us put away this unknown, and concern ourselves with the known. Put aside for the moment your beliefs, your slavery to traditions, your dependence on your Bhagavad-Gita, your scriptures, your Masters. I am not attacking your favorite beliefs, your favorite societies: I am telling you that if you would understand the truth of what I say, you must try to listen without bias.

Through our various systems of education—which may be university training, or the following of a guru, or the dependence on the past in the form of tradition and habit, which creates incompleteness of the present—through these systems of education we have been encouraged to acquire, to worship success. Our whole system of thought, as well as our whole social structure, is based on the idea of gain. We look to the past because we cannot understand the present. To understand the present, which is experience, mind must be unburdened of past traditions and habits. As long as the weight of the past overwhelms us, we cannot understand, we cannot gather the perfume of an experience fully. So there must be incompleteness as long as there is the search for gain. That our whole system of thought is based on gain is no mere hypothetical assumption on my part; it is a fact. And the central idea of our social structure is also one of gain, achievement, success.

But because I have said that your pursuit of this idea of gain will not result in complete living, do not therefore think in terms of the opposite. Don't say, "Must we not seek? Must we not gain? Must we not succeed?" This shows very limited thinking. What I want you to do is to question the very idea of gain. As I have said, the whole social, economic, and so-called spiritual structure of our world is based on this central idea of gain: gain from experience, gain from living, gain from teachers. And from this idea of gain you gradually cultivate in yourself the idea of fear, because in your looking for gain you are always in fear of loss. So, having this fear of loss, this fear of losing an opportunity, you create the exploiter, whether it be the man who guides you morally, spiritually, or an idea to which you cling. You are afraid and you want courage; therefore courage becomes your exploiter. An idea becomes your exploiter.

Your attempt at achievement, at gain, is merely a running away, an escape from insecurity. When you talk of gain you are thinking of security; and after establishing the idea of security, you want to find a method of obtaining and keeping that security. Isn't that so? If you consider your life, if you examine it critically, you will find that it is based on fear. You are always looking to gain; and after searching out your securities, after establishing them as your ideals, you turn to someone who offers you a method, a plan, by which to achieve and to guard your ideals. Therefore you say, "In order to achieve that security, I must behave in a certain way, I must pursue virtue, I must serve and obey, I must follow gurus, teachers and systems; I must study and practice in order to obtain what I want." In other words, since your desire is for security, you find exploiters who will help you to obtain that which you want. So you, as individuals, establish religions to serve as securities, to serve as standards for conventional conduct; because of the fear of loss, the fear of missing something that you want, you accept such guides or ideals as religions offer.

Now, having established your religious ideals, which are really your securities, you must have particular ways of conduct, practices, ceremonials and beliefs, in order to attain those ideas. In trying to carry them out, there arises division in religious thought, resulting in' schisms, sects, creeds. You have your beliefs, and another has his; you hold to your particular form of religion and another to his; you are a Christian, another is a Mohammedan, and yet another a Hindu. You have these religious dissensions and distinctions, but yet you talk of brotherly love, tolerance, and unity—not that there must be uniformity of thought and ideas. The tolerance of which you speak is merely a clever invention of the mind; this tolerance merely indicates the desire to cling to your own idiosyncrasies, your own limited ideas and prejudices, and allow another to pursue his own. In this tolerance there is no intelligent diversity, but only a kind of superior indifference. There is utter falsity in this tolerance. You say, "You continue in your own way, and I shall continue in mine; but let us be tolerant, brotherly." When there is true brotherliness, friendliness, when there is love in your heart, then you will not talk of tolerance. Only when you feel superior in your certainty, in your position, in your knowledge, only then do you talk of tolerance. You are tolerant only when there is distinction. With the cessation of distinction, there will be no talk of tolerance. Then you will not talk of brotherhood, for then in your hearts you are brothers.

So you, as individuals, establish various religions which act as your security. No teacher has established these organized, exploiting religions. You yourselves, out of your insecurity, out of your confusion, out of your lack of comprehension, have created religions as your guides. Then, after you have established religions, you seek out gurus, teachers; you seek out Masters to help you.

Don't think that I am trying to attack your favorite belief; I am simply stating facts, not for you to accept, but for you to examine, to criticize, and to verify.

You have your Master, and another has his particular guide; you have your savior, and another has his. Out of such division of thought and belief grows the contradiction and conflict of the merits of various systems. These disputes set man against man; but since we have intellectualized life, we no longer openly fight: we try to be tolerant.

Please think about what I am saying. Don't merely accept or reject my words. To examine impartially, critically, you must put aside your prejudices and idiosyncrasies, and approach the whole question openly.

Throughout the world, religions have kept men apart. Individually, each one is seeking his own little security and is concerned about his own progress; individually, each one desires to grow, to expand, to succeed, to achieve, and so he accepts any teacher who offers to help him towards his advancement and growth. As a result of this attitude of acceptance, criticism and true inquiry have ceased. Stagnation has set in. Though you move along a narrow groove of thought and of life, there is no longer true thinking, no longer full living, but only a defensive reaction. As long as religion keeps men apart there can be no brotherhood, any more than there can be brotherhood as long as there is nationality, which must ever cause conflict among men.

Religion with its beliefs, its disciplines, its enticements, its hopes, its punishments, forces you towards righteous behavior, towards brotherliness, towards love. And since you are compelled, you either obey the external authority which it sets up, or—which amounts to the same thing—you begin to develop your own inner authority as a reaction against the outer, and follow that. Where there is belief, where there is a following of an ideal, there cannot be complete living. Belief indicates the incapacity to understand the present.

Now don't look to the opposite and say, "Must we have no beliefs? Must we have no ideals at all?" I am simply showing you the cause and the nature of belief. Because you cannot understand the swift movement of life, because you cannot gather the significance of its swift flow, you think that belief is necessary. In your dependence on tradition, on ideals, on beliefs, or on Masters, you are not living in the present, which is the eternal.

Many of you may think that what I am saying is very negative. It is not, for when you really see the false, then you understand the true. All that I am trying to do is to show you the false, that you may find the true. This is not negation. On the contrary, this awakening of creative intelligence is the only positive help that I can give you. But you may not think of this as positive; you would probably call me positive only if I gave you a discipline, a course of action, a new system of thought. But we cannot go further into this today. If you will ask questions about this tomorrow or on the following days, I shall try to answer them.

Individuals have created society by grouping themselves together for purposes of gain, but this does not bring about real unity. This society becomes their prison, their mold, yet each individual wants to be free to grow, to succeed. So each becomes an exploiter of society and is, in turn, exploited by society. Society becomes the apex of their desire, and government the instrument for carrying out that desire by conferring honors upon those who have the greatest power to possess, to gain. The same stupid attitude exists in religion: religious authority considers the man who has conformed entirely to its dogma and beliefs a truly spiritual person. It confers honor on the man who possesses virtue. So in our desire to possess—and again I am not talking in terms of opposites, but rather, I am examining the very thing that causes the desire for possession—in our pursuit of possession, we create a society to which we unconsciously become slaves. We become cogs in that social machine, accepting all its values, its traditions, its hopes and longings, and its established ideas, for we have created society, and it helps us to attain what we want. So the established order, either of government or of religion, puts an end to inquiry, to search, to doubt. Hence, the more we unite in our various possessions, the more we tend to become nationalistic.

After all, what is a nation? It is a group of individuals living together for the purpose of economic convenience and self-protection, and exploiting similar units. I am not an economist, but this is an obvious fact. From this spirit of acquisitiveness arises the idea of "my family," "my house," "my country." So long as this possessiveness exists there cannot be true brotherhood or true internationalism. Your boundaries, your customs, your tariff walls, your traditions, your beliefs, your religions are separating man from man. What has been created by this mentality of gain, of separativeness, safety, security?—nationalities; and where there is nationalism there must be war. It is the function of nations to prepare for wars, otherwise they cannot be true nations.

That is what is happening all over the world, and we are finding ourselves on the verge of another war. Every newspaper upholds nationalism and the spirit of separativeness. What is being said in almost every country, in America, England, Germany, Italy? "First ourselves and our individual security, and then we will consider the world." We do not seem to realize that we are all in the same boat. Peoples can no longer be separated as they were some centuries ago. We ought not to think in terms of separation, but we insist on thinking nationalistically or class-consciously because we still cling to our possessions, to our beliefs. Nationalism is a disease; it cannot bring about world unity or human unity. We cannot attain health through disease; we must first free ourselves from disease. Education, society, religion, help to keep nations apart, because individually each is seeking to grow, to gain, to exploit.

Now, out of this desire to grow, to gain, to exploit, we create innumerable beliefs—beliefs concerning life after death, reincarnation, immortality—and we find people to exploit us through our beliefs. Please understand that in saying this I am referring to no particular leader or teacher; I am not attacking any of your leaders. Attacking anyone is a sheer waste of time. I am not interested in attacking any particular leader, I have something more important to do in life. I want to act as a mirror, to make clear to you the perversions and deceptions that exist in society, in religion.

Our whole social and intellectual structure is based on the idea of gain, of achievement; and when mind and heart are held by the idea of gain, there cannot be true living, there cannot be the free flow of life. Isn't that so? If you are constantly looking to the future, to an achievement, to a gain, to a hope, how can you live completely in the present? How can you act intelligently as a human being? How can you think or feel in the fullness of the present when you are always keeping your eye on the distant future? Through our religion, through our education, we are made as nothing, and being conscious of that nothingness, we want to gain, to succeed. So we constantly pursue teachers, gurus, systems.

If you really understand this, you will act; you will not merely discuss it intellectually.

In the pursuit of gain you lose sight of the present. In your pursuit of gain, in your reliance on the past, you don't fully understand the immediate experience. That experience leaves a scar, a memory which is the incompleteness of that experience, and out of that increasing incompleteness grows the consciousness of the 'I', the ego. Your divisions of the ego are but the superficial refinement of selfishness in its search for gain. Intrinsically, in that incompleteness of experience, in that memory, the ego has its roots. However much it may grow, expand, it will always retain the center of selfishness. Thus, when you are looking for gain, for success, each experience increases self-consciousness. But we shall discuss this at another time. In this talk I want to present as much of my thought as I can, so that during the following talks I shall have time to answer the questions that you may ask.

When mind is caught up in the past or in the future, it cannot understand the significance of the present experience. This is obvious. When you are looking to gain, you cannot understand the present. And since you do not understand the present, which is experience, it leaves its scar, its incompleteness in the mind. You are not free from that experience. This lack of freedom, of completeness, creates memory, and the increase of that memory is but self-consciousness, the ego. So when you say, "Let me look to experience to give me freedom," what you are really doing is increasing, intensifying, expanding that self-consciousness, that ego; for you are looking to gain, to accumulation, as the means of getting happiness, as the means of realizing truth.

After establishing in your mind the consciousness of 'I', your mind feeds that consciousness, and from that arises the question of whether or not you shall live after death, whether you may hope for reincarnation. You want to know categorically whether reincarnation is a fact. In other words, you utilize the idea of reincarnation as a means of postponement, taking comfort therein. You say, "Through progress I shall gain understanding; what I have not understood today I shall understand tomorrow. Therefore let me have the assurance that reincarnation is true."

So you hold to this idea of progress, this idea of gaining more and more until you arrive at perfection. That is what you call progress, acquiring more and more, accumulating more and more. But to me, perfection is fulfillment, not this progressive accumulation. You use the word progress to mean accumulation, gain, achievement; that is your fundamental idea of progress. But perfection does not lie through progress; it is fulfillment. Perfection is not realized through the multiplication of experiences, but it is fulfillment in experience, fulfillment in action itself. Progress apart from fulfillment, leads to utter superficiality.

Such a system of escape is prevalent in the world today. Your theory of reincarnation makes man more and more superficial, in that he says, "As I cannot fulfill today, I shall do so in the future." If you cannot fulfill in this life, you take comfort in the idea that there is always a next life. From this comes the inquiry into the hereafter, and the idea that the man who has acquired the most in knowledge, which is not wisdom, will attain perfection. But wisdom is not the result of accumulation; wisdom is not possession; wisdom is spontaneous, immediate.

While the mind is escaping from emptiness through gain, that emptiness increases, and you have not a day, not a moment, when you can say, "I have lived." Your actions are always incomplete, unfulfilled, and hence your search to continue. With this desire, what has happened? You have become more and more empty, more and more superficial, thoughtless, uncritical. You accept the man who offers you comfort, assurance, and you, as an individual, have created him as your exploiter. You have become his slave, the slave to his system, to his ideals. From this attitude of acceptance there is no fulfillment, but postponement. Hence the necessity for the idea of your continuity, the belief in reincarnation, and from that arises the idea of progress, accumulation. In whatever you do, there is no harmony, there is no significance, because you are constantly thinking in terms of gain. You think of perfection as an end, not as fulfillment.

Now, as I have said, perfection lies in comprehension, in understanding the significance of an experience completely; and that understanding is fulfillment, which is immortality. So you have to become fully aware of your action in the present. The increase of self-consciousness comes through superficiality of action and through ceaseless exploitation, beginning with families, husbands, wives, children, and extending to society, ideals, religion; for they are all based on this idea of gain. What you are really pursuing is acquisitiveness, even though you may be unconscious of it, and of your exploitation. I want to make it clear that your religions, your beliefs, your traditions, your self-discipline are based on the idea of gain. They are but enticements for righteous behavior, and from them spring the exploiter and the exploited. If you are pursuing acquisitiveness, pursue it consciously—not hypocritically. Do not say that you are seeking truth, for truth is not come at in this way.

Now, this idea of growing more and more is to me false, for that which grows is not eternal. Has it ever been shown that the more you have, the more you understand? In theory it may be so, but in actuality it is not so. One man increases his property and encloses it; another increases his knowledge and is bound by it. What is the difference? This process of accumulative growth is shallow, false from the very beginning, because that which is capable of growth is not eternal. It is an illusion, a falsity that has in it nothing of reality. But if you are pursuing this idea of accumulative growth, pursue it with all your mind and heart. Then you will discover how superficial, how vain, how artificial it is. And when you perceive that it is false, then you will know the truth. Nothing need substitute it. Then you no longer seek truth to substitute for the false; for in your direct perception there is no longer the false. And in that understanding there is the eternal. Then there is happiness, creative intelligence. Then you will live naturally, completely, as the flower; and in that there is immortality.

December 29, 1933

Second Talk at Adyar

As I was saying yesterday, thought is crippled, stultified, when it is bound by belief, yet most of our thinking is a reaction based on belief, on a particular belief or an ideal. So our thinking is never true, flowing, creative. It is always held in check by a particular belief, tradition or an ideal. One can realize truth, that enduring understanding, only when thought is continuously in movement, unfettered by a past or by a future. This is so simple that we often do not perceive it. A great scientist has no objective in his research; if he were merely seeking a result, then he would cease to be a great scientist. So it must be with our thinking. But our thought is crippled, bound, hedged in by a belief, by a dogma, by an ideal, and so there is no creative thinking.

Please apply what I say to yourselves; then you can easily follow my meaning. If you merely listen to it as an entertainment, then what I say is wholly futile, and there will be only further confusion.

On what is our belief based? On what are most of our ideals founded? If you consider, you will find that belief has for its motive either the idea of gain, reward, or that it serves as an enticement, a guide, a pattern. You say, "I shall pursue virtue, I shall act in this or in that way, in order to obtain happiness; I shall find out what truth is, in order to overcome confusion, misery; I shall serve in order to have the blessings of heaven." But this attitude towards action as a means to future acquisition is constantly crippling your thought.

Or again, belief is based on the result of the past. Either you have external, imposed principles, or you have developed inner ideals by which you are living. External principles are imposed by society, by tradition, by authority, all of which are based on fear. These are the principles that you are constantly using as your standard: "What will my neighbor think?" "What does public opinion maintain?" "What do the sacred books or the teachers say?" Or you develop an inner law, which is nothing more than a reaction to the outward; that is, you develop an inner belief, an inner principle, based on the memory of experience, on reaction, in order to guide yourself in the movement of life.

So belief is either of the past or of the future. That is, when there is a want, desire creates the future; but when you are guiding yourself in the present according to an experience that you have had, that standard is in the past; it is already dead. So we develop resistance against the present, which we call will. Now to me, will exists only where there is lack of understanding. Why do we want will? When I understand and live in an experience, I do not have to combat it; I do not have to resist it. When I understand an experience completely there is no longer a spirit of imitation, of adjustment, or the desire to resist it. I understand it completely, and hence I am free from the burden of it. You will have to think over what I am saying; my words are not as confusing as they may sound.

Belief is based on the idea of acquisition, and the desire to obtain results through action. You are seeking gain; you are being molded by sets of beliefs based on the idea of gain, on the search for reward, and your action is the result of that search. If you were in the movement of thought, not seeking an end, a goal, a reward, then there would be results, but you would not be concerned with them. As I have said, a scientist who is seeking results is not a true scientist; and a true scientist who is profoundly seeking, is not concerned with the results he attains, even though these results may be useful to the world. So be concerned with the movement of action itself, and in that there is the ecstasy of truth. But you must become aware that your thought is bound by belief, that you are merely acting according to certain sets of beliefs, that your action is crippled by tradition. In this freedom of awareness there is completeness of action.

Suppose, for instance, that I am a teacher in a school. If I try to mold the pupil's intelligence toward a particular action, then it is no longer intelligence. How the pupil shall employ his intelligence is his own affair. If he is intelligent he will act truly, because he is not acting from motives of gain, of reward, of enticement, of power.

To understand this movement of thought, this completeness of action, which can never be static as a standard, as an ideal, mind must be free from belief; for action that seeks reward cannot understand its own completeness, its own fulfillment. Yet most of your actions are based on belief. You believe in the guidance of a Master, you believe in an ideal, you believe in religious dogmas, you believe in the established traditions of society. But with that background of belief you will never understand, you will never fathom the experience with which you are confronted, because belief prevents you from living that experience wholly, with all your being. Only when you are no longer bound by belief will you know the completeness of action. Now you are unconscious of this burden which is perverting the mind. Become fully aware in action of this burden, and that awareness alone shall free the mind from all perversions.

Now I shall answer some of the questions that have been put to me.

Question: By the sanction of the scriptures and the concurrence of many teachers, doubt has been regarded throughout the ages as a fetter to be destroyed before truth can dawn upon the soul. You, on the contrary, seem to look upon doubt in quite a different light. You have even called it a precious ointment. Which of these contradictory views is the right one?

KRISHNAMURTI: Let us leave the scriptures out of this discussion; for when you begin to quote scriptures in support of your opinions, be sure the Devil can also find texts in scripture to support quite the opposite view! In the Upanishads, in the Vedas, I am sure there can be found quite the opposite of what you say the scriptures teach: I am sure there can be found texts saying that one should doubt. So let us not quote scripture at each other; that is like hurling bricks at each other's heads.

As I have said, your actions are based on beliefs, ideals, which you have inherited or acquired. They have no reality. No belief is ever a living reality. To the man who is living, beliefs are unnecessary.

Now, since the mind is crippled by many beliefs, many principles, many traditions, false values and illusions, you must begin to question them, to doubt them. You are not children. You cannot accept whatever is offered to you or forced upon you. You must begin to question the very foundation of authority, for that is the beginning of true criticism; you must question so as to discover for yourselves the true significance of traditional values. This doubt, born of intense conflict, alone will free the mind and give you the ecstasy of freedom, an ecstasy liberated from illusion.

So the first thing is to doubt, not cherish your beliefs. But it is the delight of exploiters to urge you not to doubt, to consider doubt a fetter. Why should you fear doubt? If you are satisfied with things as they are, then continue living as you are. Say that you are satisfied with your ceremonies; you may have rejected the old and accepted the new, but both amount to the same thing in the end. If you are satisfied with them, what I say will not disturb you in your stagnant tranquillity. But we are not here to be bound, to be fettered; we are here to live intelligently, and if you desire so to live, the first thing you must do is to question.

Now, our so-called education ruthlessly destroys creative intelligence. Religious education which authoritatively holds before you the idea of fear in various forms, keeps you from questioning, from doubting. You may have discarded the old religion of Mylapore, but you have taken on a new religion which has many "don'ts" and "do's." Society, through the force of public opinion which is strong, vital, also prevents you from doubting; and you say that if you stood up against this public opinion, it would crush you. Thus, on all sides, doubt is discouraged, destroyed, put aside. Yet you can find truth only when you begin to question, to doubt the values by which society and religion, ancient and modern, have surrounded you.

So don't compare what I am saying with what is said in the scriptures: in that way we shall never understand. Comparison does not lead to understanding. Only when we take an idea by itself and examine it profoundly, not comparatively or relatively, but with the purpose of finding out its intrinsic value, only then shall we understand.

Let us take an example. You know it is the custom here to marry very young, and it has become almost sacred. Now, must you not question that custom? You question this traditional habit if you really love your children. But public opinion is so strongly in favor of early marriage that you dare not go against it and so you never honestly inquire into this superstition.

Again, you have discarded certain ceremonies and have taken up new ones. Now, why did you give up the old ceremonies? You gave them up because they did not satisfy you; and you have taken up new ceremonies because they are more promising, more enticing, they offer greater hope. You have never said, "I am going to find out the intrinsic value of ceremonies, whether they are Hindu, Christian, or of any other creed." To discover their intrinsic value, you must put aside the hopes, enticements, they offer, and critically examine the whole question. There cannot be this attitude of acceptance. You accept only when you desire to gain, when you are seeking comfort, shelter, security, and in that search for security, comfort, you make of doubt a fetter, an illusion to be banished and destroyed.

A person who would live truly, understand life completely, must know doubt. Don't say, "Will there ever be an end to doubt?" Doubt will exist as long as you suffer, as long as you have not found out true values. To understand true values, you must begin to doubt, to be critical of the traditions, the authority, in which your mind has been trained. But this does not mean that your attitude must be one of unintelligent opposition. To me, doubt is a precious ointment. It heals the wounds of the sufferer. It has a benign influence. Understanding comes only when you doubt, not for the purpose of further acquisition or substitution, but to understand. Where there is the desire for gain, there is no longer doubt. Where there is the desire for gain, there is the acceptance of authority—whether it be the authority of one, of five, or of a million. Such authority encourages acceptance and calls doubt a fetter. Because you are continually seeking comfort, security, you find exploiters who assure you that doubt is a fetter, a thing to be banished.

Question: You say that one cannot work for nationalism and at the same time for brotherhood. Do you mean to suggest that (1) we who are a subject nation and firmly believe in brotherhood should cease striving to become self-governing, or that (2) as long as we are attempting to rid ourselves of the foreign yoke we should cease to work for brotherhood?

KRISHNAMURTI: Do not let us look at this question from the point of view of a subject nation or of an exploiting nation. When we call ourselves a subject nation, we are creating an exploiter. Let us not look at the question in this way for the moment. To me, the solution of an immediate problem is not the point, for if we fully understand the ultimate purpose toward which we are working, then in working for that purpose we solve the immediate problem without great difficulty.

Now please follow what I am going to say; it may be new to you, but don't reject it for that reason. I know that most of you are nationalists and that at the same time you are supposed to be for brotherhood. I know that you are trying to maintain the spirit of nationalism and the spirit of brotherhood at the same time. But please put this nationalistic attitude aside for the moment, and look at the question from another point of view.

The ultimate solution of the problem of employment and of starvation, is world or human unity. You say that there are millions of people starving and suffering in India, and that if you can get rid of the English, you will find ways and means to satisfy the starving people. But I say, don't tackle the problem from this point of view. Don't consider the immediate sufferings of India, but consider the whole question of the starving millions in the world. Millions of Chinese are dying from lack of food. Why don't you think of these? "No, no," you say, "my first duty is at home." That is also what the Chinese say, "My first duty is at home." It is what the English, the Germans, the Italians proclaim; it is what every nationalist maintains. But I say, don't look at the problem from this point of view—I won't call it either a narrow or a broad point of view. I say, consider the whole cause of starvation throughout the world, not why a particular people have not sufficient food.

What causes starvation?—lack of organized planning for the whole of mankind. Isn't that so? There is enough food. There are some excellent methods which can be used for the distribution of food and clothes, and for the employment of man. There is enough of all things. Then what prevents our making intelligent use of these things? Class distinctions, national distinctions, religious and sectarian distinctions—all these prevent intelligent cooperation. At heart each one of you is striving for gain; each is ruled by the possessive instinct. That is why you ruthlessly accumulate, you bequeath your possessions to your families, and this has become a bane to the world.

As long as this spirit exists, no intelligent system will work satisfactorily because there are not enough intelligent people to use it wisely. When you talk of nationalism you mean, "My country, my family, and myself first." Through nationalism you can never come to human unity, to world unity. The absurdity and cruelty of nationalism is beyond doubt, but the exploiters use nationalism to their own ends.

Those of you who talk of brotherhood are generally nationalistic at heart. What does brotherhood mean as an idea or a reality? How can you really have the feeling of brotherly love in your hearts when you hold a certain set of dogmatic beliefs, when you have religious distinctions? And that is what you are doing in your various societies, in your various groups. Are you acting in accord with the spirit of brotherhood when there are these distinctions? How can you know that spirit when you are class-minded? How can there be unity or brotherhood when you think only in terms of your family, of your nationality, of your God?

As long as you are trying to solve merely the immediate problem—here, the problem of starvation in India—you are faced with insurmountable difficulties. There is no process, no system, no revolution that can alter that condition at once. Getting rid of the English immediately, or substituting a brown bureaucracy for a white bureaucracy, will not feed the starving millions in India. Starvation will exist as long as there is exploitation. And you, individually, are involved in this exploitation, in your craving for power, which creates distinctions, in your desire for individual security, spiritual as well as physical. I say that as long as the spirit of exploitation exists, there will ever be starvation.

Or, what may happen is this: You may be ruthlessly driven to accept another set of ideas, to adopt a new social order, whether you like it or not. At present it is the custom—and it is recognized as legitimate—to exploit, to possess and to increase your possessions, to hold, to gather, to hoard up, to inherit. The more you have, the greater your power for exploitation. In recognition of your possessions, of your power, the government honors you, conferring titles and monopolies; you are called "Sir"; you become a K.C.S.I., Rao Bahadur. This is what is happening in your material existence, and in your so-called spiritual life exactly the same condition exists. You are acquiring spiritual honors, spiritual titles; you enter into the spiritual distinctions of disciples, Masters, gurus. There is the same struggle for power, the same possessiveness, the same appalling cruelty of exploitation through religious systems and their exploiters, the priests. And this is thought to be spiritual, moral. You are slaves to this present existing system.

Now another system is springing up, called communistic. This system is inevitably making its appearance because those who possess are so inhuman, so ruthless in their exploitation, that those who feel the cruelty and the ugliness of it must find some way of resistance. So they are beginning to awaken, to revolt, and they will sweep you into their system of thought because you are inhuman. (Laughter)

No, don't laugh. You don't realize the appalling cruelty brought about by your petty systems of possession. A new system is coming, and whether you like it or not, you will be dispossessed; you will be driven like sheep towards nonpossession, as you are now being driven towards possession. In that system honor goes to those who are not possessive. You will be slaves to that new system as you are slaves to the old. One forces you to possess, the other not to possess. Perhaps the new system will benefit the multitudes, the masses of people; but if you are forced, individually, to accept it, then creative thought ceases. So I say, act voluntarily, with understanding. Be free from possessiveness as well as its opposite, nonpossessiveness.

But you have lost all sense of true feeling. That is why you are struggling for nationalism—yet you are not concerned with the many implications of nationalism. When you are occupied with class distinctions, when you are fighting to keep what you have, you are really being exploited individually and collectively, and this exploitation will inevitably lead to war. Isn't that blatantly obvious in Europe now? Every nation continues the piling up of armaments, and yet talks of peace and attends disarmament conferences. (Laughter)

You are doing exactly the same thing in another way. You talk about brotherhood, and yet you hold to caste distinctions; religious prejudices divide you; social customs have become cruel barriers. By your beliefs, ideals, prejudices, the unity of man is ever being broken up. How can you talk of brotherhood when you do not feel it in your hearts, when your actions are opposed to the unity of man, when you are constantly pursuing your own self-expansion, your own self-glorification? If you were not pursuing your own selfish ends, do you mean to say that you would belong to organizations which promise you spiritual and temporal rewards? That is what your religions, your selective groups, your governments are doing, and you belong to them to them for your own self-expansion, your own self-glorification.

If you become intelligent about this whole question of nationalism, if you give it real thought and so act truly with regard to it, you can create a world unity which will be the only real solution for the immediate problem of starvation. But it is hard for you to think along these lines because you have been trained for years to think along the nationalistic groove. Your histories, your magazines, your newspapers all emphasize nationalism. You are trained by your political exploiters not to listen to anyone who calls nationalism a disease, anyone who says that it is not a means to world unity. But you must not separate the means from the end; the end is directly connected with the means; it is not distinct from it. The end is world unity, an organized plan for the whole, though this does not mean equalization of individuality. Yet a lifeless, mechanical equalization will come about if you do not act voluntarily, intelligently.

I wonder how many of you feel the urgency, the necessity of these things? The end is human unity, of which you talk so much; but you merely talk without willing and intelligent action; you don't feel, and your actions deny your words. The end is human unity, and organized planning for the whole of man, not the conditioning of man. The purpose is not to force man to think in any one particular direction, but to help him to be intelligent so that he shall live fully, creatively. But there must be organized planning for the well-being of man, and that can be brought about only when nationalism and class distinction, with their exploitation, no longer exist.

Sirs, how many of you feel the great necessity of such action? I am well aware of your attitude. "Millions are starving in India," you say. "Isn't it important to tackle that problem immediately?" But what are you doing even about that? You talk about doing something, but what you really do is to argue and debate as to how your plans shall be organized, what system shall be adopted, and who shall be its leader. That is in your hearts. You are not really concerned with the starving millions throughout the world. That is why you talk of nationalism. If you tackled the problem as a whole, if you really felt for the whole of mankind, you would then see the immense necessity for a complete human action, which can come about only when you cease to talk in terms of nationalities, of classes, of religions.

Question: Are you still inclined flatly to deny that you are the genuine product of Theosophical culture?

KRISHNAMURTI: What do you mean by Theosophical culture? You see how this question is connected with the previous one of nationalism. You ask, "Has not our society, our religion, our country brought you up?" And the next question follows, "Why are you ungrateful to us?"

Intelligence is not the product of any society, though I know that societies and groups like to exploit it. If I agreed that I am the "genuine product of Theosophical culture," whatever that may mean, you would say, "See what a marvelous man he is! We have produced him; so follow us and our ideas." (Laughter) I know I am putting this crudely, but that is how many of you think. Don't laugh. You laugh too easily, you laugh superficially, showing that you don't feel vitally. I want you to consider why you ask me this question, not whether I am or am not the result of Theosophical culture.

Culture is universal. True culture is infinite; it does not belong to any one society, to any one nation, to any one religion. A true artist is neither Hindu nor Christian, American nor English, for an artist who is conditioned by tradition or by nationalism is not a true artist. So let us not discuss whether I am the result of Theosophical culture or whether I am not. Let us consider why you ask this question. That is more important.

Because you are clinging to your particular beliefs, you say that your way is the only way, that it is better than all other ways. But I say that there is no way to truth. Only when you are free from this idea of paths which are but temperamental illusions, will you begin to think intelligently and creatively.

Now, I am not attacking your society. You have been kind enough to invite me to speak here, and I am not abusing that kindness. Your society is like thousands of other societies throughout the world, each holding to its own beliefs, each thinking, "Ours is the best way; our belief is right, and other beliefs are wrong." In the old days, people whose beliefs differed from the accepted orthodoxy were burned or tortured. Today we have become what we call tolerant; that is, we have become intellectualized. That is what tolerance amounts to.

You ask me this question because you want to convince yourselves that your culture, your belief, is the best; you want to bring others to that belief, to that culture. Today Germany holds that it shall be a country only of Nordic peoples, that there shall be but one culture. You say exactly the same thing in a different way. You say, "Our beliefs will solve the problems of the world." And that is what the Buddhists and Mohammedans say; that is what the Roman Catholics and others say: "Our beliefs are the best; our institution is the most precious." Every sect and group believes in its own superiority, and from such beliefs spring schisms, quarrels and religious wars over things that do not matter a scrap.

For a man who is living fully, completely, for a man who is truly cultured, beliefs are unnecessary. He is creative. He is truly creative, and that creativeness is not the outcome of a reaction to a belief. The truly cultured man is intelligent. In him there is no separation between his thought and his emotion, and therefore his actions are complete, harmonious. True culture is not nationalistic nor is it of any group. When you understand this, there will be the true spirit of brotherhood; you will no longer think in terms of Roman Catholicism or Protestantism, in terms of Hinduism or Theosophy. But you are so conscious of your possessions and your struggle for further acquisition that you cause distinctions, and from this there arise the exploiter and the exploited.

Some of you, I know, have shut your minds against what I am saying and what I am going to say. It is obvious from your faces.

Comment: We doubt you, that is all.

KRISHNAMURTI: It is perfectly right that you should doubt me. I am glad if you doubt. But you are not doubting. If you were really doubting, how could you ask me a question such as this, whether I am the result of Theosophical culture or not? Thought is not to be conditioned, shaped, yet I know that this is happening; but surely you cannot accept things as they are. You accept only when you are satisfied, contented. You do not accept when you are suffering. When you suffer you begin to question. So why should you not doubt? Have I not invited you from the beginning to examine, to challenge everything that I say, so that you will become intelligent, affectionate, human? Have you arrived at that intelligent understanding of life? I am asking you to question, to doubt, not only what I am saying, but also the past values and those in which you are now caught up.

Doubt brings about lasting understanding; doubt is not an end in itself. What is true is revealed only through doubt, through questioning the many illusions, traditional values, ideals. Are you doing that? If you know you are sincerely doing this, then you will also know the enduring significance of doubt. Are the mind and heart freeing themselves from possessiveness? If you are truly awakened to the wisdom of doubt, the instinct of acquisitiveness should be completely destroyed, for that instinct is the cause of much misery. In that there is no love, but only chaos, conflict, sorrow. If you truly doubt, you will perceive the falsity of the instinct of possession.

If you are critical, questioning, why do you cling to ceremonies? Now, do not compare one ceremony with another in order to decide which is the better, but find out if ceremonies are worthwhile at all. If you say, "The ceremonies which I perform are very satisfying to me," then I have nothing more to say. Your statement merely shows that you do not know of doubt. You are only concerned with being satisfied. Ceremonies keep people apart, and each believer in them says, "Mine are the best. They have more spiritual power than others." This is what the members of every religion, of every religious sect or society maintain, and over these artificial distinctions there have been quarrels for generations. These ceremonies and such other thoughtless barriers have separated man from man.

May I say something else? If you doubt, that is, if you desire greatly to find out, you must let go of those things which you hold so dearly. There cannot be true understanding by keeping what you have. You cannot say, "I shall hold on to this prejudice, to this belief, to this ceremony, and at the same time I shall examine what you say." How can you? Such an attitude is not one of doubt; it is not one of intelligent criticism. It shows that you are merely looking for a substitute.

I am trying to help you to understand truly the completeness of life. I am not asking you to follow me. If you are satisfied with your life as it is, then continue it. But if you are not, then try what I am saying. Don't accept, but begin to be intelligently critical. To live completely you must be free from the perversions, the illusions in which you are held. To find out the lasting significance of ceremony, you must examine it critically, objectively, and to do this you must not be enticed into it, entangled in it. Surely this is obvious. Examine both the performance and the nonperformance of ceremonies. Doubt, question, ponder over this profoundly. When you begin to relinquish the past, you will create conflict in yourself, and out of that conflict there must come action born of understanding. Now you are afraid to let go, because that act of relinquishment will bring turmoil; out of that act might come the decision that ceremonies are of no avail, which would go against your family, your friends, and your past assertions. There is fear behind all this, so you merely doubt intellectually. You are like the man who holds to all his possessions, to his ideas, his beliefs, his family, and yet talks about nonpossession. His thought has nothing to do with his action. His life is hypocritical.

Please don't think that I am talking harshly; I am not. But neither am I going to be sentimental or emotional in order to rouse you to action. In fact, I am not interested in rousing you to action; you will rouse yourself to action when you understand. I am interested in showing you what is happening in the world. I want to awaken you to the cruelty, to the appalling oppression, exploitation, that is about you. Religion, politics, society are exploiting you, and you are being conditioned by them; you are being forced in a particular direction. You are not human beings; you are mere cogs in a machine. You suffer patiently, submitting to the cruelties of environment, when you, individually, have the possibilities of changing them.

Sirs, it is time to act. But action cannot take place through mere reasoning and discussions. Action takes place only when you feel intensely. True action takes place only when your thoughts and your feelings are harmoniously linked together. But you have divorced your feelings from your thoughts, because from their harmony, action must create conflict which you are unwilling to face. But I say, free yourself from the false values of society, of traditions; live completely, individually. By this I do not mean individu- alistically. When I talk about individuality, I mean by that the understanding of true values liberating you from the social, religious machine which is destroying you. To be truly individual, action must be born of creative intelligence, without fear, not caught up in illusion.

You can do this. You can live completely—not only you, but the people about you—when you become creatively intelligent. But now you are out to gain, ever seeking for power. You are driven by enticements, by beliefs, by substitutes. In this there is no happiness, in this there is no creative intelligence, in this there is no truth.

December 30, 1933

Third Talk at Adyar

If one can find an absolute guarantee of security, then one has fear of nothing. If one can be certain of anything, then fear ceases wholly, fear either of the present or of the future. Therefore we are always seeking security, consciously or unconsciously, security that eventually becomes our exclusive possession. Now, there is physical security which, in the present state of civilization, a man can amass through his cunning, his cleverness, through exploitation. Physically he may thus make himself secure, while emotionally he turns for security to so-called love, which is for the most part possessive- ness; he turns to the egoistic emotional distinctions of family, of friends, and of nationality. Then there is the constant search for mental security in ideas, in beliefs, in the pursuit of virtue, systems, certainties, and so-called knowledge.

So we entrench ourselves continually; through possessiveness we build around ourselves securities, comforts, and try to feel assured, safe, certain. That is what we are constantly doing. But though we entrench ourselves behind the securities of knowledge, virtue, love, possession, though we build up many certainties, we are but building on sand, for the waves of life are constantly beating against their foundations, laying open the structures that we have so carefully and sedulously built. Experiences come, one after another, which destroy all previous knowledge, all previous certainties, and all our securities are swept away, scattered like chaff before the wind. So, though we may think that we are secure, we live in continual fear of death, fear of change and loss, fear of revolution, fear of gnawing uncertainty. We are constantly aware of the transiency of thought. We have built up innumerable walls behind which we seek security and comfort, but fear is still gnawing at our hearts and minds. So we continually look for substitution, and that substitution becomes our goal, our aim. We say, "This belief has proved to be of no value, so let me turn to another set of beliefs, another set of ideas, another philosophy." Our doubt ends merely in substitution, not in the questioning of belief itself. It is not doubt that questions, but the desire for securities. Hence your so-called search for truth becomes merely a search for more permanent securities, and you accept as your teacher, your guide, anyone who offers to give you absolute security, certainty, comfort.

That is how it is with most people. We want and we search. We try to analyze the substitutes which others suggest to take the place of the securities which we know and which are steadily being eaten away, corroded, by the experience of life. But fear cannot be got rid of by substitution, by removing one set of beliefs and replacing it by another. Only when we find out the true value of the beliefs that we hold, the lasting significance of our possessive instincts, our knowledge, the securities that we have built up, only in that understanding can we put an end to fear. Understanding comes not from seeking substitutes, but from questioning, from really coming into conflict with traditions, from doubting the established ideas of society, of religion, of politics. After all, the cause of fear is the ego and the consciousness of that ego, which is created by lack of understanding. Because of this lack of understanding we seek securities, and thereby strengthen that limited self- consciousness.

Now, as long as the ego exists, as long as there is consciousness of the 'my', there must be fear; and this ego will exist as long as we desire substitutes, as long as we do not understand the things about us, the things that we have established, the very monuments of tradition, the habits, ideas, beliefs in which we take shelter. And we can understand these traditions and beliefs, find out their true significance, only when we come into conflict with them. We cannot understand them theoretically, intellectually, but only in the fullness of thought and emotion, which is action.

To me, the ego represents the lack of perception which creates time. When you understand a fact completely, when you understand the experiences of life wholly, unreservedly, time ceases. But you cannot understand experience completely if you are constantly seeking certainty, comfort, if your mind is entrenched in security. To understand an experience in all its significance, you must question, you must doubt the securities, the traditions, the habits, which you have built up, for they prevent the completeness of understanding. Out of that questioning, out of that conflict, if that conflict is real, dawns understanding; and in that understanding, self-consciousness, limited consciousness, disappears.

You must discover what you are seeking, security or understanding. If you are seeking security, you will find it in philosophy, in religions, traditions, authority; but if you desire to understand life, in which there is no security, comfort, then there is enduring freedom. And you can discover what you are seeking only by being aware in action; you cannot find out by merely questioning action. When you question and analyze action, you put an end to action. But if you are aware, if you are intense in your action, if you give to it your whole mind and heart, then that action will reveal whether you are thereby seeking comfort, security, or that infinite understanding which is the eternal movement of life.

Question: In her autobiography Dr. Besant has said that she entered from storm into peace for the first time in her life when she met her great Master. Her magnificent life from then onwards had its motive power in her unstinted and ceaseless devotion to her Master, expressed through the joy of service to him. You yourself, in your poetic words, have declared your inexpressible joy in the union with the Beloved and in seeing his face wherever you turned. Could not the influence of a Master, such as was evident in the great life of Dr. Besant and in your own, be equally significant in other lives?

KRISHNAMURTI: You are asking me, in other words, whether Masters are necessary, whether I believe in Masters, whether their influence is beneficial, and whether they exist. That is the whole question, is it not? Very well, sirs. Now, whether or not you believe in Masters (and some of you do believe in them), please don't close your minds against what I am going to say. Be open, critical. Let us examine the question comprehensively, rather than discuss whether you or I believe in Masters.

First of all, to understand truth you must stand alone, entirely and wholly alone. No Master, no teacher, no guru, no system, no self-discipline will ever lift for you the veil which conceals wisdom. Wisdom is the understanding of enduring values and the living of those values. No one can lead you to wisdom. That is obvious, isn't it? We need not even discuss it. No one can force you, no system can urge you to free yourself from the instinct of possessiveness until you yourself voluntarily understand, and in that understanding there is wisdom. No Master, no guru, no teacher, no system can force you to that understanding. Only the suffering that you yourself experience can make you see the absurdity of possession from which arises conflict; and out of that suffering comes understanding. But when you seek escape from that suffering, when you seek shelter, comfort, then you must have Masters, you must have philosophy and belief; then you turn to such refuges of safety as religion.

So with this understanding I am going to answer your question. Let us forget for the moment what Dr. Besant has said and done, or what I have said and done. Let us leave that aside. Don't bring Dr. Besant into the discussion; if you do, you will react emotionally, those of you who are in sympathy with her ideas, and those of you who are not. You will say that she has brought me up, that I am disloyal, and such words which you use to show your disapproval. Let us put aside all this for the present and look at the question quite plainly and simply.

First of all, you want to know whether Masters exist. I say that whether they exist or not is of very little importance. Now please do not think that I am attacking your beliefs. I realize that I am speaking to members of the Theosophical Society, and that I am your guest here. But you have asked me a question, and I am simply answering it. So let us consider why you want to know whether or not Masters exist. "Because," you say to yourselves, "Masters can guide us through the turmoil as a beacon from the lighthouse guides the mariner." But your saying that shows that you are merely seeking a harbor of safety, that you are afraid of the open sea of life.

Or, again, you may ask the question because you want to strengthen your belief; you want substantiation, corroboration of your belief. Sirs, a thing that is a toy, though made beautiful by the corroboration of thousands of people, remains a toy. You say to me, "Our teachers have given us faith, but now you come to cast doubt on that faith. Therefore we want to know whether Masters exist or not. Please strengthen us in our belief that they exist; tell us whether or not you yourself were guided by them."

If you merely desire to be strengthened in your faith, then I cannot answer your question because I don't hold with faith. Faith is mere authority, blindness, hope, longing; it is a means of exploitation, whether here or in the Roman Catholic church, or in any other religion. It is a means of forcing man to action, to righteous or unrighteous action. Strengthening of faith does not yield understanding; rather, the very doubting of that faith and the finding out of its significance brings understanding. What difference would it make if you were to see the Masters physically every day? You would still hold to your prejudices, your traditions, your habits; you would still be slaves to your cruelties, your bigoted, narrow beliefs, your lack of love, your pride in nationality, but these you would keep secretly under lock and key.

Then out of the first question arises a second: "Do you doubt the messengers of the Masters?" I doubt everything, for it is only through doubt that one can discover, not through the placing of one's faith in something. But you have carefully, sedulously avoided doubt; you have discarded it as a fetter.

Then again you will say, "If I come in contact with the Masters, I can find out their plan for humanity." Do you mean a social plan, a plan for the physical welfare of man? Or do you refer to the spiritual welfare of man? If you reply, "Both," then I say that man cannot attain spiritual welfare through the agency of someone else. That lies entirely in his own hands. No one can plan that for another. Each man must find out for himself, he must understand; there is completeness in fulfillment, not in progress. But if you say, "We seek a plan for the physical welfare of man," then you must study economics and sociology. Then why not make Harold Laski your master, or Keynes, or Marx, or Lenin? Each of these offers a plan for the welfare of man. But you don't want that. What you want, when you seek Masters, is shelter, a refuge of safety; you want to protect yourself from suffering, hide yourself from turmoil and conflict.

I say that there is no such thing as shelter, comfort. You can make only an artificial shelter, intellectually created. Because you have done this for generations, you have lost your creative intelligence. You have become authority-bound, crippled with beliefs, with false traditions and habits. Your hearts are dry, hard. That is why you support all manner of cruel systems of thought, leading to exploitation. That is why you encourage nationalism, why you lack brotherhood. You talk of brotherhood, but your words are meaningless as long as your hearts are bound by class distinctions. You, who believe so profoundly in all these ideas, what have you, what are you? Empty shells resounding with words, words, words. You have lost all sense of feeling for beauty, for love; you support false institutions, false ideas. Those of you who believe in Masters and are following the system of these Masters, their plan, their messengers, what are you? In your exploitation, your nationalism, your ill-treatment of women and children, your acquisitiveness, you are just as cruel as the man who does not believe in Masters, in their plan, in their messengers. You have simply instituted new traditions for the old, new beliefs for the old; your nationalism is as cruel as of old, only you have more subtle arguments for your cruelties and exploitation.

As long as mind is caught up in belief, there is no understanding, there is no freedom. So to me, whether or not Masters exist is quite irrelevant to action, to fulfillment, with which we should concern ourselves. Even though their existence be a fact, it is of no importance; for to understand, you must be independent, you must stand by yourself, completely naked, stripped of all security. This is what I said in my introductory talk. You must find out whether you are seeking security, comfort, or whether you are seeking understanding. If you really examine your own hearts, most of you will find that you are seeking security, comfort, places of safety, and in that search you provide yourselves with philosophies, gurus, systems of self-discipline; thus you are thwarting, continually narrowing down thought. In your efforts to escape from fear, you are entrenching yourselves in beliefs, and thereby increasing your own self-consciousness, your own egotism; you have merely grown more subtle, more cunning.

I know that I have said all these things previously in a different way, but apparently my words have had no effect. Either you want to understand what I say, or you are satisfied with your own beliefs and miseries. If you are satisfied with them, why have you invited me to talk here? Why do you listen to me? No, fundamentally you are not satisfied. You may profess to be satisfied; you may join institutions, perform new ceremonies, but inwardly you feel an uncertainty, a ceaseless gnawing that you never dare to face. Instead, you seek substitutes; you want to know whether I can give you new shelters, and that is why you have asked me this question. You want me to support you in those beliefs of which you are uncertain. You want inward stability, but I tell you that there is no such stability. You want me to give you certainties, assurances. I say that you have such certainties, such assurances by the hundreds in your books, in your philosophies, but they are worthless to you; they are dust and ashes because in your own selves there is no understanding. You can have understanding, I assure you, only when you begin to doubt, when you begin to question the very shelters in which you are taking comfort, in which you are taking refuge.

But this means that you must come into conflict with the traditions and habits that you have set up. Perhaps you have discarded old traditions, old gurus, old ceremonies, and have taken on new ones. What is the difference? The new traditions, gurus, ceremonies are just the same as the old, except that they are more exclusive. By constantly questioning you will find out the real, the inherent value of traditions, gurus, ceremonies. I am not asking you to abandon ceremonies, to cease following the Masters. That is a very minor and unintelligent point; whether you perform ceremonies or look to Masters for guidance is not important. But as long as there is lack of understanding there is fear, there is sorrow, and the mere attempt to cover up that fear, that sorrow, through ceremonies, through the guidance of Masters, will not free you.

You have asked me this question before; you asked me the same question last year. And each time you ask it because you want to take shelter behind my answer; you want to feel safe, to put an end to doubt. Now I may contradict your belief; I may say that there are no Masters. Then another comes to tell you that Masters do exist. I say, doubt both answers, question both; don't merely accept them. You are not children, monkeys imitating someone else's action; you are human beings, not to be conditioned by fear. You are supposed to be creatively intelligent, but how can you be creatively intelligent if you follow a teacher, a philosophy, a practice, a system of self-discipline? Life is rich only to the man who is in the constant movement of thought, to the man whose actions are harmonious. In him there is affection, there is consideration. He whose actions are harmonious will utilize an intelligent system to heal the festering wounds of the world.

I know that what I am saying today I have said innumerable times; I have said it again and again. But you don't feel these things because you have explained away your suffering, and in these explanations, beliefs, you are taking shelter, comfort. You are concerned only with yourselves, with your own security, comfort, like men who struggle for government titles. You do the same thing in different ways, and your words of brotherhood, of truth, mean nothing; they are but empty talk.

Question: The one regret of Dr. Besant is said to have been the fact that you failed to rise to her expectations of you as the World Teacher. Some of us frankly share that regret and that sense of disappointment, and feel that it is not altogether without some justification. Have you anything to say?

KRISHNAMURTI: Nothing, sirs. (Laughter) When I say "Nothing," I mean nothing to relieve your disappointment or Dr. Besant's disappointment—if she were disappointed, for she often expressed to me the contrary. I am not here to justify myself; I am not interested in justifying myself. The question is, why are you disappointed, if you are? You had thought to put me in a certain cage, and since I did not fit into that cage, naturally you were disappointed. You had a preconceived idea of what I should do, what I should say, what I should think.

I say that there is immortality, an eternal becoming. The point is not that I know, but that it is. Beware of the man who says, "I know." Ever-becoming life exists, but to realize that, your mind must be free of all preconceived ideas of what it is. You have preconceived ideas of God, of immortality, of life. "This is written in books," you say, or, "Someone has told me this." Thus you have built an image of truth, you have pictured God and immortality. You want to hold to that image, that picture, and you are disappointed in anyone whose idea differs from yours, anyone whose ideas do not conform to yours. In other words, if he does not become your tool, you are disappointed in him. If he does not exploit you—and you create the exploiter in your desire for security—then you are disappointed in him. Your disappointment is based not on thought, not on intelligence, not on deep affection, but on some image of your own making, however false it may be.

You will find people who will tell you that I have disappointed them, and they will create a body of opinions holding that I have failed. But in a hundred years' time I don't think it will matter much whether you are disappointed or not. Truth, of which I speak, will remain—not your fantasies or your disappointments.

Question: Do you consider it a sin for a man or a woman to enjoy illegitimate sexual intercourse? A young man wants to get rid of such illegitimate happiness which he considers wrong. He tries continually to control his mind but does not succeed. Can you show him any practical way to be happy?

KRISHNAMURTI: In such things there is no "practical way." But let us consider the question; let us try to understand it, though not from the point of view of whether a certain act is a sin or not a sin. To me there is no such thing as sin.

Why has sex become a problem in our life? Why are there so many distortions, perversions, inhibitions, suppressions? Is it not because we are starving mentally and emotionally, we are incomplete in ourselves, we have but become imitative machines, and the only creative expression left to us, the only thing in which we can find happiness, is the thing which we call sex? As individuals we have mentally and emotionally ceased to be. We are mere machines in society, in politics, in religion. We as individuals have been utterly, ruthlessly destroyed through fear, through imitation, through authority. We have not released our creative intelligence through social, political, and religious channels. Therefore the only creative expression left to us as individuals is sex, and to that we naturally assign tremendous importance, on that we place tremendous emphasis. That is why sex has become a problem, isn't it?

If you can release creative thought, creative emotion, then sex will no longer be a problem. To release that creative intelligence completely, wholly, you must question the very habit of thought, you must question the very tradition in which you are living, those very beliefs that have become automatic, spontaneous, instinctive. Through questioning you come into conflict, and that conflict and the understanding of it will awaken creative intelligence; in that questioning you will gradually release creative thought from imitation, from authority, from fear.

That is one side of the question. There is also another side to this question, which concerns food and exercise, and love of the work that you do. You have lost the love of your work. You have become clerks, slaves to a system, working for fifteen rupees or ten thousand rupees, not for the love of what you are doing.

With regard to illegitimate sexual intercourse, let us first consider what you mean by marriage. In most cases marriage is but the sanctification of possessiveness, by religion and by law. Suppose that you love a woman; you want to live with her, to possess her. Now society has innumerable laws to help you to possess, and various ceremonies which sanctify this possessiveness. An act that you would have considered sinful before marriage, you consider lawful after that ceremony. That is, before the law legalizes and religion sanctifies your possessiveness, you consider the act of intercourse illegal, sinful.

Where there is love, true love, there is no question of sin, of legality or illegality. But unless you really think deeply about this, unless you make a real effort not to misunderstand what I have said, it will lead to all kinds of confusion. We are afraid of many things. To me the cessation of sex problems lies not in mere legislation, but in releasing that creative intelligence, in being complete in action, not separating mind and heart. The problem disappears only in living completely, wholly.

As I have been trying to make clear, you cannot cultivate nationalism and at the same time talk of brotherhood. I think it was Hitler who banished the idea of brotherhood from Germany because, he said, it was antagonistic to nationalism. But here you are trying to cultivate both. At heart you are nationalistic, possessive; you have class distinctions, and yet you talk about universal brotherhood, about world peace, about the unity and the oneness of life. As long as your action is divided, as long as there is no intimate connection between thinking, feeling, and action, and the full awareness of that intimate connection, there will be innumerable problems which take such predominance in your lives that they become a constant source of decay.

Question: What you say as to the necessity for freedom from all conformity, from all leadership and authority, is a useful teaching for some of us. But society and perhaps even religion, together with their institutions and a wise government, are essential for the vast majority of mankind and hence useful to them. I speak from years of experience. Do you disagree with this view?

KRISHNAMURTI: What is poison to you is poison to another. If religious belief, if authority is false to you, it is false to everyone else. When you consider man as the questioner regards him, then you retain and cultivate a slavish mentality in him. That is what I call exploitation. That is the acquisitive or capitalistic attitude: "What is beneficial and useful for me is dangerous for you." So you keep as slaves those who are bound to authority, to religious beliefs. You do not bring into being new organizations, new institutions, to help these slaves to free themselves and not become slaves again to the new organizations and institutions.

Now I am not opposed to organizations, but I hold that no organization can lead man to truth. Yet all religious societies, sects, and groups are based on the idea that man can be guided to truth. Organizations should exist for the welfare of man, organizations not divided by nationalities, by class distinctions. This is the ultimate thing that will solve the immediate problem that confronts each people, the problem of exploitation, the problem of starvation.

You may insist that, as people are, they must be subjected to authority. But if you perceive that authority is perverting, crippling, then you will combat authority; you will discover new methods of education that will help man to free himself, without this curse of distinction. But when you look at life from a narrow, selfish, bigoted point of view, you inevitably ask such a question as this; you ask it because you are afraid that those over whom you have authority will no longer obey you. This consideration for the mass, for the many, is very superficial, false; it springs from fear, and must inevitably lead to exploitation. But if you truly perceived the significance of authority, of conforming to tradition, of shaping yourself after a pattern, of conditioning your mind and heart by a principle or ideal, then you would intelligently help man to free himself from them. Then you would see their shallowness and their degenerating effect, not only upon yourself or upon a few men, but upon the whole of mankind. Thereby you would help to release the creative power in man, whether in yourself or in someone else; you would no longer maintain this artificial distinction between man and man, as high and low, evolved and unevolved. But this does not mean that there is or that there will be equality; there is no such thing. There is only man in fulfillment. But the mind that creates distinction because it thinks of itself as separate is an exploiting mind, is a cruel mind, and against such a mind intelligence must ever be in revolt.

December 31, 1933

Fourth Talk at Adyar

(Krishnamurti was garlanded by a member of the audience who wished him a happy new year.)

KRISHNAMURTI: Thank you. I had forgotten that it is a new year. I wish you all a happy new year too.

In my brief talk this morning I want to explain how one may discover for oneself what is true satisfaction. Most people in the world are caught up in some kind of dissatisfaction, and they are constantly seeking satisfaction. That is, their search for satisfaction is a search for an opposite. Now dissatisfaction, discontent, arises from the feeling of emptiness, the feeling of loneliness, of boredom, and when you have this dissatisfaction you seek to fill the void, the emptiness in your life. When you are dissatisfied you are constantly seeking something to replace that which causes dissatisfaction, something to serve as a substitute, something that will give you satisfaction. You look to a series of achievements, a series of successes, to fill the aching void in your mind and in your heart. That is what most of you are trying to do. If there is fear, you seek courage which you hope will give you contentment, happiness.

In this search for the opposite, profound feelings are gradually being destroyed. You are becoming more and more superficial, more and more empty, because your whole conception of satisfaction, happiness, is one of substitution. The longing, the hunger of most people is for the opposite. In your hunger for attainment you pursue spiritual ideals, or you seek to have worldly titles conferred upon you, and both amount to exactly the same thing.

Let us take an example which may perhaps make the matter clearer; though, for the most part, examples are confusing and disastrous to understanding, for they give no clear perception of the abstract, from which alone can one come to the practical. Suppose that I desire something, and that through my endeavors I finally possess it. But this possession does not give me the satisfaction that I had hoped for; it does not give me lasting happiness. So I change my desire to something else, and I possess that. But even this new thing does not give me permanent satisfaction. Then I look to affection, to friendship; then to ideas, and finally I turn to the search for truth or God. This gradual process of the change of the objects of desire is called evolution, growth towards perfection.

But if you will really think about it, you will see that this process is nothing more than the process of satisfaction, and therefore an ever increasing emptiness, shallowness. If you consider, you will see that this is the substance of your lives. There is no joy in your work, in your environment; you are afraid, you are envious of the possessions of others. From that there arises struggle, and from that struggle comes discontent. Then, to overcome that discontent, to find satisfaction, you turn to the opposite.

In the same way, when you change your desire from the so-called transient, the unessential, to the permanent, the essential, what you have done is you have merely changed the object of your satisfaction, the object of your gain. First it was a concrete thing, and now it is truth. You have merely changed the object of your desires, thereby becoming more superficial, more vain, more empty. Life has become unsatisfactory, shallow, transient.

I don't know whether you agree or disagree with what I am saying, but if you are willing to think about it, to discuss and question it, you will see that your hunger for truth, as I have been trying to explain during these talks, is merely the desire for gratification, satisfaction, the longing for safety, for security. In that hunger there is never reality. That hunger is superficial, passive; it results in nothing else but cunning, emptiness, and unquestioning belief.

There is a true hunger, a true longing; it is not the desire for an opposite, but the desire to understand the cause of the very thing in which one is caught up. Now you are constantly seeking opposites; when you are afraid you seek courage as a substitute for fear, but that substitute does not really free you from fear. Fundamentally you are still afraid; you have merely covered that basic fear with the idea of courage. The man who pursues courage, or any other virtue, is acting superficially, whereas if he tried to understand intelligently this pursuit of courage, he would be led to the discovery of the very cause of fear, which would set him free from fear as well as from its opposite. And that is not a negative state; it is the only dynamic, positive way of living.

What, for instance, is your immediate concern when you have physical pain? You want immediate relief, don't you? You are not thinking of the moment when you felt no pain, or of the moment when you will have no pain. You are concerned only with the immediate relief from that pain. You are seeking the opposite. You are so consumed with that pain that you want to be free from it. The same attitude exists when your whole being is consumed with fear. When such fear arises, do not run away from it. Deal with it completely, with all your being, do not try to develop courage. Then only will you understand its fundamental cause, thereby freeing the mind and heart from fear.

Modern civilization has helped to train your mind and heart not to feel intensely. Society, education, religion have encouraged you toward success, have given you hope in gain. And in this process of success and gain, in this process of achievement and spiritual growth, you have sedulously, carefully destroyed intelligence, depth of feeling.

When you are really suffering, as when someone dies whom you really love, what is your reaction? You are so caught up in your emotions, in your sufferings, that for the moment you are paralyzed with pain. And then what happens? You long to have your friend back again. So you pursue all the ways and means of reaching that person. The study of the hereafter, the belief in reincarnation, the use of mediums—all these you pursue in order to get into contact with the friend whom you have lost. So what has happened? The acuteness of mind and heart which you felt in your sorrow has become dull, has died.

Please try to follow intelligently what I am saying. Even though you may believe in the hereafter, please do not close your mind and heart against what I have to say.

You desire to have the friend whom you have lost. Now that very want destroys the acuteness, the fullness of perception. For, after all, what is suffering? Suffering is a shock to awaken you, to help you to understand life. When you experience death, you feel utter loneliness, the loss of support; you are like the man who has been deprived of his crutches. But if you immediately seek crutches again in the shape of comfort, companionship, security, you deprive the shock of its significance. Another shock comes, and again you go through the same process. Thus, though you have many experiences during your life, shocks of suffering that should awaken your intelligence, your understanding, you gradually dull those shocks by your desire and pursuit after comfort.

Thus you use the idea of reincarnation, belief in the hereafter, as a kind of drug or dope. In your turning to this idea there is no intelligence. You are merely seeking an escape from suffering, a relief from pain. When you talk about reincarnation you are not helping another to understand truly the cause of pain; you are not helping him to free himself from sorrow. You are only giving him a means of escape. If another accepts the comfort, the escape which you offer him, his feelings become shallow, empty, for he takes shelter in the idea of reincarnation. Because of this placid assurance that you have given him, he no longer feels deeply when someone dies, for he has dulled his feelings, he has deadened his thoughts.

So in this search for contentment, comfort, your thoughts and feelings become shallow, barren, trivial, and life becomes an empty shell. But if you see the absurdity of substitution and perceive the illusion of contentment, with its achievement, then there is great depth to thought and feeling; then action itself reveals the significance of life.

Question: There are many systems of meditation and self-discipline adapted to varying temperaments, and all of them are intended to cultivate and sharpen the mind or emotions, or both; for the usefulness and value of an instrument is great or small according to whether it is sharp or blunt. Now: (1) Do you think that all these systems are alike futile and harmful without exception? (2) How would you deal with the temperamental differences of human beings? (3) What value has meditation of the heart to you?

KRISHNAMURTI: Let us differentiate between concentration and meditation. Now when you talk of meditation, most of you mean the mere learning of the trick of concentration. But concentration does not lead to the joy of meditation. Consider what happens in what you call meditation, which is merely the process of training the mind to concentrate on a particular object or idea. You exclude from your mind all other thoughts or images except the one which you have deliberately chosen; you try to focus your mind on that one idea, picture, or word. Now that is merely contraction of thought, limitation of thought. When other thoughts arise during this process of contraction, you dismiss them, you brush them aside. So your mind becomes more and more narrow, less and less elastic, less and less free.

Why do you want to concentrate? Because you see an enticement, a reward, awaiting you as the result of concentration. You want to become a disciple, you want to find the Master, you want to develop spiritually, you want to understand truth. So your concentration becomes utterly destructive of thought and emotion because you consider meditation, concentration, in terms of gain, in terms of escape from turmoil. Just think about it for a moment, those of you who have practiced meditation, concentration, for years. You have been forcing your mind to adjust itself to a particular pattern, to conform itself to a particular image or idea, to shape itself according to a particular idiosyncrasy or prejudice. Now, all beliefs, ideals, idiosyncrasies depend on personal like and dislike. Your self-discipline, your so-called meditation, is merely a process by which you try to obtain something in return. And this assurance of something in return, this looking for a reward, also accounts for the large membership of churches and religious societies: these institutions promise a reward, a recompense to their followers who faithfully adhere to their discipline.

Where there is control, there is no meditation of the heart. When you are searching with an eye to gain, to recompense, your search has already ended. Take, for instance, the case of a scientist, a great scientist, not a pseudo-scientist. A true scientist is continually experimenting without seeking results. In his search there are what we call results, but he is not bound by these results, for he is constantly experimenting. In that very movement of experiment he finds joy. That is true meditation. Meditation is not the seeking for a result, a by-product. Such a result is merely incidental, an outward expression of that great search which is ecstatic, eternal.

Now instead of banishing each thought that arises, as you do when you practice so-called meditation, try to understand and live in the significance of each thought as it comes to you; do this not at a particular period, at a particular hour or moment of the day, but throughout the day, continuously. In that awareness you will understand the cause of each thought and its significance. That awareness will release the mind from opposites, from pettiness, shallowness; in that awareness there is freedom, completeness of thought. It is in eternal movement, without limitation, and in that there is the true joy of meditation; in that there is living peace. But when you seek a result, your meditation becomes shallow, empty, as is shown by your acts.

Many of you have meditated for years. What has it availed you? You have banished your thought from your action. In temples, in shrines, in chapels of meditation you have filled your minds with the supposed image of truth, God, but when you go out into the world, your actions exhibit nothing of those qualities which you are trying to attain. Your actions are quite the opposite; they are cruel, exploiting, possessive, destructive. So in this search for reward, recompense, you have differentiated between thought and action, you have made a division between the two, and your so-called meditation is empty, without depth, without profundity of feeling or greatness of thought.

If you are constantly aware, fully aware as each thought and emotion arises, in that flame your action will be the harmonious outcome of thought and feeling. That is the joy, the peace of true meditation, not this process of self-discipline, twisting, training the mind to conform to a particular attitude. Such discipline, such distortion, means only decay, boredom, routine, death.

Question: During the Theosophical convention last week several leaders and admirers of Dr. Besant spoke, paying her high tributes. What is your tribute to and your opinion of that great figure who was a mother and friend to you? What was her attitude toward you through the many years of her guardianship of you and your brother, and also subsequently? Are you not grateful to her for her guidance, training, and care?

KRISHNAMURTI: Mr. Warrington kindly asked me to speak about this matter, but I told him that I did not want to. Now don't condemn me by using such words as "guardianship," "gratitude," and so on. Sirs, what can I say? Dr. Besant was our mother, she looked after us, she cared for us. But one thing she did not do. She never said to me, "Do this," or "Don't do that." She left me alone. Well, in these words I have paid her the greatest tribute. (Cheers)

You know, followers destroy leaders, and you have destroyed yours. In your following of a leader, you exploit that leader; in your use of Dr. Besant's name so constantly you are merely exploiting her. You are exploiting her and other teachers. The greatest disservice you can ever do to a leader is to follow that leader. I know you wisely nod your heads in approval. Let me but quote her name and sanctify her memory, and I can exploit you because you want to be exploited; you want to be used as instruments, for that is easier than thinking for yourselves. You are all cogs, parts of machines, being used by exploiters. Religions use you in the name of God, society uses you in the name of law, politicians and educators use and exploit you. So-called religious teachers and guides exploit you in the name of ceremonies, in the name of Masters. I am merely awakening you to these facts. You can do about them what you will; with that I am not concerned, because I don't belong to any society, and I shall probably not come here again.

Comment: But we want you to come.

KRISHNAMURTI: Please don't get sentimental about this. Probably some of you will be glad that I shall not come again.

Comment: No.

KRISHNAMURTI: Wait a moment, please. I don't want you to ask me or not to ask me to return. That doesn't matter at all.

Sirs, these two things are wholly different: what you are thinking and doing, and what I am talking and doing. The two cannot combine. Your whole system is based on exploitation, on the following of authority, on the belief in religion and faith. Not only your system, but the systems of the entire world. I cannot help those of you who are content with this system. I want to help those who are eager to break away, to understand. Naturally you will reject me, for I am opposed to all that you hold dear, sacred and worthwhile. But your rejection will not matter to me. I am not attached to this or any place. I repeat, what you are doing and what I am doing are two totally different things that have nothing in common.

But I was answering the question about Dr. Besant. Human mind is lazy, lethargic. It has been so dulled by authority, so shaped, controlled, conditioned, that it cannot stand by itself. But to stand by oneself is the only way to understand truth. Now are you really, fundamentally interested in understanding truth? No, most of you are not. You are only interested in supporting the system that you now hold, in finding substitutes, in seeking comfort and security; and in that search you are exploiting others and being exploited yourselves. In that there is no happiness, no richness, no fullness. Because you follow this way of life you have to choose. When you base your life either on the authority of the past or the hope of the future, when you guide your actions by the past greatness or the past ideas of a leader, you are not living; you are merely imitating, acting as a cog in a machine. And woe to such a person! For him life holds no happiness, no richness, but only shallowness, emptiness. This seems so clear to me that I am surprised that the question arises again and again.

Question: You have spoken in clear terms on the subject of the existence of Masters and the value of ceremonies. May I ask you a straightforward question? Are you disclosing to us your own genuine point of view without any mental reservation? Or is the ruthless manner of the presentation of your view merely a test of our devotion to the Masters and our loyalty to the Theosophical Society to which we belong? Please state your answer frankly, even though it may be hurtful to some of us.

KRISHNAMURTI: What do you think I am? I have not given you a momentary reaction, I have told you what I really think. If you wish to use that as a test to fortify yourselves, to entrench yourselves in your old beliefs, I cannot help it. I have told you what I think, frankly, straightly, without dissimulation. I am not trying to make you act in one way or another, I am not trying to entice you into any society or into a particular form of thought, I don't dangle a reward in front of you. I have told you frankly that Masters are unessential, that the idea of Masters is nothing more than a toy to the man who really seeks truth. I am not trying to attack your beliefs, I realize that I am a guest here; this is merely my frank opinion, as I have stated it over and over again.

I hold that where there is unrighteousness there are ceremonies, whether it be in Mylapore or in Rome or here. But why discuss this matter any longer? You know my point of view, as I have stated it repeatedly. I have given you my reasons for my opinion regarding Masters and ceremonies. But because you want Masters, because you like to perform ceremonies, because such performance gives you a certain sense of authority, of security, of exclusiveness, you continue in your practices. You continue them with blind faith, blind acceptance, without reason, without real thought or emotion behind your acts. But in that way you will never understand truth; you will never know the cessation of sorrow. You may find forgetfulness, oblivion, but you will never discover the root, the cause of sorrow and be free from it.

Question: You rightly condemn a hypocritical attitude of mind and such feelings and actions as are born from it. But since you say that you do not judge us, but somehow seem to regard the attitude of some of us as hypocritical, can you say what it is that gives you such an impression?

KRISHNAMURTI: Very simple. You talk about brotherhood, and yet you are nationalists. I call that hypocrisy, because nationalism and brotherhood cannot exist together. Again, you talk about the unity of man, talk about it theoretically, and yet you have your particular religions, your particular prejudices, your class distinctions. I call that hypocrisy. Or again, you turn to self-glorification, subtle self-glorification, instead of what you call the gross self-glorification of the men of the world who seek distinctions, concessions, and government honors. You also are men of the world, and your self-glorification is just the same, only a little more subtle. You, with your distinctions, your secret meetings, your exclusiveness, are also trying to become nobles, to attain honors and degrees, but in a different world. That I call hypocrisy. It is hypocrisy because you pretend to be open, you speak of the brotherhood and the unity of man, while at the same time your acts are quite the opposite of your words.

Whether you do this consciously or unconsciously is of no importance. The fact is that you do it. If you do it consciously, with fully awakened interest, then, at least, you are doing it without hypocrisy. Then you know what you are doing. If you say, "I want to glorify myself, but since I cannot attain distinctions and honors in this world, I shall try to acquire them in another; I shall become a disciple, I shall be called this and that, I shall be honored as a man of quality, a man of virtue," then, at least, you are perfectly honest. Then there is some hope that you will find out that this process leads nowhere.

But now you are trying to do two incompatible things at one time. You are possessive, and at the same time you talk about freedom from possession. You talk about tolerance, and yet you are becoming more and more exclusive in order "to help the world." Words, words, without depth. That is what I call hypocrisy. At one moment you talk of love for a Master, of reverence for an ideal, for a belief, for a God, and yet in the next moment you act with appalling cruelty. Your acts are acts of exploitation, possessiveness, nationalism, ill-treatment of women and children, cruelty to animals. To all this you are insensitive, yet you talk of affection. Is that not hypocrisy? You say, "We don't notice these conditions." Yes, that is just why they exist. Then why talk of love?

So to me, your societies, your meetings in which you talk of your beliefs, ideals, are gatherings of hypocrisy. Isn't that so? I am not speaking harshly, on the contrary; you know what I feel about the state of the world. Yet you who can help, you who say that you want to help, you who are trying to help, are becoming more and more narrow, more and more bigoted, sectarian. You have ceased to cry, to weep, to smile. Emotion means nothing to you. You are concerned only with ceaseless gain, gain of knowledge which is suffocating, which is merely theoretical, which is blind emptiness. Knowledge has nothing to do with wisdom. Wisdom cannot be bought; it is natural, spontaneous, free. It is not merchandise that you can buy from your guru, teacher, at the price of discipline. Wisdom, I say, has nothing to do with knowledge. Yet you search for knowledge, and in that search for knowledge, for gain, you are losing love, all sense of feeling for beauty, all sensitivity to cruelty. You are becoming less and less impressionable.

That brings us to another question which we shall perhaps discuss later, the question of impressions and reactions. You are emphasizing ego-consciousness, limitation. When you say, "I am doing this because I like it, because it gives me satisfaction, pleasure," I am entirely with you, for then you will understand. But if you say, "I am seeking truth; I am trying to help mankind," and if at the same time you increase your self-consciousness, your glory, then I call your attitude and your life a hypocrisy because you are seeking power through exploiting others.

Question: True criticism, according to you, excludes mere opposition, which amounts to the same thing as saying that it excludes all carping, faultfinding, or destructive criticism. Is not then criticism in your sense the same as pure thought directed toward that which is under consideration? If so, how can the capacity for true criticism or pure thinking be aroused or developed?

KRISHNAMURTI: To awaken such true criticism without opposition you must first know that you are not truly critical, that you are not thinking clearly. That is the first consideration. To awaken clear thinking, I must first know that I am not thinking openly. In other words, I must become aware of what I am thinking and feeling. Only then can I know that I am thinking truly or falsely. Isn't that so? When you say that you are critical, you are merely opposing through prejudice, through personal like and dislike, through emotional reactions. In that state you say that you are thinking clearly, that you are critical. But I say that to be intelligently critical you must be free from this personal bias, this personal opposition. And to be intelligently critical, you must first realize that your thinking is influenced, narrow, bigoted, personal, even though you have not been conscious of this bondage. So you have first to become aware of this.

You see how the tension of this audience has gone down. Either you are tired, or you are not as much interested in this subject as you are in ceremonies and Masters. You don't see the importance of criticism because your capacities to doubt, to question, have been destroyed through education, through religion, through social conditions. You are afraid that doubt and criticism will wreck the structure of belief that you have so carefully built up. You know that the waves of doubt will undermine the foundation of the house which you have built on the sands of faith. You are afraid of doubt and questioning. That is why your interest, your tension, has subsided. But tension is necessary for action; without such tension you will do nothing either in the physical world or in the world of thought and feeling, which is all one.

So first of all you must become aware that you are thinking very personally, that your thought is dominated by like and dislike, by reactions of pleasure and pain. Now you say to yourself, "I like your appearance; therefore I shall follow what you teach." Or, of another, "I don't like his beliefs; therefore I won't listen to him. I shall not even try to find out if what he says has any intrinsic value, I shall simply oppose him." Or, again, "He is a teacher of authority, and therefore I must obey him." Through such thinking, by such attitudes, you are gradually but surely destroying all sense of true intelligence, all creative thinking. You are becoming machines whose only activity is routine, whose only end is boredom and decay. Yet you question why you suffer, and seek a discipline whereby you can escape from that suffering.

Question: What are the rules and principles of your life? Since, presumably, they are based on your own conception of love, beauty, truth, and God, what is that conception?

KRISHNAMURTI: What are my rules and principles of life? None. Please follow what I say, critically and intelligently. Don't object, "Must we not have rules? Otherwise our lives would be chaos." Don't think in terms of opposites. Think intrinsically with regard to what I am saying. Why do you want rules and principles? Why do you want them, you who have so many principles by which you are shaping, controlling, directing your lives? Why do you want rules? "Because," you reply, "we cannot live without them. Without rules and principles we would do exactly the things that we want to do; we might overeat or overindulge in sex, possess more than we should. We must have principles and rules by which to guide our lives." In other words, to restrain yourselves without understanding, you must have these principles and rules. This is the whole artificial structure of your lives—restraint, control, suppression—for behind this structure is the idea of gain, security, comfort, which causes fear.

But the man who is not pursuing acquisitiveness, the man who is not caught up in the promise of reward or the threat of punishment, does not require rules; the man who tries to live and understand each experience completely does not need principles and rules, for it is only conditioning beliefs which demand conformity. When thought is unbound, unconditioned, it will then know itself as eternal. You try to control thought, to shape and direct it, because you have established a goal, a conclusion towards which you wish to go, and that end is always what you desire it to be, though you may call it God, perfection, reality.

You ask me concerning my conception of God, truth, beauty, love. But I say, if someone describes truth, if someone tells you the nature of truth, beware of that person. For truth cannot be described; truth cannot be measured by words. You nod your heads in agreement, but tomorrow you will again be trying to measure truth, to find a description of it. Your attitude towards life is based on the principle of creating a mold, and then fitting yourselves into that mold. Christianity offers you one mold, Hinduism offers another, Mohammedanism, Buddhism, Theosophy offer still others. But why do you want a mold? Why do you cherish preconceived ideas? All that you can know is pain, suffering, and passing joys. But you want to escape from them; you don't try to understand the cause of pain, the depth of suffering. Rather, you turn to its opposite for your consolation. In your sorrow, you say that God is love, that God is just, merciful. Mentally and emotionally you turn to this ideal of love, justice, and shape yourselves after that pattern. But you can understand love only when you are no longer possessive; from possessiveness arises all sorrow. Yet your system of thought and emotion is based on possessiveness, so how can you know of love?

So your first concern is to free the mind and heart from possessiveness, and you can do that only when that possessiveness becomes a poison to you, when you feel the suffering, the agony which that poison causes. Now you are trying to escape from that suffering. You want me to tell you what my ideal of love is, my ideal of beauty, so that you can make of it another pattern, another standard, or compare my ideal with yours, hoping thereby to understand. Understanding does not come through comparison. I have no ideal, no pattern. Beauty is not divorced from action. True action is the very harmony of your whole being. What does that mean to you? It means nothing but empty words, because your actions are disharmonious, because you think one thing and act another.

You can find enduring freedom, truth, beauty, love, which are one and the same, only when you no longer seek them. Please try to understand what I am saying. My meaning is subtle only in the sense that it can be carried out infinitely. I say that your very search is destroying your love, destroying your sense of beauty, of truth, because your search is but an escape, a flight from conflict. And beauty, love, truth, that Godhead of understanding, is not found by running away from conflict; it lies in the very conflict itself.

January 1, 1934

Fifth Talk at Adyar

This morning I want to explain something that requires very delicate thinking; and I hope you will listen, or rather, try to understand what I am going to say, not with opposition but with intelligent criticism. I am going to talk on a subject which, if understood, if thoroughly gone into, will give you an entirely new outlook on life. Also I would beg you not to think in terms of opposites. When I say that certainty is a barrier, don't think that you must therefore be uncertain; when I speak of the futility of assurance, please do not think that you must seek insecurity.

When you really consider, you will perceive that mind is constantly seeking certainties, assurances; it is seeking the certainty of a goal, of a conclusion, of a purpose in life. You inquire, "Is there a divine plan, is there predetermination, is there not free will? Cannot we, realizing that plan, trying to understand it, guide ourselves by that plan?" In other words, you want assurance, certainty, so that mind and heart can shape themselves after it, can conform to it. And when you inquire for the path to truth, you are really seeking assurance, certainty, security.

When you speak of a path to truth, it implies that truth, this living reality, is not in the present, but somewhere in the distance, somewhere in the future. Now to me, truth is fulfillment, and to fulfillment there can be no path. So it seems, to me at least, that the first illusion in which you are caught is this desire for assurance, this desire for certainty, this inquiry after a path, a way, a mode of living whereby you can attain the desired goal, which is truth. Your conviction that truth exists only in the distant future implies imitation. When you inquire what truth is, you are really asking to be told the path which leads to truth. Then you want to know which system to follow, which mode, which discipline, to help you on the way to truth.

But to me there is no path to truth; truth is not to be understood through any system, through any path. A path implies a goal, a static end, and therefore a conditioning of the mind and the heart by that end, which necessarily demands discipline, control, acquisitiveness. This discipline, this control, becomes a burden; it robs you of freedom and conditions your action in daily life. Inquiry after truth implies a goal, a static end, which you are seeking. And that you are seeking a goal shows that your mind is searching for assurance, certainty. To attain this certainty, mind desires a path, a system, a method which it can follow, and this assurance you think to find by conditioning mind and heart through self-discipline, self-control, suppression.

But truth is a reality that cannot be understood by following any path. Truth is not a conditioning, a shaping of the mind and heart, but a constant fulfillment, a fulfillment in action. That you inquire after truth implies that you believe in a path to truth, and this is the first illusion in which you are caught. In that there is imitativeness, distortion. Now please don't say, "Without an end, a purpose, life becomes chaotic." I want to explain to you the falseness of this conception. I say that everyone must find out for himself what truth is, but this does not mean that each one must lay down a path for himself, that each one must travel an individual path. It does not mean that at all, but it does mean that each one must understand truth for himself. I hope that you see the distinction between the two. When you have to understand, to discover, to experiment with life, a path becomes a hindrance. But if you must hew out a path for yourself, then there is an individual point of view, a narrow, limited point of view. Truth is the movement of eternal becoming, so it is not an end, it is not static. Hence the search for a path is born of ignorance, of illusion. But when mind is pliable, freed from beliefs and memories, freed from the conditioning of society, then in that action, in that pliability, there is the infinite movement of life.

A true scientist, as I said the other day, is one who is continually experimenting, without a result in view. He does not seek results, which are merely the byproducts of his search. So when you are seeking, experimenting, your action becomes merely a byproduct of this movement. A scientist who seeks a result is not a true scientist. He is not truly seeking. But if he is searching without the idea of gain, then, though he may have results in his search, these results are of secondary importance to him. Now you are concerned with results, and therefore your search is not living, dynamic. You are seeking an end, a result, and therefore your action becomes increasingly limited. Only when you search without desire for success, achievement, does your life become continuously free, rich. This does not mean that in your search there will be no action, no result; it means that action, results, will not be your first consideration.

As a river waters the trees that grow on its banks, so this movement of search nourishes our actions. Cooperative action, action bound together, is society. You want to create a perfect society. But there can be no such perfect society, because perfection is not an end, a culmination. Perfection is fulfillment, constantly in movement. Society cannot live up to an ideal; nor can man, for society is man. If society tries to fashion itself according to an ideal, if man tries to live according to an ideal, neither is truly fulfilling; both are in decay. But if man is in this movement of fulfillment, then his action will be harmonious, complete; his action will not be mere imitation of an ideal.

So to me, civilization is not an achievement but a constant movement. Civilizations reach a certain height, exist for a time, and then decline, because in them there is no fulfillment for man, but only the constant imitation of a pattern. There is completeness, fulfillment, only when mind and heart are in this constant movement of fulfillment, of search. Now don't say, "Will there never be an end to search?" You are no longer searching for a conclusion, a certainty; therefore living is not a series of culminations, but a continual movement, fulfillment. If society is merely approxi- mating to an ideal, society will soon decay. If civilization is merely an achievement of individuals collected as a group, it is already in the process of decay. But if society, if civilization, is the outcome of this constant movement in fulfillment, then it will endure, it will be the completeness of man.

To me, perfection is not the achievement of a goal, of an ideal, of an absolute, through this idea of progress. Perfection is the fulfillment of thought, of emotion, and therefore of action—fulfillment which can exist at any time. Therefore perfection is free of time; it is not the result of time.

Well, sirs, there are many questions, and I shall try to answer them as concisely as possible.

Question: If a war breaks out tomorrow and the conscription law comes into force at once to compel you to take up arms, will you join the army and shout, "To arms, to arms!" as the Theosophical leaders did in 1914, or will you defy war?

KRISHNAMURTI: Don't let us concern ourselves with what the Theosophical leaders did in 1914. Where there is nationalism there must be war. Where there are several sovereign governments there must be war. It is inevitable. Personally, I would not affiliate myself with war activities of any kind because I am not a nationalist, class-minded, or possessive. I would not join the army, nor give help in any way. I would not join any organization that exists merely for the purpose of healing the wounded and sending them back to the field to get wounded again. But I would come to an understanding about these matters before war threatened.

Now, for the moment at least, there is no actual war. When war comes, inflaming propaganda is made, lies are told against the supposed enemy; patriotism and hatred are stirred up, people lose their heads in their supposed devotion to their country. "God is on our side," they shout, "and evil with the enemy." And throughout the centuries they have shouted these same words. Both sides fight in the name of God; on both sides priests bless—marvelous idea—the armaments. Now they will even bless the bombing planes, so eaten up are they with that disease which creates war: nationalism, their own class, or individual security. So while we are at peace—though "peace" is an odd word to describe the mere cessation of armed hostilities—while we are, at all events, not actually killing each other on the field of battle, we can understand what are the causes of war, and disentangle ourselves from those causes. And if you are clear in your understanding, in your freedom, with all that that freedom implies—that you may be shot for refusing to comply with war mania—then you will act truly when the moment comes, whatever your action may be.

So the question is not what you will do when war comes, but what you are doing now to prevent war. You, who are always shouting at me for my negative attitude, what are you doing now to wipe out the very cause of war itself? I am talking about the real cause of all wars, not only of the immediate war that inevitably threatens while each nation is piling up armaments. As long as the spirit of nationalism exists, the spirit of class distinction, of particularity, and possessiveness, there must be war. You cannot prevent it. If you are really facing the problem of war, as you should be now, you will have to take a definite action, a definite, positive action; and by your action you will help to awaken intelligence, which is the only preventive of war. But to do that, you must free yourself of this disease of "my God, my country, my family, my house."

Question: What is the cause of fear, particularly of the fear of death? Is it possible ever to be completely rid of that fear? Why does fear universally exist, even though common sense speaks against it, considering that death is inevitable and is a perfectly natural occurrence?

KRISHNAMURTI: To him who is constantly fulfilling there is no fear of death. If we are really complete each moment, each day, then we know no fear of tomorrow. But our minds create incompleteness of action, and so the fear of tomorrow. We have been trained by religion, by society, to incompleteness, to postponement, and this serves us as an escape from fear, because we have tomorrow to complete that which we cannot fulfill today.

But just a moment, please. I wish you would look at this problem neither from the background of your traditions, modern or ancient, nor through your commitment to reincarnation, but very simply. Then you will understand truth, which will free you wholly from fear. To me, the idea of reincarnation is mere postponement. Even though you may believe profoundly in reincarnation, you still have fear and sorrow when someone dies, or fear of your own death. You may say, "I shall live on the other side; I shall be much happier, and shall do better work there than I can do here." But your words are merely words. They cannot quiet the gnawing fear that is always in your heart. So let us tackle this problem of fear rather than the question of reincarnation. When you have understood what fear is, you will see the unimportance of reincarnation; then we shall not even need to discuss it. Don't ask me what happens after death to the man who is crippled, to the man who is blind in this life. If you understand the central point, you will then consider such questions intelligently.

You are afraid of death because your days are incomplete, because there is never fulfillment in your actions. Isn't that so? When your mind is caught up in a belief, belief in the past or in the future, you cannot understand experience fully. When your mind is prejudiced, there can be no complete understanding of experience in action. Hence you say that you must have tomorrow in which to complete that action, and you are afraid that tomorrow will not come. But if you can complete your action in the present, then infinity is before you. What prevents you from living completely? Please don't ask me how to complete action, which is the negative way of looking at life. If I tell you how, then you will merely make your action imitative, and in that there is no completeness. What you will have to do is to discover what prevents you from living completely, infinitely; and that, you will find, is this illusion of an end, of a certainty, in which your mind is caught, this illusion of attaining a goal. If you are constantly looking to the future in which to achieve, to gain, to succeed, to conquer, your action in the present must be limited, must be incomplete. When you are acting according to your beliefs or principles, naturally your action must be limited, incomplete. When your action is based on faith, that action is not fulfillment; it is merely the result of faith.

So there are many hindrances in our minds; there is the instinct of possessiveness, cultivated by society, and the instinct of non-possessiveness, also cultivated by society. When there is conformity and imitation, when mind is bound by authority, there can be no fulfillment, and from this there arises fear of death and the many other fears that lie hidden in the subconscious. Have I made my answer clear? We shall deal with this problem again, in a different way.

Question: How does memory arise, and what are the different kinds of memory? You have said, "In the present is contained the whole of eternity." Please go more fully into this statement. Does it mean that the past and the future have no subjective reality to the man who lives wholly in the present? Can past errors, or, as one might call them, gaps in understanding, be adjusted or remedied in the ever continuous present in which the idea of a future can have no place?

KRISHNAMURTI: If you have followed the previous answer you will understand the cause of memory; you will see how memory arises. If you don't understand an incident, if you don't live completely in an experience, then the memory of that incident, experience, lingers in your mind. When you have an experience that you cannot fully fathom, the significance of which you cannot see, then your mind returns to that experience. Thus memory is created. It is born, in other words, from incompleteness in action. And since you have many layers of memories arising from incomplete actions, there comes into being that self-consciousness which you call the ego, and which is nothing but a series of memories, an illusion without reality, without substance either here or in the highest plane.

There are various kinds of memory. For instance, there is the memory of the past, as when you recollect a beautiful scene. But are you interested in this? I see so many people looking all around. If you are not really interested in following this, we shall discuss nationalism and golf or tennis. (Laughter)

Now, there is the memory which is associated with the pleasure of yesterday. That is, you have enjoyed a beautiful scene; you have admired the sunset or the moonlight on the waters. Then later, say when you are in your office, your mind returns to that scene. Why? Because when you are in an unpleasant and ugly environment, when your mind and heart are caught up in what is not pleasant, your mind tends automatically to return to the pleasant experience of yesterday. This is one type of memory. Instead of changing conditions around you, instead of altering the environment about you, you retrace the steps of a pleasant experience and dwell on that memory, supporting and tolerating the unpleasant because you feel that you cannot alter it. Therefore the past lingers in the present. Have I made that clear?

Then there is the memory, pleasant or unpleasant, which precipitates itself into the mind even though you do not want it. Uninvited past incidents come into your mind because you are not vitally interested in the present, because you are not fully alive to the present.

Another kind of memory is that concerned with beliefs, principles, ideals. All ideals and principles are really dead, things of the past. The memory of ideals persists when you cannot meet or understand the full movement of life. You want a measure to gauge that movement, a standard by which to judge experience; and acting in the measure of that standard you call living up to an ideal. Because you cannot understand the beauty of life, because you cannot live in its fullness, its glory, you want an ideal, a principle, an imitative pattern, to give significance to your living.

Again, there is the memory of self-discipline, which is will. Will is nothing else but memory. After all, you begin to discipline yourself through the pattern of memory. "I did this yesterday," you say, "and I have made up my mind not to do it today." So action, thought, emotion, in the vast majority of cases, is entirely the result of the past; it is based on memory. Therefore such action is never fulfillment. It always leaves a scar of memory, and the accumulation of many such scars becomes self-consciousness, the 'I', which is always preventing you from understanding completely. It is a vicious circle, this consciousness of the 'I'.

So we have innumerable memories, memories of discipline and will, of ideals and beliefs, of pleasant attractions and unpleasant disturbances. Please follow what I am saying. Don't be disturbed by others. If this does not interest you, if your mind is constantly wandering, you may as well leave. I can go on, but what I say will mean nothing to you if you are not listening.

We are constantly acting through this veil of memories, and therefore our action is always incomplete. Hence we take comfort in the idea of progress; we think of a series of lives tending towards perfection. Thus we have never a day, never a moment, of rich, full completeness, because these memories are always impeding, curtailing, limiting, trammeling our action.

To return to the question, "Does it mean that the past and the future have no subjective reality to the man who lives wholly in the present?" Don't ask me that question. If you are interested, if you want to eradicate fear, if you really want to live richly, worship the day in which the mind is free of the past and of the future, then you will know how to live completely.

"Can past errors, or, as one might call them, gaps in understanding, be adjusted or remedied in the ever-continuous present in which the idea of a future can have no place?" Do you understand the question? As I have not previously read this question, I must think as I go along. You can remedy past gaps in understanding only in the present, at least, that is my view. Introspection, the process of analysis of the past, does not yield understanding, because you cannot have understanding from a dead thing. You can have understanding only in the ever-active, living present. This question opens up a wide field, but I don't want to go into that now. It is only in the moment of the present, in the moment of crisis, in the moment of tremendous, acute questioning born of full action, that past gaps in understanding can be remedied, destroyed; this cannot be done by looking into the past, examining your past actions.

Let me take an example which will, I hope, make the matter clear to you. Suppose that you are class-minded and are unconscious of this. But the training in that class consciousness, the memory of it, still remains with you, is still a part of you. Now to free the mind from that memory or training, don't turn back to the past and say, "I am going to examine my action to see if that action is bound by class consciousness." Don't do this, but rather, in your feelings, actions, be fully aware, and then this class-conscious memory will precipitate itself in your mind; in that moment of awakened intelligence, mind begins to free itself of this bondage.

Again, if you are cruel—and most people are unconscious of their cruelty—don't examine your actions to find out whether you are cruel or not. In that way you will never find out, you will never understand; for then the mind is constantly looking to cruelty and not to action, and is therefore destroying action. But if you are fully aware in your action, if your mind and heart are wholly alive in action, in the moment of action you will see that you are cruel. Thus you will find out the actual cause, the very root of cruelty, not the mere incidents of cruelty. But you can do this only in the fullness of action, when you are fully aware in action. Gaps in understanding cannot be bridged over through introspection, through examination, or through analysis of a past incident. This can be done only in the moment of action itself, which must ever be timeless.

I don't know how many of you have understood this. The problem is really very simple, and I shall try to explain it more simply. I am not using philosophical or technical terms, because I don't know any. I am speaking in everyday language.

Mind is accustomed to analyze the past, to dissect action in order to understand action. But I say you cannot understand in this way, for such analysis always limits action. Concrete examples of such limitation of action can be seen here in India and elsewhere, cases where action has almost ceased. Don't try to analyze your action. Rather, if you want to find out whether you are class-conscious, whether you are self-righteous, whether you are nationalistic, bigoted, authority-bound, imitative—if you are really interested in discovering these hindrances, then become fully aware, become conscious of what you are doing. Don't be merely observant, don't merely look at your action objectively, from the outside, but become fully aware, both mentally and emotionally, aware with your whole being in the moment of action. Then you will see that the many impeding memories will precipitate themselves in your mind and prevent you from acting fully, completely. In that awareness, in that flame, the mind will be able without effort to free itself from these past hindrances. Don't ask me, "How?" Simply try. Your minds are always asking for a method, asking how to do this or that. But there is no "how." Experiment, and you will discover.

Question: Since temple entry for Harijans helps to break down one of the many forms of division between man and man which exist in India, do you support this movement which is being zealously advocated in this country just now?

KRISHNAMURTI: Now please understand that I am not attacking any personality. Don't ask, "Are you attacking Gandhiji?" and so on. I do not think that the problem of class distinction in India or elsewhere is going to be solved by allowing Harijans to enter temples. Class distinction ceases only when there are no more temples, no more churches, when there are no more mosques and no more synagogues; for truth, God, is not in a stone, in a carved image; it is not contained within four walls. That reality is not in any of these temples, nor does it lie in any of the ceremonies performed in them. So why bother about who enters and who does not enter these temples?

Most of you smile and agree, but you don't feel these things. You don't feel that reality is everywhere, in yourselves, in all things. To you, reality is personified, limited, confined in a temple. To you, reality is a symbol, whether it be Christian or Buddhist, whether it is associated with an image or with no image. But reality is not a symbol. Reality has no symbol. It is. You cannot carve it into an image, limit it by a stone or by a ceremony or by a belief. When these things no longer exist, the quarrels between man and man will cease, as when nationalism—which has been cultivated through centuries for purposes of exploitations—no longer exists, there will be no more wars. Temples, with all their superstitions, with their exploiters, the priests, have been created by you. Priests cannot exist by themselves. Priestcraft may exist as a means of livelihood, but that will soon disappear when economic conditions change, and the priests will alter their calling. The cause, the root of all these things, of temples, nationalism, exploitation, possessiveness, lies in your desire for security, comfort. Out of your own acquisitiveness, you create innumerable exploiters, whether they are capitalists, priests, teachers, or gurus, and you become the exploited. As long as this acquisitiveness, this self-security exists, there will be wars, there will be caste distinctions.

You cannot get rid of poison by merely discussing, by talking, by organizing. When you as individuals awaken to the absurdity, the falseness, the hideousness of all these things, when you really feel within you the gross cruelty of all this, only then will you create organizations of which you will not become slaves. But if you don't awaken, organizations will come into being that will make of you their slaves. That is what is happening now throughout the world. For God's sake, awaken to these things, at least those of you who think! Don't invent new ceremonies, create new temples, new secret orders. They are merely other forms of exclusiveness. There cannot be understanding, wisdom, as long as this spirit of exclusiveness exists, as long as you are looking for gain, for security. Wisdom is not in proportion to progress. Wisdom is spontaneous, natural; it cannot result from progress; it exists in fulfillment.

So even though all of you, Brahmins and non-Brahmins, are allowed to enter temples, that will not dissolve class distinctions. For you will go at a later hour than the Harijans; you will wash yourselves more carefully or less carefully. That poison of exclusiveness, that canker in your hearts, has not been rooted out, and nobody is going to root it out for you. Communism and revolution may come and sweep away all the temples in this country, but that poison will continue to exist, only in a different form. Isn't that so? Don't nod your heads in agreement, because the next moment you will be doing the very thing against which I am talking. I am not judging you.

There is only one way to tackle all these problems, and that is fundamentally, not superficially, symptomatically. If you approach them fundamentally, there must be tremendous revolution; father will stand against son, brother against brother. It will be a time of the sword, of warfare, not of peace, because there is so much corruption and decay. But you all want peace, you want tranquillity at any price, with all this cankerous poison in your hearts and minds. I tell you that when a man seeks truth he is against all these cruelties, barriers, exploitations; he does not offer you comfort; he does not bring you peace. On the contrary, he turns to the sword because he sees the many false institutions, the corrupt conditions that exist. That is why I say that if you are seeking truth you must stand alone—it may be against society, against civilization. But unfortunately very few people are truly seeking. I am not judging you. I am saying that your own actions should reveal to you that you are building up rather than destroying those walls of class distinction; that you are safeguarding rather than demolishing them, cherishing rather than tearing them down, because you are continually seeking self-glorification, security, comfort, in one form or another.

Question: Can one not attain liberation and truth, this changing, eternal movement of life, even though one belongs to a hundred societies? Can one not have inward freedom, leaving the links outwardly unbroken?

KRISHNAMURTI: Realization of truth has nothing to do with any society. Therefore you may belong or you may not. But if you are using societies, social or religious bodies, as a means to understand truth, you will have ashes in your mouth.

"Can one not have inward freedom, leaving the links outwardly unbroken?" Yes, but along that way lie deceit, self-deception, cunning, and hypocrisy, unless one is supremely intelligent and constantly aware. You can say, "I perform all these ceremonies, I belong to various societies, because I don't want to break my connection with them. I follow gurus, which I know is absurd, but I want to have peace with my family, live harmoniously with my neighbor and not bring discord to an already confused world." But we have lived in such deceptions so long, our minds have become so cunning, so subtly hypocritical, that now we cannot discover or understand truth unless we break these ties. We have so dulled our minds and hearts that, unless we break the bonds that bind us and thereby create a conflict, we cannot find out if we are truly free or not. But a man of true understanding—and there are very few—will find out for himself. Then there will be no links that he desires either to retain or to break. Society will despise him, his friends will leave him, his relations will have nothing to do with him; all the negative elements will break themselves away from him, he will not have to break away from them. But that course means wise perception; it means fulfillment in action, not postponement. And man will postpone as long as mind and heart are caught up in fear.

January 2, 1934

Sixth Talk At Adyar

As this is my last talk here, I shall first answer the questions that have been asked me, and then conclude with a brief talk. But before I proceed to answer the questions, I should like again to thank Mr. Warrington, the president pro tem, for inviting me to speak at Adyar and for his great friendliness.

As I said at the beginning of my talks, I am really not interested in attacking your society. In saying this I am not going back on what I have said. I think that all spiritual organizations are a hindrance to man, for one cannot find truth through any organization.

Question: Which is the wiser course to take—to protect and shelter the ignorant by advice and guidance, or to let them find out through their own experience and suffering, even though it may take them a whole lifetime to extricate themselves from the effects of such experience and suffering?

KRISHNAMURTI: I would say neither; I would say help them to be intelligent, which is quite a different thing. When you want to guide and protect the ignorant, you are really giving them a shelter which you have created for yourself. And to take the opposite point of view, that is, to let them drift through experiences, is equally foolish. But we can help another by true education—not this modern disease we call education, this passing through examinations and universities. I don't call that education at all. It is merely stultifying the mind. But that is a different question.

If we can help another to become intelligent, that is all we need do. But that is the most difficult thing in the world, for intelligence does not offer shelter from the struggles and turmoils of life, nor does it give comfort; it only creates understanding. Intelligence is free, untrammelled, without fear or superficiality. We can help another to free himself from acquisitiveness, from the many illusions and hindrances which bind him, only when we begin to free ourselves. But we have this extraordinary attitude of wanting to improve the masses while we ourselves are still ignorant, still caught up in superstition, in acquisitiveness. When we begin to free ourselves, then we shall help another naturally and truly.

Question: While I agree with you as to the necessity for the individual to discover superstitions, and even religions as such, do you not think that an organized movement in that direction is useful and necessary, particularly as in its absence the powerful vested interests, namely, the high priests in all the principal places of pilgrimage, will continue to exploit those who are still caught up in superstitions and religious dogmas and beliefs? Since you are not an individualist, why don't you stay with us and spread your message instead of going to other lands and returning to us when your words will probably have been forgotten?

KRISHNAMURTI: So you conclude organizations are necessary. I shall explain what I mean by organizations. There must be organizations for the welfare of man, the physical welfare of man, but not for the purpose of leading him to truth. For truth is not to be found through any organization, by any path, by any method. Merely helping man, through an organization, to destroy his superstitions, his beliefs, his dogmas, will not give him understanding. He will but create new beliefs in place of the old which you have destroyed. That is what is happening throughout the world. You destroy one set of beliefs, and man creates another; you take away a particular temple, and he creates another.

But if individuals, out of their understanding, create intelligence about them, create understanding about them, then organizations will come into being naturally. Now we start first with organizations and then say, "How can we live and adjust ourselves to all the demands of these organizations?" In other words, we put organization first and individuals afterwards. I have seen this in every society: individuals go to the wall while organization, that mysterious thing in which you are all working, becomes a force, a crushing power for exploitation. That is why I feel that freedom from superstition, from beliefs and dogmas, can begin only with the individual. If the individual truly understands, then through his understanding, through the action of that understanding, he will naturally create organizations which will not be instruments of exploitation. But if we put organization first, as most people do, we are not destroying superstition but only creating substitutions.

Take, for example, the possessive instinct. Law sanctifies you, blesses you, in the possession of your wife, your children, and your properties; it honors you. Then if communism comes, it honors the person who possesses nothing. Now to me, both systems are the same; they are the same in contrary terms, in opposition. When you are forced to a certain action, shaped, molded by circumstance, by society, by an organization, in that action there is no understanding. You are merely exchanging masters. Organizations will result naturally if there are people who truly feel and are intelligent about these things. But if you are concerned merely with organization, you destroy that vital feeling, that intelligent, creative thinking, because you have to consider the organization, the revenue of the organization, and the beliefs on which the organization is founded. You have to consider all the commitments, and therefore neither you nor the organization will ever be fluidic, alive, pliable. Your organization is much more important to you than freedom. If you really think about this, you will see.

A few individuals create organizations out of their enthusiasm, their enlivened interest, and the rest of the people fit into these organizations and become slaves to them. But if there were creative intelligence— which hardly exists in this country, because you are all followers, saying, "Tell me what to do, what discipline, what method to follow," like so many sheep—if you were truly free, if you had creative intelligence, then out of that would come action; you would tackle the problem fundamentally, that is, through education, through schools, through literature, through art; not through this perpetual talk about organizations. To have schools, to have the right kind of education, you must have organization; but all that will come naturally if individuals, if a few people are truly awake, are truly intelligent.

"Since you are not an individualist, why don't you stay with us and spread your message instead of going away to other lands and returning to us when your words will probably have been forgotten?" I have promised this time to go to other countries, South America, Australia, the United States. But when I come back I intend to stay a long time in India. (Applause) Don't bother to applaud. Then I want to do things quite differently.

Question: Which comes first, the individual or organization?

KRISHNAMURTI: That is very simple. Are you concerned with patchwork, which implies the modification of nationalism, of class distinction, of possessiveness, of inheritance, fighting over who should enter temples, doing a little bit of alteration here and there: or do you desire a complete, radical change? That change means freedom from self-consciousness, from the limited 'I' which creates nationalism, fear, distinctions, possessiveness. If you perceive fundamentally the falseness of these things, then there comes true action. So you have to understand and act. As you are, you are merely glorifying self-consciousness, and I feel that basically all religious societies are doing that, though in theory, in books, their teachings may be different. You know, I have often been told that the Upanishads agree with what I say. People tell me, "You are saying exactly what Buddha said, what Christ said," or, "Fundamentally you are teaching what Theosophists stand for." But that is all theory. You must really think about this, you must be really honest, frank. When I say "honest," "frank," I do not mean sincere, for a fool can be sincere. (Replying to an interruption) Please just follow this. A lunatic who holds steadfastly to one idea, one belief, is sincere. Most people are sincere, only they have innumerable beliefs. Instead of one, they have many, and they are trying to be sincere in holding to them.

If you are really frank, honest, you will see that your whole thought and action is based on this patchwork, this limited consciousness, this self-glorification, this desire to become somebody either spiritually or in the physical world. If you act and work with that attitude, then what you do must inevitably lead to patchwork; but if you act truly, then for you this whole structure has collapsed. For yourself you want glorification, you want safety, you want security, you want comfort; so you have to decide to do one thing or the other; you cannot do both. If frankly, honestly, you pursue security and comfort, then you will find out their emptiness. If you are really honest with regard to this self-glorification, then you will perceive its shallowness.

But unfortunately our minds are not clear. We are biased, we are influenced; tradition and habit bind us. We have innumerable commitments. We have organizations to keep up. We have committed ourselves to certain ideas, to certain beliefs. And economics play a large part in our lives. We say, "If I think differently from my associates, from my neighbors, I may lose my job. Then how could I earn a living?" So we go on as before. That is what I call hypocrisy, not facing facts directly.

Perceive truly and act; action follows perception, they are inseparable. Find out what you desire to do, patchwork or complete action. Now you are laying emphasis on work, and therefore primarily on patchwork.

Question: Reincarnation explains much that is otherwise full of mystery and puzzle in life. It shows, among other things, that highly cherished personal relationships of any one incarnation do not necessarily continue in the next. Thus, strangers are in turn our relations and vice versa; this reveals the kinship of the human soul, a fact which, if properly understood, should make for true brotherhood. Hence, if reincarnation is a natural law and you happen to know that it is such; or, equally, if you happen to know that there is no such law, why do you not say so? Why do you always prefer in your answers to leave this highly important and interesting subject surrounded with the halo of mystery?

KRISHNAMURTI: I don't think it is important; I don't think it solves anything fundamentally. I don't think it makes you understand that fundamental, living, unique unity, which is not the unity of uniformity. You say, "I was married to someone last life, and I am married to a different person in this life; does not this bring about a feeling of brotherhood, or affection, or unity?" What an extraordinary way of thinking! You prefer the brotherhood of a mystery to the brotherhood of reality. You would be affectionate because of relationship, not because affection is natural, spontaneous, pure. You want to believe because belief comforts you. That is why there are so many class distinctions, wars, and the constant use of that absurd word *tolerance.* If you had no divisions of beliefs, no sets of ideals, if you were really complete human beings, then there would be true brotherhood, true affection, not this artificial thing that you call brotherhood.

The question of reincarnation I have dealt with so often that I shall speak of it only briefly now. You may not consider at all what I say; or you may examine it, just as you like. I am afraid you will not consider it—though that does not matter—because you are committed to certain ideas, to certain organizations, bound by authority, by traditions.

To me, the ego, that limited consciousness, is the result of conflict. Inherently it has no value; it is an illusion. It comes into being through lack of understanding which in turn creates conflict, and out of this conflict grows self-consciousness or limited consciousness. You cannot perfect that self-consciousness through time; time does not free the mind from that consciousness. Please make no mistake; time will not free you from this self-consciousness, because time is merely postponement of understanding. The further you postpone an action, the less you understand it. You are conscious only when there is conflict; and in ecstasy, in true perception, there is spontaneous action in which there is no conflict. You are then not conscious of yourself as an entity, as the 'I'. Yet you desire to protect that accumulation of ignorance which you call the 'I', that accumulation from which springs this idea of more and more, that center of growth which is not life, which is but an illusion. So while you are looking to time to bring about perfection, self-consciousness merely increases. Time will never free you from that self-consciousness, that limited consciousness. What will free the mind is the completeness of understanding in action; that is, when your mind and heart are acting harmoniously, when they are no longer biased, tethered to a belief, bound by a dogma, by fear, by false value, then there is freedom. And that freedom is the ecstasy of perception.

You know, it would really be of great interest if one of you who believe so fundamentally in reincarnation would discuss the subject with me. I have discussed it with many, but all they can say is, "We believe in reincarnation, it explains so many things," and that settles the question. One cannot discuss with people who are convinced of their beliefs, who are positive of their knowledge. When a man says that he knows, the matter is finished; and you worship the man who says, "I know," because his positive statement, his certainty, gives you comfort, shelter.

Whether you believe in reincarnation or not seems to me a very trivial matter; that belief is like a toy, it is pleasant; it does not solve a thing, because it is merely a postponement. It is merely an explanation, and explanations are as dust to the man who is seeking. But unfortunately you are choked with dust, you have explanations for everything. For every suffering you have a logical, suitable explanation. If a man is blind, you account for his hard lot in this life by means of reincarnation. Inequalities in life you explain away by reincarnation, by the idea of evolution. So, with explanations, you have settled the many questions concerning man, and you have ceased to live. The fullness of life precludes all explanations. To the man who is really suffering, explanations are like so much dust and ashes. But to the man who is seeking comfort, explanations are necessary and excellent. There is no such thing as comfort. There is only under- standing, and understanding is not bound by belief or by certainties.

You say, "I know that reincarnation is true." Well, what of it? Reincarnation, that is, the process of accumulation, of growth, of gain, is merely the burden of effort, the continuance of effort; and I say there is a way of living spontaneously, without this continual struggle, and that is by understanding, which is not the result of accumulation, growth. This understanding, perception, comes to him who is not bound by fear, by self-consciousness.

Question: The man who remains unmoved in the face of dangers and trials in life, such as the opposition of his fellow men to a course of action, is always a man of steadfast will and sterling character. Public schools in England and elsewhere recognize the importance of developing will and character, which are commonly regarded as the best equipment with which to embark on life, for will insures success, and character insures a moral sanction. What have you to say about will and character, and what is their true value to the individual?

KRISHNAMURTI: The first part of this question serves as the background of the question itself which is, "What have you to say about will and character, and what is their true value to the individual?" None, from my point of view. But that does not mean that you must be without will, without character. Don't think in terms of opposites. What do you mean by will? Will is the outcome of resistance. If you don't understand a thing, you want to conquer it. All conquering is but slavery and therefore resistance; and out of that resistance grows will, the idea of "I must and I must not.'' But perception, understanding, frees the mind and heart from resistance, and so from this constant battle of ''I must and I must not.''

The same thing applies to character. Character is only the power to resist the many encroachments of society upon you. The more will you have, the greater is self-consciousness, the 'I', because the 'I' is the result of conflict, and will is born out of resistance which creates self-consciousness. When does resistance come into being? When you pursue acquisition, gain, when you desire to succeed, when you are pursuing virtue, when there is imitation and fear.

All this may sound absurd to you because you are caught up in the conflict of acquisition, and you will naturally say, ''What can a man be without will, without conflict, without resistance?'' I say that is the only way to live, without resistance, which does not mean nonresistance; it does not mean having no will, no purposefulness, being blown hither and thither. Will is the outcome of false values; and when there is understanding of what is true, conflict disappears and with it the developing of resistance which is called will. Will and the development of character, which are as the colored glass that perverts the clear light, cannot free man; they cannot give him understanding. On the contrary, they will limit man.

But a mind that understands, a mind that is pliable, alert—which does not mean the cunning mind of a clever lawyer, a type which is so prevalent in India, a type which is destructive—the mind that is pliable, I say, the mind that is not bound, not possessive, to such a mind there is no resistance because it understands; it perceives the falseness of resistance, for it is like water. Water will assume any shape, and still it remains water. But you want to be shaped after a particular pattern because you have not complete understanding. I say that when you fulfill, act completely, you will no longer seek a pattern and exert your will to fit into that pattern, for in true understanding there is constant movement which is eternal life.

Question: You said yesterday that memory, which is the residue of accumulated actions, gives rise to the idea of time and hence progress. Please develop the idea further with special reference to the contribution of progress to human happiness.

KRISHNAMURTI: There is progress in the field of mechanical science, progress with regard to machines, motorcars, modern conveniences, and the conquering of space. But I am not referring to that kind of progress, because progress in mechanical science must ever be transient; in that there can never be fulfillment for man. I must talk very briefly because I have many questions to answer. I hope that what I say will be clear; if not, we shall continue at a later time.

There can be no fulfillment for man in mechanical progress. There will be better cars, better airplanes, better machines, but fulfillment is not to be realized through this continual process of mechanical perfection—not that I am against machines. When we talk of progress as applied to what we call individual growth, what do we mean? We mean the acquiring of more knowledge, greater virtue, which is not fulfillment. What is called virtue here may be considered vice in another society. Society has developed the concepts of good and bad. Inherently there is no such thing as good or bad. Don't think in terms of opposites. You have to think fundamentally, intrinsically.

To me, through progress there cannot be completeness of action, because progress implies time, and time does not lead to fulfillment. Fulfillment lies in the present only, not in the future. What prevents you from living completely in the present? The past, with its many memories and hindrances.

I shall put it differently. While there is choice, there must be this so-called progress in things essential and unessential; but the moment you possess the essential, it has already become the unessential. And so we go on, continually moving from unessential to essential, which in its turn becomes the unessential, and this substitution we call progress. But perfection is fulfillment, which is the harmony of mind and heart in action. There cannot be such harmony if your mind is caught up by a belief, by a memory, by a prejudice, by a want. Since you are caught up in these things, you must become free of them, and you can become free only when you as an individual have found out their true significance. That is, you can act harmoniously only when you discover their true significance by questioning, by doubting their existing values.

I am sorry but I must now stop answering questions. Many questions have been asked me with regard to the Theosophical Society, whether I would accept the presidency if it were offered me, and what would be my policy if I were elected; whether the Theosophical Society, which strives to educate the masses and raise the ethical standard, should be disbanded; what policy I would advocate for the Indo-British commonwealth, and so on. I do not propose to stand for the presidency of the Theosophical Society because I do not belong to that society. That does not interest me—not that I think myself superior—for I do not believe in religious organizations, and also I don't want to guide a single man. Please believe me, sirs, when I say that I don't want to influence one single person; for the desire to guide shows inherently that one has an end, a goal, towards which he thinks all humanity must come like a band of sheep. That is what guidance implies. Now I do not want to urge any man towards a particular goal or an end; what I want to do is to help him to be intelligent, and that is quite a different thing. So I have not time to answer these innumerable questions based on such ideas.

Since it is rather late, I should like to make a résumé of what I have been saying during the last five or six days, and naturally I must be paradoxical. Truth is paradoxical. I hope that those of you who have intelligently followed what I have been saying will understand and act, but not make a standard of me for your actions. If what I have said is not true to you, you will naturally forget it. Unless you have really fathomed, unless you have thought over what I have said, you will simply repeat my phrases, learn my words by heart, and that is of no value. For understanding, the first requirement is doubt, doubt not only with regard to what I say, but primarily with regard to the ideas which you yourselves hold. But you have made an anathema of doubt, a fetter, an evil to be banished, to be put away; you have made of doubt an abominable thing, a disease. But to me, doubt is none of these; doubt is an ointment that heals.

But what do you generally doubt? You doubt what the other says. It is very easy to doubt someone else. But to doubt the very thing in which you are caught up, that you hold, to doubt the very thing that you are seeking, pursuing, that is more difficult. True doubt will not yield to substitution. When you doubt another, as when someone said during one of these talks the other day, "We doubt you," that shows you are doubting what I am giving, what I am trying to explain. Quite right. But your doubt is but the search for substitution. You say, "I have this, but I am not satisfied. Will that satisfy me, that other thing which you are offering? To find out, I must doubt you." But I am not offering you anything. I am saying, doubt the very thing that is in your hands, that is in your mind and heart; then you will no longer seek substitution.

When you seek substitution there is fear, and therefore increase of conflict. When you are afraid you seek the opposite of fear, which is courage, you proceed to acquire courage. Or, if you decide that you are unkind, you proceed to acquire kindness, which is merely substitution, a turning to the opposite. But if, instead of seeking a substitution, you really begin to inquire into that very thing in which your mind is caught—fear, unkindness, acquisitiveness—then you will discover the cause. And you can find out the cause only by continually doubting, by questioning, by a critical and intelligent attitude of mind, which is a healthy attitude, but which has been destroyed by society, by education, by religions that admonish you to banish doubt. Doubt is merely an inquiry after true values, and when you have found out true values for yourself, doubt ceases. But to find out, you must be critical, you must be frank, honest.

Since most people are seeking substitution, they are merely increasing their conflict. And this increase of conflict, with its desire for escape, we call progress, spiritual progress, because to us substitution or escape is further acquisition, further achievement. So what you call the search for truth is merely the attempt to find substitutes, the pursuit of greater securities, safer shelters from conflict. When you seek shelters you are creating exploiters, and having created them, you are caught up in that machine of exploitation which says, "Don't do this, don't do that, don't doubt, don't be critical. Follow this teaching, for this is true and that is false." So when you are talking of truth, you are really wanting substitution; you want repose, tranquillity, peace, assured escapes, and in this want you create artificial and empty machines, intellectual machines, to provide this substitution, to satisfy this want. Have I made my meaning clear?

First of all, you are caught up in conflict, and because you cannot understand that conflict you want the opposite, repose, peace, which is an intellectual concept. In that want you have created an intellectual machine, and that intellectual machine is religion; it is utterly divorced from your feelings, from your daily life, and is therefore merely an artificial thing. That intellectual machine may also be society, intellectually created, a machine to which you have become slaves and by which you are ruthlessly trodden down.

You have created these machines because you are in conflict, because through fear and anxiety you are driven to the opposite of that conflict, because you are seeking repose, tranquillity. Desire for the opposite creates fear, and out of that fear arises imitation. So you invent intellectual concepts such as religions, with their beliefs and standards, their authority and disciplines, their gurus and Masters, to lead you to what you want, which is comfort, security, tranquillity, escape from this constant conflict. You have created this vast machine which you call religion, this intellectual machine which has no validity, and you have also created the machine that is called society, for in your social as well as in your religious life you want comfort, shelter. In your social life you are held by traditions, habits, unquestioned values; public opinion acts as your authority; and unquestioned opinion, habit, and tradition eventually lead to nationalism and war.

You talk of searching for truth, but your search is merely a search for substitution, the desire for greater security and greater certainty. Therefore your search is destroying that which you are seeking, which is peace, not the peace of stagnation, but of understanding, of life, of ecstasy. You are denied that very thing because you are looking for something that will help you to escape.

So to me the whole purpose—if I may use that word without your misunderstanding me—lies in destroying this false intellectual machine by means of intelligence, that is, by true awareness. You can understand, put away tradition, which has become a hindrance; you can understand, put away Masters, ideas, beliefs. But do not destroy them merely to take up new ones; I don't mean that. You must not merely destroy, merely put away, you must be creative; and you can be creative only when you begin to understand true values. So question the significance of traditions and habits, of nationality, of discipline, of gurus and Masters. You can understand only when you are fully aware, aware with your whole being. When you say, "I am seeking God," fundamentally you mean, "I want to run away, to escape." When you say, "I am seeking truth, and an organization might help me to find it," you are merely seeking a shelter. Now I am not being harsh; I only want to emphasize and make clear what I am saying. It is for you to act.

We have created artificial hindrances. They are not real, fundamental hindrances; they are artificial. We have created them because we are seeking something, rewards, security, comfort, peace. To gain security, to help us avoid conflict, we must have many aids, many supports. And these aids, these supports, are self-discipline, gurus, beliefs.

I have gone into all this more or less fully. Now when I am speaking about these things, please don't think in terms of opposites, for then you will not understand. When I say that self-discipline is a hindrance, don't think that therefore you must not have discipline at all. I want to show you the cause of self-discipline. When you understand that, there is neither this self-imposed discipline nor its opposite, but there is true intelligence. In order to realize what we want—which is fundamentally false, because it is based on the idea of the opposite as a substitution—we have created artificial means, such as self-discipline, belief, guidance. Without such belief, without such authority, which is a hindrance, we feel lost; thus we become slaves and are exploited.

A man who lives by belief is not truly living; he is limited in his actions. But the man who, because he understands, is really free from belief and from the burden of knowledge, to him there is ecstasy, to him there is truth. Beware of the man who says, "I know," because he can know only the static, the limited, never the living, the infinite. Man can only say, "There is," which has nothing to do with knowledge. Truth is ever becoming; it is immortal; it is eternal life.

We have these hindrances, artificial hindrances, based on imitation, on acquisitiveness which creates nationalism, on self-discipline, gurus, Masters, ideals, beliefs. Most of us are enslaved by one of these, consciously or unconsciously. Now please follow this; otherwise you will say, "You are merely destroying and not giving us any constructive ideas."

We have created these hindrances; and we can be free from them only by becoming aware of them, not through the process of discipline, not by substitution, not by control, not by forgetfulness, not by following another, but only by becoming aware that they are poisons. You know, when you see a poisonous snake in your room, you are fully aware of it with your whole being. But these things, disciplines, beliefs, substitutions, you do not regard as poisons. They have become mere habits, sometimes pleasurable and sometimes painful, and you put up with them as long as pleasure outweighs pain. You continue in this manner until pain overwhelms you. When you have intense bodily pain, your only thought is to get rid of that pain. You don't think of the past or the future, of past health, of the time when you are not going to have any more pain. You are only concerned with getting rid of pain.

Likewise, you have to become fully and intensely aware of all these hindrances, and you can do that only when you are in conflict, when you are no longer escaping, no longer choosing substitutes. All choice is merely substitution. If you become fully aware of one hindrance, whether it be a guru, memory, or class consciousness, that awareness will uncover the creator of all hindrances, the creator of illusions, which is self-consciousness, the ego. When mind awakens intelligently to that creator, which is self-consciousness, then in that awareness the creator of illusions dissolves itself. Try it, and you will see what happens.

I am not saying this as an enticement for you to try. Don't try with the purpose of becoming happy. You will try it only if you are in conflict. But as most of you have many shelters in which you take comfort, you have altogether ceased to be in conflict. For all your conflicts you have explanations—so much dust and ashes—and these explanations have eased your conflict. Perhaps there are one or two among you who are not satisfied with explanations, not satisfied with ashes, whether dead ashes of yesterday, or future ashes of belief, of hope.

If you are really caught up in conflict you will find the ecstasy of life, but there must be intelligent awareness. That is, if I tell you that self-discipline is a hindrance, don't immediately reject or accept my statement. Find out if your mind is caught up in imitation, if your self-discipline is based on memory, which is but an escape from the present. You say, "I must not do this," and out of that self-imposed prohibition grows imitation; so self-discipline is based on imitation, fear. Where there is imitation there cannot be the fruition of intelligence. Find out if you are imitative; experiment. And you can experiment only in action itself. These are not just so many words; if you think it over, you will see. You cannot understand after action has taken place, which would be self-analysis, but only in the moment of action itself. You can be fully aware only in action. Don't say, "I must not be class-conscious," but become aware to discover if you are class-minded. That discovery in action will create conflict, and that conflict itself will free the mind from class consciousness, without your trying to overcome it.

So action itself destroys illusions, not self-imposed discipline. I wish you would think this over and act; then you would see what it all means. It opens immense avenues to the mind and heart, so that man can live in fulfillment without seeking an end, a result; he can act without a motive. But you can live completely only when you have direct perception, and direct perception is not attained through choice, through effort born of memory. It lies in the flame of awareness, which is the harmony of mind and heart in action. When your mind is freed from religions, gurus, systems, from acquisitiveness, then only can there be completeness of action, then only can mind and heart follow the swift wanderings of truth.

January 3, 1934

Questions

Italy, 1933

Ommen, 1933

Norway, 1933

Adyar, 1933–1934

Index

For further information about Krishnamurti Libraries, Retreats, Study Centers, Schools and events world-wide, as well as other publications, please contact the following:

Krishnamurti Foundation of America
P.O. Box 1560
Ojai, California 93024 U.S.A.
E-mail: kfa@kfa.org
www.kfa.org

Krishnamurti Foundation Trust, Ltd.
Brockwood Park
Bramdean, Hampshire
England SO24 0LQ
E-mail: info@brockwood.org.uk
www.brockwood.org.uk

Krishnamurti Foundation India
64-65 Greenways Road
Vasanta Vihar
Chennai
India 600 028
E-mail: kfihq@vsnl.com
www.kfionline.org